Shine Bright 3e

Cycle 4 A2>B1

Sous la direction de **Corinne Escales**

Corinne Escales
IA – IPR
Académie de Versailles

Aurélie Caumartin
Professeure certifiée
Collège Guy de Maupassant, Houilles (78)
Formatrice, Académie de Versailles

Soline Gommez-Despres
Professeure certifiée
Collège Descartes,
Soisy-sous-Montmorency (95)
Formatrice à l'INSPE,
Académie de Versailles

Marine Kerebel
Professeure certifiée
Collège de la Paix, Issy-les-Moulineaux (92)

Patrick Moore
Professeur certifié
Collège François Verdier, Lézat-sur-Lèze (09)
Formateur, Académie de Toulouse

Hadrien Morand
Professeur agrégé
Collège de Sèvres (92)
Formateur, Académie de Versailles

Emma Newman
Professeure agrégée
Collège Henri Matisse, Nice (06)
Formatrice, Chargée de mission d'inspection,
Académie de Nice

Odette Toneatti
Professeure agrégée
Collège-lycée Le Caousou, Toulouse (31)

Nathan

Bienvenue dans Shine Bright 3e

La 3e est la dernière année du cycle 4 instauré par les programmes en vigueur depuis la rentrée 2016.
Ce cycle regroupe les classes de 5e, 4e et 3e. En anglais LV1, le niveau visé en fin de cycle 4 est A2 dans les cinq activités langagières et B1 dans plusieurs activités langagières.

	ÉCOUTER ET COMPRENDRE	LIRE	RÉAGIR ET DIALOGUER	PARLER EN CONTINU	ÉCRIRE ET RÉAGIR À L'ÉCRIT
A2	Je peux comprendre une intervention brève si elle est claire et simple.	Je peux comprendre de courts textes simples sur des sujets concrets courants avec une fréquence élevée de langue quotidienne.	Je peux interagir avec une aisance raisonnable dans des situations bien structurées et de courtes conversations à condition que le locuteur apporte de l'aide le cas échéant.	Je peux décrire ou présenter simplement des gens, des conditions de vie, des activités quotidiennes, ce qu'on aime ou pas, par de courtes séries d'expressions ou de phrases.	Je peux écrire une série d'expressions et de phrases simples reliées par des connecteurs simples.
B1	Je peux comprendre une information factuelle sur des sujets simples en distinguant l'idée générale et les points de détail, à condition que l'articulation soit claire et l'accent courant.	Je peux lire des textes factuels directs sur des sujets relatifs à mon domaine et à mes intérêts avec un niveau satisfaisant de compréhension.	Je peux exprimer un avis, manifester un sentiment et donner quelques éléments simples de contexte sur un sujet abstrait ou culturel.	Je peux assez aisément mener à bien une description directe et non compliquée de sujets variés dans mon domaine en la présentant comme une succession linéaire de points.	Je peux écrire un énoncé simple et bref sur des sujets familiers ou déjà connus.

Le **Socle commun de connaissances, de compétences et de culture** en vigueur depuis la rentrée 2016 se décline en cinq domaines, tous pris en compte dans *Shine Bright 3e*.

Domaine 1 Les langages pour penser et communiquer
Domaine 2 Les méthodes et outils pour apprendre
Domaine 3 La formation de la personne et du citoyen
Domaine 4 Les systèmes naturels et les systèmes techniques
Domaine 5 Les représentations du monde et de l'activité humaine

L'éditeur et les auteurs remercient Fanny Hory, professeure certifiée et formatrice (Académie de Versailles), pour sa relecture pédagogique.

ISBN 978-2-09-178181-5

Shine Bright 3e Cycle 4 A2>B1

va te permettre d'approfondir ta connaissance du monde anglophone grâce à des **supports authentiques**, des **tâches variées** et des **outils innovants**.

Apprends en agissant avec Shine Bright 3e

La première partie de ton manuel est constituée de **12 chapitres de deux longueurs différentes** (***Files et Snapfiles***). Grâce à **des documents variés et authentiques** (vidéo, audio, textes littéraires et journalistiques, supports iconographiques, etc.), tu construiras les **compétences culturelles et linguistiques** nécessaires à la réalisation de la tâche finale.

Apprends en te cultivant avec Shine Bright 3e

Les **12 chapitres** du manuel te feront découvrir la **diversité du monde anglophone** : de l'émission *Spy School* à la lutte pour les droits des femmes en Nouvelle-Zélande, en passant par la musique afro-américaine et les problématiques écologiques à la Barbade, c'est **une véritable plongée dans les pays anglophones** qui t'est proposée. *Dive in!*

Apprends en partageant avec Shine Bright 3e

Une langue est par définition un moyen d'échange, c'est pourquoi nous avons proposé dans le manuel beaucoup d'**activités à faire en groupes**, que tu repéreras facilement grâce au picto TEAMWORK. En effet, on est plus fort à plusieurs !

Apprends en jouant avec Shine Bright 3e

Le jeu est un puissant moteur d'apprentissage. Dans chaque *File*, mets tes connaissances culturelles à l'épreuve grâce à la page ***Game on!***

Découvre également le plaisir de faire un ***Escape game*** en anglais pour plonger dans *Treasure Island* de R. L. Stevenson.

Apprends en variant les outils avec Shine Bright 3e

Nous avons eu à cœur de proposer une **palette d'outils diversifiés** qui puissent s'adresser à tout type d'élève.

Ainsi, **des parcours différenciés** sont proposés pour l'étude de certains documents et la réalisation de certaines tâches intermédiaires (***Your mission***).

Tu pourras aussi développer tes **compétences linguistiques et langagières** :

- Pour la grammaire, des infographies et des ***Grammar tutos*** t'aideront à comprendre et maîtriser les outils linguistiques nécessaires pour bien comprendre et t'exprimer.
- Pour le vocabulaire, tu auras à disposition des **cartes mentales** récapitulatives dans chaque chapitre.
- Enfin, des rubriques ***Yes you can!*** dédiées à la méthodologie et l'ensemble des pages ***How to shine***... à la fin de ton manuel t'accompagneront dans la réalisation des tâches.

Évalue tes acquis avec Shine Bright 3e

Afin de t'accompagner pas à pas dans ta progression et te permettre d'évaluer tes acquis, le manuel te propose plusieurs outils :

- **Des quiz numériques** sont disponibles régulièrement au fil des pages pour faire le point sur tes connaissances grammaticales, lexicales, phonologiques et culturelles.
- **Les pages *Test your skills*** à la fin de chaque *File* proposent des documents pour t'auto-évaluer.

We wish you a very SHINY year!

Les auteurs

Sommaire

▶ **Have you got what it takes to be a British spy?**

1. Discover the show
2. The perfect spy's profile
3. Spy skills needed

YOUR SNAP MISSION

Discover the *Spy School* show and **submit** your video application.

Build your English!

- Le superlatif
- La capacité au présent
- Les qualités et compétences
- L'accentuation des adjectifs et des adverbes

Je vais apprendre à…

- Parler de soi et convaincre.
- Exprimer la capacité.

▶ **How have British Indians helped shape today's UK?**

EXPLORE

1. A rich cultural mix
2. A strong legacy
3. Cultural fusion

GAME ON!

Snakes and ladders

Build your English!

- Le présent simple et le présent en *be* + *V-ing*
- Les tournures exclamatives
- Le quartier, la ville, le multiculturalisme
- La prononciation du <s> final
- L'accentuation des tournures exclamatives

YOUR FINAL MISSION

Write an enthusiastic travel blog post.

Je vais apprendre à…

- Présenter un quartier.
- Exprimer l'enthousiasme.
- Décrire un événement.

TEST YOUR SKILLS! ➜ p. 31

▶ **How are New Zealand women leading the way in terms of gender equality?**

1. Purple Power Week
2. Leading the way
3. Getting there
4. Lord – with an 'e'

YOUR SNAP MISSION

Write the life story of an inspiring New Zealand woman.

Build your English!

- Le prétérit simple et le prétérit en *be* + *V-ing*
- Les pronoms relatifs
- L'égalité des sexes, les métiers et l'engagement
- La prononciation de la terminaison *-ed*

Je vais apprendre à…

- Décrire une scène passée.
- Rédiger une biographie.

EDD Éducation au développement durable

▶ **How are Barbadians trying to preserve their marine treasures?**

1. Diving into paradise
2. Paradise lost?
3. Environmental policies
4. Take action!

YOUR SNAP MISSION

Make a video to encourage the protection of the marine environment in Barbados.

Build your English!

- Le conseil et l'obligation (*should, must, have to* et *need to*)
- L'hypothèse avec *if* et *will*
- L'environnement, le tourisme et le bénévolat
- L'accentuation des mots possédant un suffixe

Je vais apprendre à...

- Décrire un futur hypothétique.
- Dire ce qu'il faut faire.

▶ **Who were the American gangsters behind the myths?**

EXPLORE

1. Gangster's paradise
2. Gangsters in the spotlight
3. The harder they fall

GAME ON!

Gangster Quiz

Build your English!

- Le prétérit et le *past perfect*
- Les questions (2)
- Le crime, la loi et les médias
- La prononciation des graphies <e> et <u>
- L'accent américain

YOUR FINAL MISSION

Write an interview with a reformed gangster.

Je vais apprendre à...

- Présenter une chronologie.
- Raconter une scène.
- Conduire un entretien journalistique.

TEST YOUR SKILLS! → p. 91

Parcours artistique

▶ **How has the superhero been shaped by American history?**

1. This is the Captain
2. A superhero for the real world
3. Reinventing the Patriot
4. Meet the new Captain

YOUR SNAP MISSION

Write and **record** a portrait of Captain America.

Build your English!

- Le gérondif
- Le comparatif
- Le patriotisme, la description physique et morale
- La prononciation du suffixe *-ing*

Je vais apprendre à...

- Décrire un personnage.
- Décrire une évolution.

▶ **How do British people assert their identities through their clothes?**

EXPLORE

1. Norms and uniforms
2. Me and my clique
3. Style as a statement

GAME ON!

The "Dressing Challenge"

Build your English!

- Les quantifieurs
- L'opposition et la concession, la cause et la conséquence
- La mode, l'apparence et les normes
- La prononciation de la graphie <o>
- Les *gap fillers*

YOUR FINAL MISSION

Take part in a talk show about fashion: "Should we wear whatever we want?"

Je vais apprendre à…

- Exprimer un point de vue.
- Comparer des styles vestimentaires.
- Argumenter pour convaincre.

TEST YOUR SKILLS! ➜ p. 111

▶ **Can reality be distorted for a good cause?**

1. Denouncing
2. Defending a cause
3. Acting positive
4. Raising awareness

YOUR SNAP MISSION

Write an article about using manipulated images to raise awareness.

Build your English!

- La probabilité (*must, may, could, might, can't*)
- Les discours direct et indirect
- Les médias, les *fake news*, la sensibilisation
- La prononciation des diphtongues

Je vais apprendre à…

- Présenter une action.
- Expliquer la stratégie d'une campagne de sensibilisation.

▶ **How is science fiction impacting our lives?**

EXPLORE

1. Changing everyday objects
2. Helping us go further
3. Fuelling our imagination

GAME ON!

Mission Shine Rocket

Build your English!

- Le conditionnel
- L'expression du futur (*will, may, be going to* et *be* + *V-ing*)
- Les innovations technologiques, les jeux vidéo et le cinéma, l'exploration spatiale
- La prononciation de la graphie <ea>
- L'accentuation des mots composés

YOUR FINAL MISSION

Design and **present** an invention that could be inspired by science fiction.

Je vais apprendre à…

- Décrire un monde fictif.
- Évoquer des événements futurs.
- Décrire des possibilités à venir.

TEST YOUR SKILLS! ➜ p. 131

ESCAPE GAME

1. Discover *Treasure Island*
2. Escape with the treasure!

YOUR MISSION

Help Jim find the treasure before the pirates and escape from Treasure Island.

HOW to shine in…

Visite guidée de ton manuel

Les pictos de ton manuel

- Compréhension orale
- Compréhension écrite
- Expression orale en continu
- Expression orale en interaction
- Expression écrite
- **Video** / **Audio** Document vidéo ou audio
- **AUDIO** Lexique ou activité de phonologie
- **Grammar tuto** Vidéo de grammaire
- **QUIZ Test de positionnement** college.nathan.fr/3sb21 — Entraînement au test de positionnement de fin de 3e
- **QUIZ Test** college.nathan.fr/3sb35 — Quiz d'auto-évaluation
- **WB** → p. 6-7 Renvoi au *workbook*
- **WB DIFFÉRENCIATION** → p. 6-7 Renvoi à des parcours différenciés dans le *workbook*
- **HOW TO SHINE IN ...** → p. 136 Renvoi aux pages de méthodologie en fin de manuel

Pour découvrir et comprendre

Chaque chapitre comporte plusieurs pages de documents pour découvrir la langue et les différents aspects de la thématique culturelle.

À quoi sert la double page d'ouverture ?

- Elle te permet de découvrir la problématique de l'unité à travers **trois documents** (une iconographie, une citation et une vidéo) et un **travail en groupes**.

Comment fonctionnent les pages de documents ?

- Chaque double page ***Explore*** propose des **documents authentiques**, accompagnés d'**activités de compréhension et de production**.
- Des encarts ***Grammar spot***, ***Vocabulary spot*** et ***Phonology spot*** t'accompagnent en contexte sur des points de langue qui te seront utiles pour les tâches.
- La rubrique ***Your mission*** contient une tâche à réaliser à la suite de l'étude des documents. Deux ***Ways*** sont parfois présentés afin de te donner le choix. Une boîte ***Build your skills*** t'aidera à améliorer ta production.
- Enfin, les rubriques ***At home*** et ***A little extra*** te fournissent des pistes pour prolonger le travail à la maison ou découvrir d'autres documents.

Comment fonctionnent les *Snapfiles* ?

- Ces chapitres **plus courts** te feront découvrir une thématique culturelle à travers une suite de documents et **une tâche à réaliser en deux temps**.

Pour maîtriser la langue et préparer la tâche finale

Quels sont les outils à ta disposition pour progresser ?

- Tu disposes d'**infographies** et de ***Grammar tutos*** pour consolider ta maîtrise de la grammaire anglaise .
- Le lexique de chaque unité n'aura plus de secret pour toi grâce aux ***cartes mentales de vocabulaire*** et aux activités de manipulation de la rubrique ***Vocabulary***.
- Savoir prononcer et écrire correctement est essentiel pour se faire comprendre : les activités de la rubrique ***Phonology*** t'y aideront.
- Pour continuer à t'entraîner, tu trouveras dans l'***Exercise bank*** en fin de manuel d'autres exercices de grammaire et de vocabulaire classés par chapitre.

Pour progresser et t'évaluer

Es-tu joueur(se) ?

Si c'est le cas, les pages ***Game on!*** vont te plaire ! Elles te permettront de faire le point sur tes connaissances culturelles.

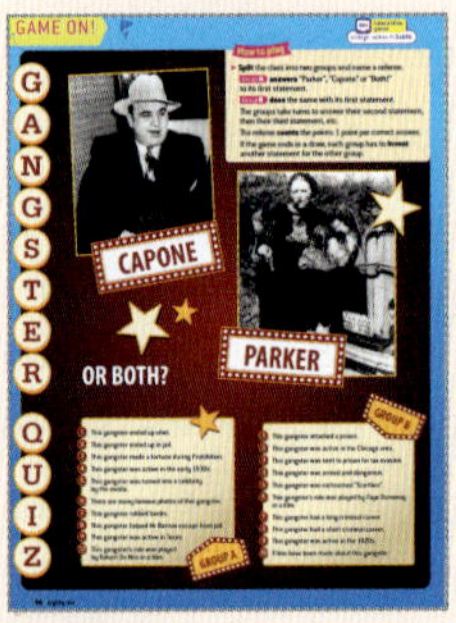

À quoi servent les pages *Your final mission* et *Test your skills* ?

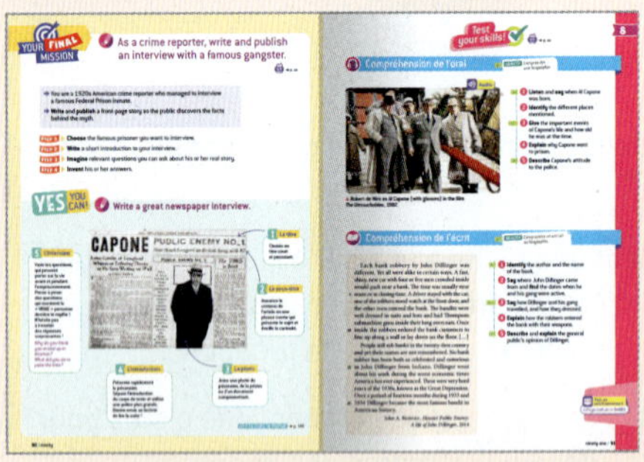

- Ces pages sont l'aboutissement de ton travail sur l'ensemble du *File*. Elles te permettront de **montrer que tu as compris et assimilé les éléments culturels et linguistiques** via une expression orale ou écrite (la tâche finale).
- La rubrique ***Yes you can*** sera un outil méthodologique précieux pour t'accompagner dans ta production finale.

Quels outils numériques sont à ta disposition ?

Au fil du manuel, tu verras des pictos qui t'indiquent la présence d'**activités numériques** complémentaires accessibles via l'appli Nathan Live! ou en tapant les mini-liens dans ton navigateur Web :

- QUIZ **Test** college.nathan.fr/**3sb35** te permet d'accéder à une série d'activités pour évaluer ta maîtrise des connaissances linguistiques et culturelles de la double page étudiée.
- QUIZ **Test de positionnement** college.nathan.fr/**3sb321** est situé en fin de chaque *File* et te propose des activités d'entraînement au test de positionnement de fin de 3e.

À quoi servent les pages *How to shine...?*

- Conçues de manière très visuelle, ces pages te fourniront des **stratégies précieuses** pour appréhender la **grammaire**, le **vocabulaire**, la **phonologie** et toutes les **activités de compréhension et de production**.

Visite guidée de ton workbook

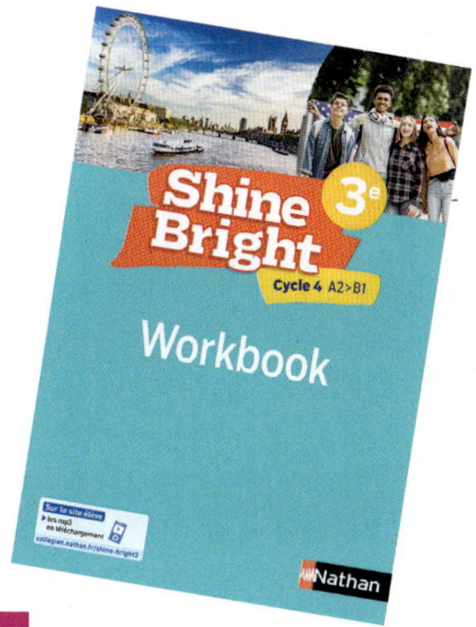

Pour t'aider à démarrer l'année

- Des **jeux et activités** pour réactiver tes connaissances avant d'attaquer les unités du manuel.

Pour t'accompagner dans la compréhension des documents

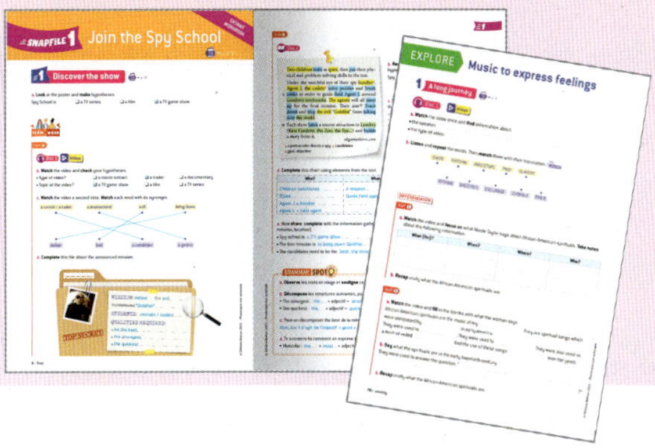

- Pour chaque document des pages ***Explore***, tu trouveras dans ton *workbook* des activités qui te guideront dans ta compréhension des documents.
- Pour certains documents, tu pourras choisir entre deux parcours différents : ***Way 1*** et ***Way 2***.

Pour t'aider à comprendre et maîtriser les points de langue

- Pour chaque encart ***Grammar spot***, ***Vocabulary spot*** ou ***Phonology spot***, ton *workbook* contient des activités t'amenant à comprendre et compléter la leçon, puis t'entraîner.

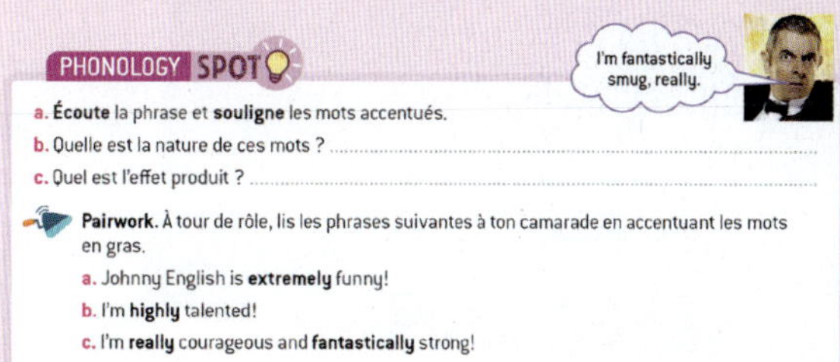

Pour te guider dans la réalisation des tâches

- Chaque ***Snap mission*** ou ***Final mission*** fait l'objet d'un accompagnement guidé pas à pas, avec des *check lists*, pour te rappeler les outils à mobiliser ou te donner des conseils.

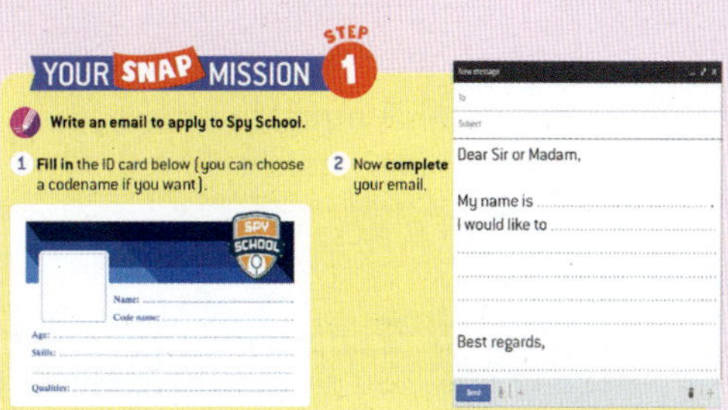

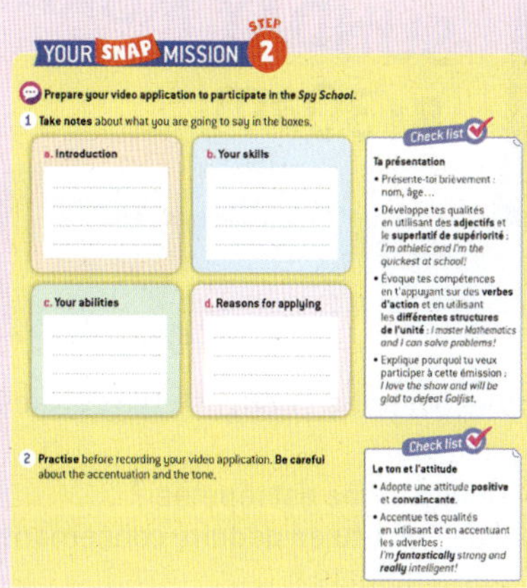

SNAPFILE 1 Join the Spy School

▶ Have you got what it takes to be a British spy?

YOUR SNAP MISSION

Discover the *Spy School* show and submit your video application.

1 Discover the show

WB → p. 7

Video

Doc 1

Doc 2

Two children train as spies, then put their physical and problem-solving skills to the test. Under the watchful eye of their spy handler[1], Agent J, the cadets[2] solve puzzles and break codes in order to guide Field Agent L around London's landmarks. The agents will all meet up for the final mission. Their aim[3]? Track down and stop the evil "Goldfist" from taking over the world.

Each show takes a tourist attraction in London (Kew Gardens, the Zoo, the Eye...) and builds a story from it.

ukgameshows.com

1. a person who directs a spy 2. candidates
3. goal, objective

TEAM WORK

a. **Look** at the poster and **guess** what *Spy School* is.

Team A

b. **Watch** the video (doc 1) and **give** information about *Spy School*.

c. **Pick out** elements about the TV programme.

Team B

b. **Read** the text (doc 2) and **find** information about *Spy School*.

c. **Say** what the cadets will do.

d. Now **share** what you have learnt with the other team. What type of show is *Spy School*?

GRAMMAR SPOT

the best, the strongest, the quickest

Quelle forme est répétée ?
Que peux-tu en déduire concernant les candidats ?

2 The perfect spy's profile

WB → p. 9

Doc 1

AUDIO VERSION

ONLY THE STRONG SURVIVE

CHERUB agents are highly trained, extremely talented – and all under the age of seventeen. For official purposes, these agents do not exist. They are sent out on missions to spy on terrorists, hack into critical documents, and gather intel[1] on global threats – all without gadgets or weapons. It is an extremely dangerous job, but these agents have one crucial advantage: Adults never suspect that teens are spying on them.

James is the latest CHERUB recruit. He's a bit of a troublemaker[2], but he's also brilliant. And CHERUB needs him. James has no idea what to expect, but he's out of options. Before he can start in the field, he must first survive one hundred gruelling[3] days of basic training, where even some of the toughest[4] recruits don't make it to the end…

WILL YOU ACCEPT THE NEXT MISSION?

Robert Muchamore, *The Recruit*, 2004

1. collect information 2. agitator 3. *épuisants* 4. strongest

HOW TO SHINE IN READING → p. 136

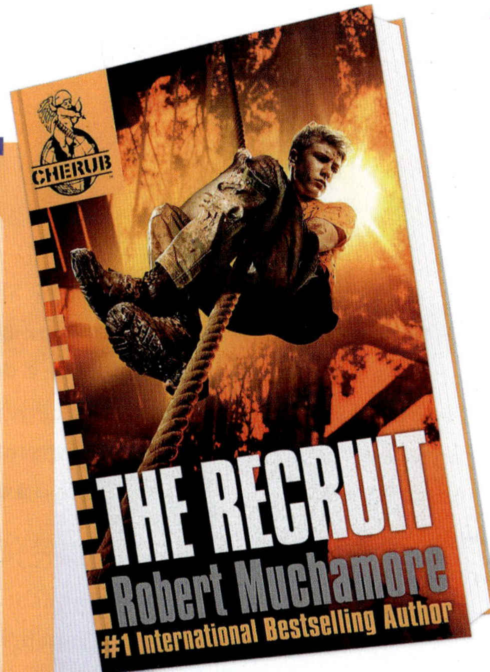

a. **Read** the text and **say** why CHERUB agents are exceptional.
b. **Say** what missions they are sent on and **explain** why.
c. **Focus** on James. Do you think that CHERUB was right to recruit him?

Doc 2

Video

PHONOLOGY SPOT AUDIO

He's fantastically smug, really.

Écoute cette phrase. Quels mots sont accentués ? Pourquoi ?

a. **Look** at the film poster and **describe** Johnny English's attitude.
b. **Watch** the video and **list** the adjectives describing him.
c. **Comment** on Johnny English's personality. Is he a "traditional" spy?

YOUR SNAP MISSION — STEP 1

Ready to challenge Goldfist? Write an email to apply to *Spy School*.

1. Briefly **introduce** yourself (name, age, origin, etc.).
2. **Write** about your personality and qualities. **Be** convincing!

WB → p. 10

Build your skills! **Parler de sa personnalité et convaincre**

- Utilise le superlatif de supériorité : *I'm **the best, the toughest, the quickest**…*
- Ajoute des adverbes en ***-ly*** : *I'm **fantastically** talented.* • *I'm **highly** determined.*

BUILD YOUR ENGLISH → p. 16

3 Spy skills needed

WB → p. 11

Doc 1 — Audio

SKILLS

MAIN SKILLS
- Secret Service: ●●●●●
- Shooting: ●●●●●
- Driving: ●●●○○
- Skiing: ●●●●○
- Combat: ●●●●○
- Diving: ●●●○○
- Swimming: ●●●●○
- Golf: ●●●●○

OTHER SKILLS
- Charm: ●●●●●
- Style: ●●●●●
- Courage: ●●●●●
- Gentleman: ●●●●●
- Taste: ●●●●●

LANGUAGE SKILLS:
- English: ●●●●●
- French: ●●●●●
- German: ●●●●●

a. **Look** at the document (doc 1) and **guess** what the audio is about.

b. **Listen** to the audio and **take** notes about the skills mentioned.

c. **Describe** James Bond's skills in a short paragraph.

GRAMMAR SPOT

He **can** fly a plane.

Qu'exprime le modal *can* ici ? Reformule la phrase en utilisant un adjectif.

Doc 2

M.I. High is a TV series following the adventures of Saint Hope's students who work as undercover spies.

CHARACTER PROFILE DAISY

Daisy is a master of disguise, and in many episodes she goes undercover. She has a lot of imagination when it comes to inventing excuses when she's being called by Lenny for missions, or for distracting someone else's attention from someone/thing. She was one of the first M.I. High agents. Socialite[1] Daisy is an undercover expert with extraordinary chameleon abilities and a master in the art of disguise, building allegiances to get closer to the enemy. She makes diversions for the team and adapts herself to every situation.

1. person who goes to prestigious social events

mihigh.fandom.com

Doc 3

AUDIO VERSION

Alex Rider, a 14-year-old boy, is in the northwest corner of Afghanistan. He is escorted by five Afghan nomads.

He had seen their astonishment when he climbed out of the helicopter, and as they had travelled together toward the mountains, they kept glancing[1] at him [...]. He couldn't have looked more different from them. He was half their size, fair-haired, European. He was wearing a black combat suit and hiking boots and a backpack.

It was unfortunate that horse riding was one of the few outdoor activities he had never fully mastered. They had given him a sleek black Egyptian colt[2] [...], but he was barely able to control it [...]. He was very glad to dismount[3] and have a rest. [...]

"English boy!" It was Faisal, the second-in-command, who had spoken. [...] Alex looked up.

"You living in London?"

Alex nodded. He didn't want to pass on any information, but there was no point denying it.

Anthony Horowitz, *Alex Rider: Secret Weapon: Seven Untold Adventures From the Life of a Teenaged Spy*, 2019

1. looking 2. horse 3. *descendre de cheval*

TEAMWORK

Team A

a. **Look** at the picture (**doc 2**) and **guess** what M.I. High is.

b. **Read** the text and **check** your hypotheses.

c. **Recap** Daisy's skills.

Team B

a. **Read** the text and **find** information about the situation.

b. **Say** why the men are surprised.

c. **Describe** Alex's strengths and weaknesses.

d. **Introduce** your character to the other team and **choose** the best spy.

YOUR SNAP MISSION — STEP 2

Now prepare your video application to participate in the *Spy School*.

1 **Prepare** your "skills sheet". Then, **express** yourself: **explain** who you are and what your skills and qualities are.

2 **Talk** about *Spy School*: why do you want to participate in this show? You want to be chosen! **Be** creative and convincing!

Build your skills! **Exprimer la capacité**

- Utilise les modaux pour dire ce qu'une personne est capable de faire ou pas :
  - *Alex Rider **cannot** ride a horse well.*
  - *James Bond **can** fly a plane.*
- Emploie des expressions pour donner des points forts :
  - *Daisy is **a master in** the art of disguise.*
    *= She is **good at** disguis**ing** herself.*
  - *James Bond is **an expert in** hand-to-hand combat.*

WB → p. 14 HOW TO SHINE IN SPEAKING → p. 144 BUILD YOUR ENGLISH → p. 16

QUIZ Test
college.nathan.fr/3sb15

EXERCISES ➜ p. 166

A Exprimer la supériorité avec le superlatif

Grammar tuto

On utilise **le superlatif de supériorité** pour parler d'un élément ou d'une personne qui est au-dessus des autres dans sa catégorie ou qui excelle dans un domaine.

Smug Spy is **the most arrogant** spy.
adjectif long

Sporty Spy is **the strongest** spy.
adjectif court

Silly Spy is **the funniest** spy.
modification orthographique

Smart Spy is **the best** spy because
adjectif irrégulier
she has **the biggest** set of skills.
modification orthographique

1 Écris le superlatif de supériorité de ces adjectifs.

Ex : *handy ➜ the handiest*

funny • intelligent • bad • mighty • silly • good • smart • powerful • young • discreet

2 Écris ces phrases en mettant les adjectifs au superlatif de supériorité.

a. Clever Spy is **intelligent** and **brave**.
b. Discreet Spy is **shy** but **determined**.
c. To be a spy, you have to be **fit** and **good** at hiding.

3 Décris chaque agent secret en utilisant les adjectifs donnés au superlatif de supériorité.

Ex : *Daisy is the worthiest recruit.*

good • worthy • able • intelligent • fast • imaginative

HOW TO SHINE IN GRAMMAR ➜ p. 147

B Exprimer la capacité au présent

Modal et équivalent		1re personne du singulier	3e personne du singulier
can/can't	+ V	*I can solve problems.* *I can't drive a car.*	*Daisy can go undercover.* *James Bond can't fly a spaceship.*
be able to		*I **am** able to gather intel.*	*Alex Rider **is** barely able to control his black Egyptian horse.*

Autres expressions		1re personne du singulier	3e personne du singulier
be capable of	+ V-ing	*I **am** capable of solving puzzles.*	*James Bond **is** capable of hacking a computer.*
be good at		*I **am** good at breaking codes.*	*Daisy **is** good at going undercover.*
master		*I have mastered swimming.*	*Alex Rider doesn't fully master horse riding.*

4 Remplace le segment en bleu par une autre structure exprimant la capacité.

a. I **can** break codes.
b. James Bond **has mastered** skiing.
c. Johnny English **is able to** go undercover.
d. Alex Rider **is not capable of** flying a plane.

5 Rédige quatre phrases afin de dire ce que tu es capable de faire en utilisant ces structures.

be able to • be capable of • master • be good at

HOW TO SHINE IN GRAMMAR ➜ p. 152

VOCABULARY

EXERCISES → p. 166

THE WORLD OF SPIES

Secret agents
AUDIO

- **es**pionage
- **ma**stermind = **ge**nius
- **mi**ssion /'mɪʃən/
- re**cruit** /rɪ'kruːt/
- spy /spaɪ/ (pl. sp**ies**)
- confi**den**tial /ˌkɒnfɪ'denʃəl/
- **se**cret /'siːkrət/
- go under**co**ver
- spy on

TV show
AUDIO

- **chal**lenge /'tʃælɪndʒ/
- con**tes**tant = ca**det**
- host
- plot
- **pro**gramme
- **chal**lenging
- ex**ci**ting /ɪk'saɪtɪŋ/
- **thril**ling
- **apply** for
- be fit for: *être compétent(e) pour*
- be trained
- par**ti**cipate in

Skills
AUDIO

- break (codes)
- de**ci**pher /dɪ'saɪfə/: *déchiffrer*
- de**tect**
- dive /daɪv/: *plonger*
- fight
- fly: *piloter*
- shoot
- solve (**puz**zles)
- swim
- train

Qualities
AUDIO

- ath**le**tic /æθ'letɪk/
- brave /breɪv/ = cou**ra**geous
- **bril**liant
- **ca**pable /'keɪpəbəl/
- **cle**ver ≠ **sil**ly
- de**ter**mined /dɪ'tɜːmɪnd/
- dis**creet**
- fast = quick
- **fun**ny
- **hum**ble ≠ smug = **ar**rogant
- per**sua**sive /pə'sweɪsɪv/
- **spor**ty
- strong
- **ta**lented
- ex**treme**ly
- fan**tas**tically
- **high**ly /'haɪli/
- **real**ly

Describe a secret agent using at least five words from the wordmap. Your classmates must guess who he/she is.

- NOUN
- ADJECTIVE
- VERB
- ADVERB

HOW TO SHINE IN VOCABULARY → p. 160

PHONOLOGY

L'accentuation des adjectifs et des adverbes

- En anglais, les **mots importants** de la phrase (noms, adjectifs, adverbes et verbes) sont **accentués**, alors que les termes qui relient les mots importants (articles, pronoms, auxiliaires, prépositions) sont en général inaccentués.
- Pour insister sur le caractère **extraordinaire** de quelque chose, l'**accent de phrase** porte souvent sur un **adjectif** ou un **adverbe**.

1 Écoute ces phrases et repère les mots accentués. AUDIO

a. Johnny English is fantastically arrogant!
b. James is highly trained and extremely talented!
c. James Bond is the strongest.
d. Daisy is the best spy.

2 Écoute et répète en accentuant les mots en bleu. AUDIO

a. I'm **really** funny and athletic.
b. I'm **extremely** brilliant and I'm **fantastically** brave!
c. I'm **highly** determined.
d. I'm the **strongest**, the **quickest** and I can be the **best** cadet!

HOW TO SHINE IN PHONOLOGY → p. 159

FILE 2

British Indian fusion

"As difficult as it can be, I'll always be grateful to have two places to call home."

Sarah Praseedom (24 years old)
Student born in the UK to Indian parents

How have British Indians helped shape today's UK?

More on SPEAKEASY NEWS
speakeasy-news.com

Celebrating Diwali in Trafalgar Square, London.

YOUR FINAL MISSION

Write an enthusiastic travel blog post to encourage visitors to discover Indian Britain.

Video

Mayor of London Sadiq Khan, the son of Pakistani immigrants, is lighting candles with other representatives to open the annual Diwali celebrations in London.

TEAM WORK

WB → p. 15

Team A
Describe the picture and **guess** what is happening.

Team B
Read the quote and **imagine** what difficulties Sarah is referring to, and why she is grateful.

Team C
Watch the video and **say** why people like Diwali.

- Now **share** what you have learnt about Indian culture in London with the other teams.

EXPLORE A rich cultural mix

1 London's Little India

WB DIFFÉRENCIATION → p. 16

Doc 1 Video

▲ A street in Southall, a large district of London nicknamed "Little India".

a. **Look** at the picture and **comment** on it.

b. **Watch** the video and **find** information about Southall.

c. **Explain** why Kamiya Jani says that Southall is "*a mini Punjab of London*".

HOW TO SHINE IN LISTENING → p. 138

CULTURE SPOT

- **Punjab** is a region of northern India and eastern Pakistan.
- India was ruled by the **British Crown** from 1858 to 1947. At Independence, India was divided into two separate countries, **India** and **Pakistan**.

Doc 2

LONDON'S SECRET LITTLE INDIA

Posted on October 20, 2016 by Alex

facebook | twitter | email

Those looking for Indian culture in London will most likely visit top-reviewed Indian restaurants or one of the religious temples such as the one in Soho. [...] A more authentic experience could be found in actual South Asian areas; one of these is Southall, a West London district which was home to the first pub in the country to accept rupees[1] as payment. Here you can listen to bhangra[2] and visit a gurdwara[3] whilst enjoying a proper curry, if you think you can handle the spice. [...]

If there's something sub-continental you're seeking, you'll probably find it. Though most of what populates the area are spice shops, there are sweet shops too, with a range of delicacies for sale: halwa, barfi, ladoo, jalebi[4], etc. [...]

For music there's Jas Musicals, which sells gig-ready sitars and Indian bansaris[5] as well as plenty of CDs covering a range of Indian traditions. [...]

Southall is also home to Sri Guru Singh Sabha Gurdwara – the largest Sikh temple outside of India. [...]

Diwali is almost definitely the best time to visit Southall, with street activities and festivities taking place all over the area.

marblearchbymontcalm.co.uk/blog

GRAMMAR SPOT

- Aadil **is making** jalebi and **serving** it to the Indian community.
- Sunny **loves** Punjabi music and **has** a store here in Southall.

Observe les groupes verbaux en gras. Quels sont les deux temps utilisés ? Pourquoi ?

a. **Read** the text and **pick out** words belonging to Indian traditions and legacy.

b. **Make** a list of all the activities you can do when you visit Southall.

c. **Say** why Southall is different from other areas in London.

1. Indian money 2. genre of Punjabi music 3. temple for Sikhs 4. Indian desserts 5. Indian flutes

2 British Indians

WB → p. 18

Doc 1

Many Indians have immigrated to the United Kingdom, and today British Indians are the country's largest ethnic minority. They have had a tremendous effect on the culture of the United Kingdom, as well as the character of its major cities. [...]

Mandavi Kaushik is but one of many immigrants who enjoys life in the United Kingdom. [...] She came to the United Kingdom fourteen years ago; nowadays she runs a popular fashion and lifestyle blog called 'The Red Notebook'. Like many British Indians she resides in London, a city with a large population of immigrants from South Asia. [...]

Despite successfully integrating into British society, immigrants from India maintain much of their cultural identity. The children of immigrants also carry on their cultural legacy, and many – such as blogger Victoria Das – consider themselves more Indian than British. [...]

British Indians have had a profound influence on British culture as a whole.

Jeremy Mancino, *jetsettimes.com*, 2019

a. Read the text and **speak** about Mandavi Kaushik.

b. Pick out information about Indian immigration to the UK.

c. Explain the author's view on British Indians' cultural identity.

CULTURE SPOT

There are nearly 1.5 million Indians or British Indians living in the UK. **British Indians** are Indian-born persons who migrated to the UK, as well as those born in the country who have Indian descent.

Doc 2 — Video

a. Watch the video and **gather** information about Britain as a land of immigration.

b. Note down elements about British Indians and the Indian diaspora in the UK.

c. How successful are British Indians?

YOUR MISSION — DIFFÉRENCIATION

In pairs, make a slide presentation to share what you know about Indian London.

WAY 1

Find three pictures showing shops, monuments or people in Southall. **Prepare** one slide per picture, with a short description of each place or person.

WAY 2

Find information about Southall. **Select** several photographs of this area and **present** the places, people and activities represented.

WB → p. 19

Build your skills! Présenter un quartier

- Utilise le présent en *be* + V-*ing* pour évoquer une action en cours :

  *He's **making** jalebi. • I'**m** really **enjoying** it. • If you'**re seeking** something sub-continental...*

- Emploie le présent simple pour parler de généralités, d'habitudes et de goûts :

  *Indians **are** extremely good business people. • Every year, the Diwali festival **takes** place in Trafalgar Square. • He clearly **loves** Punjabi music.*

BUILD YOUR ENGLISH → p. 27

QUIZ Test
college.nathan.fr/3sb21

EXPLORE A strong legacy

1 The jewel in the Crown

WB DIFFÉRENCIATION → p. 20

Doc 1

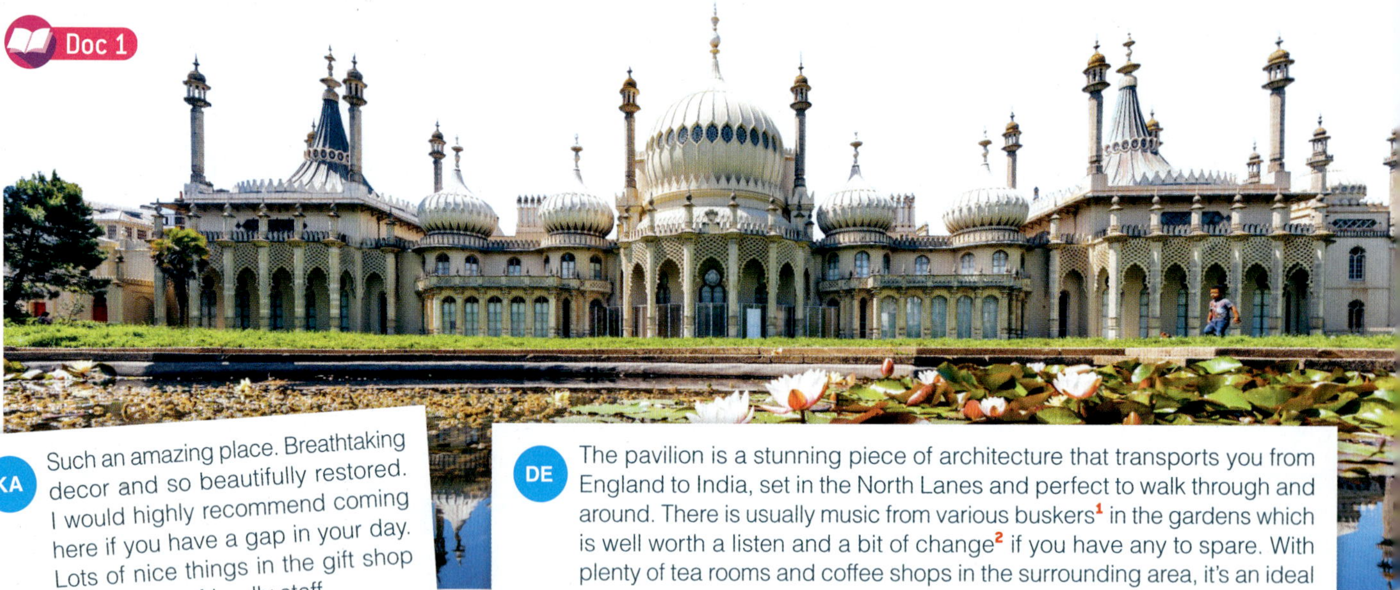

KA Such an amazing place. Breathtaking decor and so beautifully restored. I would highly recommend coming here if you have a gap in your day. Lots of nice things in the gift shop too, and very friendly staff.

DE The pavilion is a stunning piece of architecture that transports you from England to India, set in the North Lanes and perfect to walk through and around. There is usually music from various buskers[1] in the gardens which is well worth a listen and a bit of change[2] if you have any to spare. With plenty of tea rooms and coffee shops in the surrounding area, it's an ideal place to stop for a drink and a relaxation.

▲ The Royal Pavilion, in Brighton, is a former royal residence built in the 19th century for King George IV.

SA So beautiful! It's just out of this world! So, so beautiful!

VI Such a beautiful landmark and lovely gardens surrounding it! A must-visit if you are in Brighton!

1. street musicians 2. money

in.worldorgs.com

a. **Look** at the picture and **find** adjectives to describe the place.

b. **Read** the reviews and **pick out** words and expressions that express admiration and enthusiasm.

c. **Explain** why tourists are so surprised when they discover this building.

GRAMMAR SPOT

- **Such a beautiful landmark!**
- **So beautiful!**

Quel intensifieur est suivi d'un groupe nominal ? D'un adjectif simple ?

Doc 2 — Video

▲ The Durbar Room at Osborne House, Queen Victoria's seaside home on the Isle of Wight.

▲ Queen Victoria of the United Kingdom and Empress of India (1837-1901).

a. **Comment** on the pictures.

b. **Watch** the video and **give** information about the Durbar Room.

c. **Explain** what "*India came to her*" means.

PHONOLOGY SPOT AUDIO

Incredible room!

Écoute cette phrase exclamative. Que remarques-tu concernant l'intonation ?

2 So British… or is it?

WB → p. 21

Doc 1 Video

CULTURE SPOT

The British East India Company (BEIC) was a British company founded in 1600 and dissolved in 1874. It did business with India and China, trading goods such as silk, cotton, spices and… tea!

a. **Watch** the video and **identify** situations when British people love drinking tea.

b. **Pick out** historical and cultural elements.

c. **Explain** what "*quintessentially British*" means. Can you give other examples?

Doc 2

Three flags fluttering[1] above the pavilion of London's Oval cricket ground neatly symbolised the interchangeable identities of Britain's ethnic minorities at the fourth Test between England and India on Thursday.

A British Union Jack flew highest in the middle, flanked by[2] England's Saint George's Cross and an Indian tricolour, as the teams resumed a gripping[3] five-match series tied at 1-1.

Despite being born and raised in the UK, many cricket fans of Indian origin came to cheer on Virat Kohli's men rather than Joe Root's England side.

timesofindia.indiatimes.com, 2021

▲ India's Virat Kohli batting against England, September 2021.

1. moving in the wind 2. between 3. fascinating

a. **Look** at the picture, **identify** the sport and **say** what you know about it.

b. **Read** the text and **say** where the match took place and which flags were present.

c. **Explain** how British Indian spectators felt during the match.

YOUR MISSION

DIFFÉRENCIATION

Write and post an enthusiastic review about three different British Indian places.

WAY 1

Find pictures of three British Indian places and **write** a sentence with "so" or "such" for each picture.

WAY 2

Choose three British Indian places you like and **write** a short review post for each.

WB → p. 22

Build your skills! **Exprimer l'enthousiasme**

- Utilise les intensifieurs ***so*** et ***such*** pour exprimer ton engouement : ***Such*** *an amazing place!* • ***So*** *beautiful!*
- Choisis des adjectifs qui vont donner du relief à ton texte : *a* ***whopping*** *165 million cups of tea every day* • *a* ***gripping*** *five-match series* • ***breathtaking*** *decor*

BUILD YOUR ENGLISH → p. 27

QUIZ **Test**
college.nathan.fr/**3sb23**

EXPLORE Cultural fusion

1 Spice up your life!

WB DIFFÉRENCIATION → p. 23

Doc 1 Video

PHONOLOGY SPOT AUDIO

houses • restaurants • friends • drinks

Écoute ces mots. Que remarques-tu concernant la prononciation du <s> final ?

a. Watch the video (doc 1) and **say** what and where Sheba is.

b. Explain what makes it so popular.

c. Read the text (doc 2) and **comment** on the relationship between Indian and British food.

Doc 2

Asian Food: The Indian Influence on British Food

Last updated Jun 5, 2021 by Everything Zany

The Indian influence on British food is so extensive and deep. It began from Victorian times and became an integral part of multicultural Britain. Indian food is sharing the top spot with fish and chips and shepherd's pie[1] as national dishes of Britain.

1. *hachis parmentier d'agneau*

everythingzany.com

▲ An Indian food truck in London.

Doc 3 Video

a. Watch the video and **identify** where and when chicken tikka masala was invented.

b. Say how people feel about the dish today.

◀ Chicken tikka masala served with rice and naan bread.

2 Bollywood, bhangra and Britishness

WB → p. 25

Doc 1

▲ Bollywood dance company Sapnay performing on the TV show *Britain's Got Talent*. Their dance act "Bollywest Fusion" mixed Bollywood and hip-hop dancing.

Home away from home

March 04, 2016 in Collaboration

In collaboration with Sapnay, Bollywood dance[1] company, I tried to document how they have retained their cultural identities over the years in the United Kingdom. While they have managed[2] to find a balance between both the Indian and the British culture, they have also connected quite well with the people of the United Kingdom. Mrs. Ash Oberoi says, "Everyone has the right to know and understand their roots and origin".

Comment *0 likes* *Share*

▲ Blog post by Shivaani Shashi, photographer.

1. dance used in Indian films 2. succeeded

TEAM WORK

Team A

a. **Look** at the picture and **say** what is special about the performance (**doc 1**).

b. **Read** the text and **identify** what the dance company has been successful in doing.

Team B

a. **Listen** and **find out** about the musician (**doc 2**).

b. **Identify** his musical inspirations and **explain** why his music has become so famous.

c. **Share** what you learned and **define** what "fusion" is.

AT HOME Watch Sapnay's "Bollywest Fusion" act and/or **listen** to Panjabi MC's famous bhangra music.

Video
college.nathan.fr/**3sb25a**
college.nathan.fr/**3sb25b**

▼ British Indian musician Panjabi MC playing his worldwide hit "Mundian To Bach Ke", from his album *Legalised* (1998).

Doc 2

Audio

YOUR MISSION

Write a review about an Indian event in the UK for a British-Indian blog site.

1. **Choose** a musical, dance or culinary event and **describe** it for the readers.
2. **Comment** on the event and **persuade** your readers to try it too!

WB → p. 27

Build your skills! Décrire un événement

➔ Utilise le présent simple pour évoquer des faits ou des généralités : *Panjabi MC's album still* ***sounds*** *fresh.* • *The Indian influence on British food* ***is*** *so extensive and deep.*

➔ Incite les lecteurs à partager cette expérience avec des impératifs : ***Relax*** *with friends!* • ***Enjoy*** *a great selection of food!*

BUILD YOUR ENGLISH → p. 27

QUIZ Test
college.nathan.fr/**3sb25c**

Snakes and ladders

EXO Interactive game
college.nathan.fr/**3sb26**

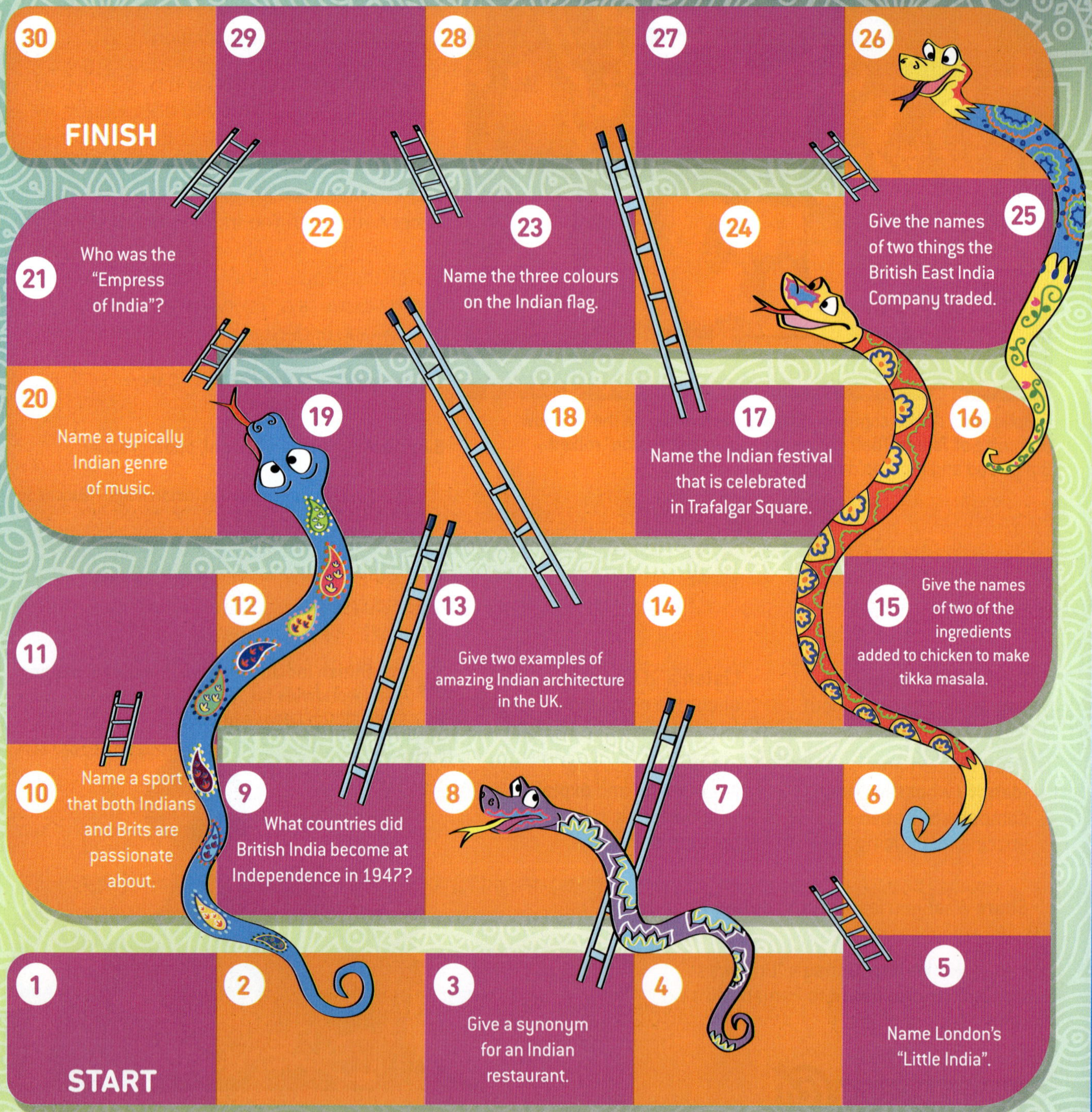

How to play

- **Get into teams** of 4 players.
- **Roll** the dice and **move** your counter forward the same number of squares.
- When you **arrive at the bottom of a ladder**, try to **answer** the question. If you answer correctly, you can **move** to the **top** of the ladder! If you get the answer wrong, you just continue to play normally.
- If you **arrive at the top of a snake** (the square with the snake's head) you have to **go down** to the bottom and continue playing from there!
- To win, you must be the first player to reach square 30.

EXERCISES ➜ p. 166

A Évoquer des faits présents à l'aide du présent simple et du présent en *be* + V-*ing*

Grammar tuto

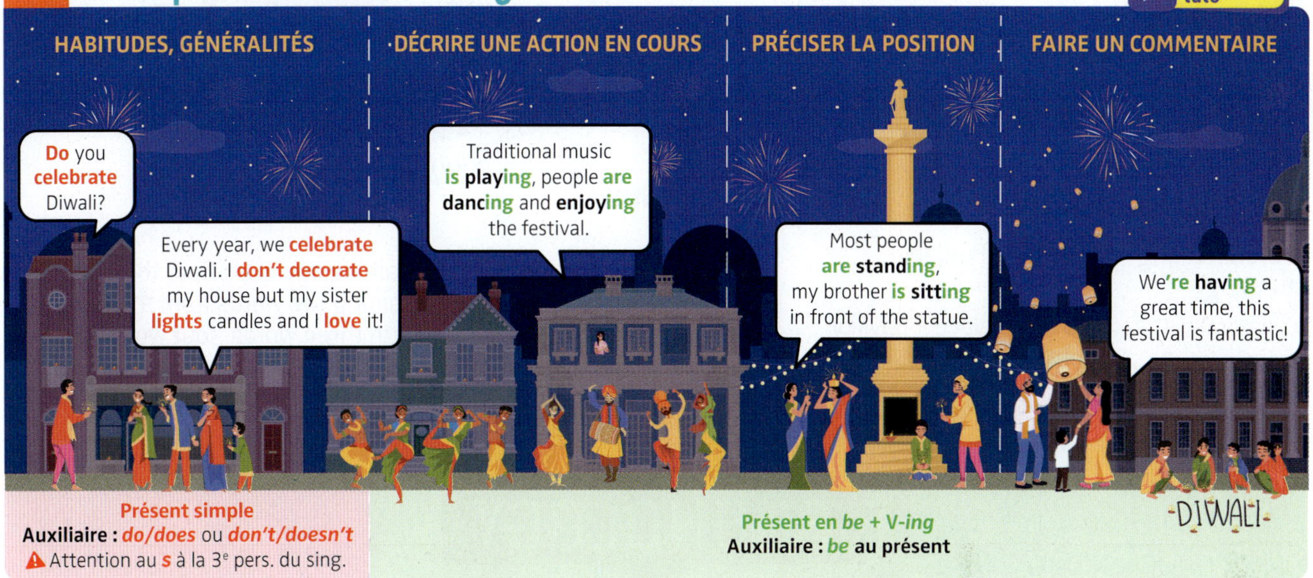

1 Choisis entre les deux formes de présent proposées et justifie ton choix.

a. A lot of British people drink / are drinking tea and eat / are eating curry because of the Indian influence.

b. Look at them! They stand / are standing in the streets, and enjoy / are enjoying the parade. They have / are having fun together.

c. Many British Indians have / are having restaurants and they cook / are cooking their specialties to perfection.

d. Today, I visit / am visiting my British Indian friends who compete / are competing in a cricket match.

2 Mets les verbes en bleu au présent simple ou en *be* + V-*ing* selon la situation.

a. I (love) learning about Indian culture. Today, I (visit) an Indian temple.

b. The Royal Pavillion (look) like an Indian monument. People (come) from all over England to visit it.

c. I usually (not / eat) curry, but this one (be) delicious! I (enjoy) it!

HOW TO SHINE IN GRAMMAR ➜ p. 150

B Exprimer l'admiration ou la surprise grâce aux tournures exclamatives

Ces tournures exclamatives se construisent avec ***so***, ***such***, ***how*** et ***what***.

	Sujet + Verbe + Tournure exclamative	Tournure exclamative (+ Sujet + Verbe)
Intensifieur + Adjectif	So + Adjectif *It is becoming so popular!*	How + Adjectif *How delicious (this curry is)!*
Intensifieur + a(n) + GN	Such + a(n) + Adjectif + Nom *It's such a great festival!*	What + a(n) + Adjectif + Nom *What an amazing temple (this is)!* *What amazing temples (these are)!*

3 Termine les phrases en montrant ton admiration à l'aide des amorces suggérées.

a. I discovered Punjabi music last week. This is such…

b. I tasted homemade curry. What…

c. Indian culture is rich. It's so…

d. My friend took me to Diwali celebrations in Trafalgar Square. How…

4 Transforme la partie en bleu en une tournure exclamative pour montrer ton admiration.

a. This festival is very colourful.

b. The Indian community in London is very present.

c. Cricket is really fun!

d. Tea is very popular.

HOW TO SHINE IN GRAMMAR ➜ p. 148

VOCABULARY

EXERCISES → p. 167

1 Name it!

a. Something you add to a dish to give it flavour: ...

b. When the elements of different cultures meet (in music, dance, cooking...): ...

c. An Indian restaurant: ...

d. Someone who comes to a new country to live there: ...

2 Find the odd one out.

a. breathtaking • amazing • Punjabi • stunning

b. festival • stately home • palace • pavilion

c. roast • heat • serve • visit

d. roots • traditions • culture • produce

3 Separate the words.

diasporacelebrateculturecommunityfestivitiescosmopolitanfusionethnicintegratelegacy

4 Word battle

In pairs:

Partner A invents a sentence containing one word from the wordmap.
Partner B invents a sentence containing two words from the wordmap.
Take turns inventing sentences with three words, four words, etc., until partner A or B capitulates.

HOW TO SHINE IN VOCABULARY → p. 160

PHONOLOGY

A La prononciation du <s> final

• **À la fin des mots, la lettre <s>** peut se prononcer soit /s/, soit /z/, soit /ɪz/. La réalisation de ce son se fait naturellement en fonction du son précédent le **<s>** final. La règle est la même pour le pluriel des noms, les verbes au présent simple et les noms finissant par **<s>**.

Son précédant le <s>	/p/, /k/, /f/, /t/	/z/ ou /s/ /tʃ/ ou /ʃ/	Tous les autres sons !
Prononciation du <s>	/s/	/ɪz/	/z/
Exemples	stops • asks • laughs • creates	organises • dances • watches • washes	signs • lives • curries

1 Écoute et répète ces mots finissant par <s> et indique leur prononciation pour chacun. AUDIO

festivals • restaurants • songs • dances • traditions • Indians • minorities • museums

2 Anticipe la prononciation des mots en bleu, puis écoute et vérifie. AUDIO

a. She loves discovering traditional dances and dishes so she tastes two different curries every week and goes to festivals every two months.

b. Monuments and traditions are keys to understanding a culture and its characteristics.

HOW TO SHINE IN PHONOLOGY → p. 156

B L'accentuation des tournures exclamatives

• Dans les tournures exclamatives, on **accentue** à l'oral les **mots-clés** sur lesquels on veut insister : ici, les adjectifs. **L'intonation** des phrases exclamatives est **descendante**.

• Such an **amazing** place! ↘

• **So** beautiful! ↘

3 Écoute et répète ces phrases en veillant à bien accentuer les tournures exclamatives. AUDIO

a. Indian culture is so rich! What an amazing country!

b. Taking part in Diwali is such an incredible experience: how stunning!

4 Lis ces phrases, repère les tournures exclamatives et anticipe leur accentuation, puis écoute et vérifie. AUDIO

a. Cricket is such a popular sport in India! People are so enthusiastic!

b. What a beautiful song! How breathtaking... I'm so moved!

HOW TO SHINE IN PHONOLOGY → p. 159

WORDMAP

WB ➜ p. 15

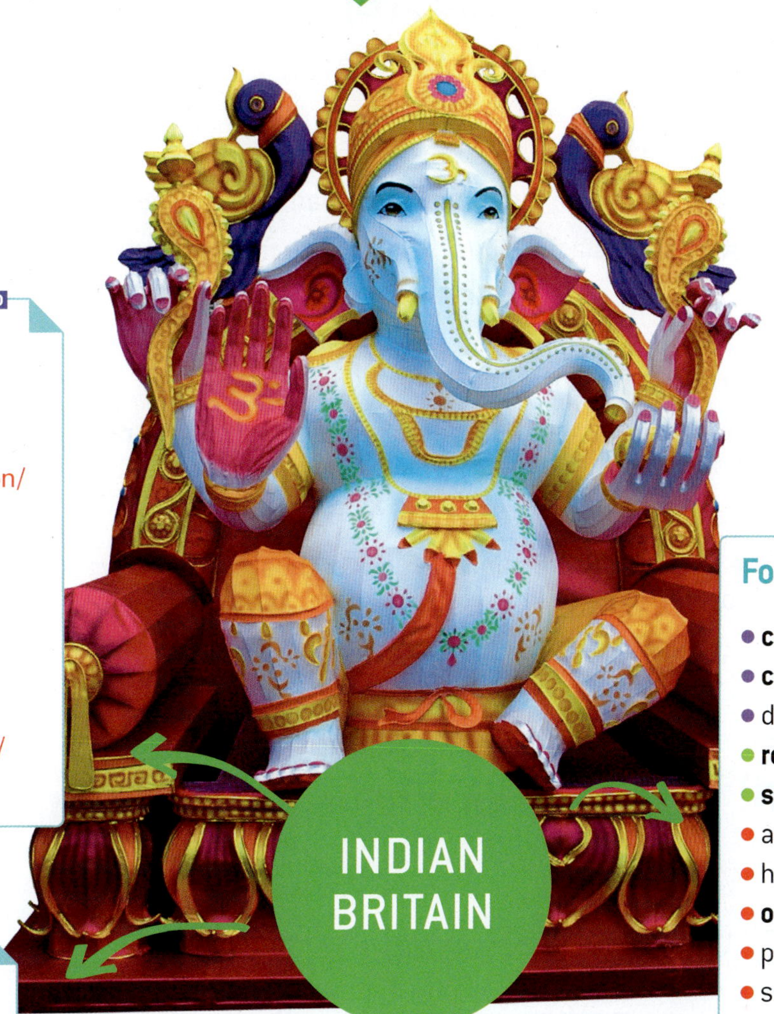

INDIAN BRITAIN

People

AUDIO

- com**mu**nity
- mi**no**rity
- popu**la**tion /ˌpɒpjə'leɪʃən/
- **A**sian /'eɪʒən/ : *indo-pakistanais (ici)*
- Bangla**desh**i
- **Bri**tish **In**dian
- **Hin**du /'hɪnduː/
- **In**dian
- Paki**sta**ni /ˌpɑːkɪ'stɑːni/
- Sikh /siːk/

Food

AUDIO

- **cor**ner shop
- **cur**ry house
- dish
- **roas**ted
- **spi**cy
- add
- heat /hiːt/
- **or**der /'ɔːdə/
- pour /pɔː/
- serve

Immigration

AUDIO

- de**scent** /dɪ'sent/
- dia**spo**ra /daɪ'æspərə/
- **imm**igrant
- immi**gra**tion /ˌɪmɪ'greɪʃən/
- mix
- roots
- cosmo**pol**itan
- **cul**tural
- **eth**nic
- over**seas**
- call home
- **in**tegrate

Tourism

AUDIO

- **ar**chitecture /'ɑːrkɪtɛktʃə/
- **gift**shop
- mu**se**um
- **must**-do
- **must**-see
- **pa**lace
- pa**vil**ion /pə'vɪliən/
- **re**sidence
- **scen**ery /'siːnəri/
- a**maz**ing
- **beau**tiful
- **breath**taking /'breθˌteɪkɪŋ/
- **stun**ning
- im**press**

Culture

AUDIO

- **bhan**gra /'bæŋgrə/
- **Bol**lywood
- **cri**cket
- faith
- **fes**tival
- fes**ti**vities
- **fu**sion /'fjuːʒən/
- **le**gacy = **her**itage
- per**for**mance
- tra**di**tion
- au**then**tic /ɔː'θentɪk/
- **ce**lebrate
- come to**geth**er

● NOUN ● ADJECTIVE ● VERB

YOUR FINAL MISSION

Write an enthusiastic travel blog post to encourage visitors to discover Indian Britain.

WB → p. 28

→ You have discovered a lot of of fascinating information about Indian Britain.
→ **Create** and **post** an enthusiastic blog article about it to inspire others!

STEP 1 ▶ **Write** a short introduction about Indian Britain. You can use information about the British Indians living in the UK.

STEP 2 ▶ **Pick** the places or things you want to concentrate on, and **research** extra information about them. What? Where? When? How? Why?

STEP 3 ▶ **Prepare** recommendations and ideas for your readers.

STEP 4 ▶ **Write** the article and **communicate** your enthusiasm using ways you discovered in the file.

YES YOU CAN!

Write an enthusiastic blog article.

1 Le titre
Choisis un titre court et percutant, qui donne envie de lire l'article.

2 L'introduction
Commence ton article en parlant de la présence indienne au Royaume-Uni.

3 La structure
Dresse une liste des activités ou visites que tu as choisies.

LONDON'S SECRET LITTLE INDIA

Posted on October 20, 2016 by Alex

facebook | twitter | email

Those looking for Indian culture in London will most likely visit top-reviewed Indian restaurants or one of the religious temples such as the one in Soho. [...] A more authentic experience could be found in actual South Asian areas; one of these is Southall, a West London district which was home to the first pub in the country to accept rupees[1] as payment. Here you can listen to bhangra[2] and visit a gurdwara[3] whilst enjoying a proper curry, if you think you can handle the spice. [...]

If there's something sub-continental you're seeking, you'll probably find it. Though most of what populates the area are spice shops, there are sweet shops too, with a range of delicacies for sale: halwa, barfi, ladoo, jalebi[4], etc. [...]

For music there's Jas Musicals, which sells gig-ready sitars and Indian bansaris[5] as well as plenty of CDs covering a range of Indian traditions. [...]

Southall is also home to Sri Guru Singh Sabha Gurdwara – the largest Sikh temple outside of India. [...]

Diwali is almost definitely the best time to visit Southall, with street activities and festivities taking place all over the area.

marblearchbymontcalm.co.uk/blog

6 Le partage
Donne la possibilité de partager ton article sur les réseaux sociaux !

5 L'illustration
Choisis une photo qui illustre bien tes propos.

4 Le style
Utilise des structures exclamatives pour montrer ton enthousiasme.
Such an amazing place!
So beautiful!

HOW TO SHINE IN WRITING → p. 140

Test your skills!

Compréhension de l'oral

B1 OBJECTIF Comprendre un reportage

Video

A2 **1** **Listen** and **identify** the topic of the video.

2 **Say** which people are concerned.

A2+ **3** **Explain** what the festival represents.

B1 **4** **Pick out** the different numbers and what they mean.

5 **Find** reasons for people to visit the site referred to during the festivities.

Compréhension de l'écrit

B1 OBJECTIF Comprendre un article historique

Cricket, curry and cups of tea: India's influence on Victorian Britain

The Victorian era saw Britons falling in love with the culture of the subcontinent, and it seems that the people took their prompt[1] from the very top. Queen Victoria herself declared a great interest in the Empire's largest possession and greatest trading[2] partner, so helping to popularise Indian delicacies, fashion, jewellery and architecture. [...]

Victoria's interest in India sprang, at least in part, from her Indian assistant Abdul Karim, who came to Britain in 1887 to serve the queen. He rose within Victoria's affections, as well as in status to the title of 'Munshi' (teacher or clerk), teaching the Queen Hindi and Urdu[3] and advising on all matters concerning India.

Karim was one of a steady stream[4] of Indian migrants coming to Britain during the 19th century (estimates suggest more than 110,000), including domestics, maritime workers, petitioners, performers, royalty, social reformers, students and travellers.

It was during the Victorian period that Britons fell in love with curry, a culinary concoction that is today Britain's favourite dish. [...] Curry wasn't the only Indian delicacy to delight the British palate. By 1900, Indian and Sri Lankan tea accounted for 90 per cent of Britain's tea imports, a fact reflected in a marketing campaign for Lipton tea, which featured an Indian female plantation worker and sandwich-board[5] men dressed as Indians.

Shompa Lahiri, *History Extra*, 2017

A2 **1** **Identify** the author and the date of publication of the article.

2 **Find** the name of Queen Victoria's Indian assistant and **say** when he came to Britain.

A2+ **3** **Make a list** of Indian things that the Victorian public loved.

B1 **4** **Describe** how Queen Victoria's assistant's role evolved.

5 **Explain** why British people adopted the Indian influence so easily.

1. example
2. commercial
3. Indian languages
4. *flot*
5. advertisement tool consisting of two boards

QUIZ Test de positionnement
college.nathan.fr/3sb31

SNAPFILE 3

Go New Zealand girls!

▶ How are New Zealand women leading the way in terms of gender equality?

YOUR SNAP MISSION

Write the life story of an inspiring New Zealand woman for Purple Power Week.

1 Purple Power Week

WB → p. 29

Doc 1 Video

a. **Look** at the picture (**doc 1**) and **guess** what Purple Power Week is about.

b. **Watch** the video and **find** information about the event.

c. **Read** the text (**doc 2**) and **comment** on the Week's evolution.

d. **Recap** what you have learnt about this event.

Doc 2

With the support of Prime Minister Jacinda Ardern, journalist Hilary Barry and dozens of other influential Kiwis[1], we here at Wellington East Girls College are launching[2] a national movement that we want you to be a part of. Our movement – Purple Power Week – which advocates for[3] the empowerment[4] of women, is now set to go nationwide.

Purple Power Week was established at Wellington East in 2015 by our then head girl Olive Brown to celebrate girl power and to encourage students to wear their feminism on their sleeve[5]. Olive recognised a few issues in the region surrounding confidence, body image and mental health, so she did something about it. Over the past five years, the Week has only become bigger and more exciting.

Hariette Boucher & Lorna Hallett, *stuff.co.nz*, 2020

1. New Zealanders 2. starting 3. supports 4. process of gaining power and freedom 5. openly show an opinion

AT HOME **Visit** this website and **write** a list of interesting facts about New Zealand.

Website
college.nathan.fr/3sb32

2 Leading the way

WB DIFFÉRENCIATION → p. 30

Doc 1 — Video

▲ Kate Sheppard, New Zealand, 1893.

a. **Study** the picture and **guess** who Kate Sheppard was.

b. **Watch** the video and **say** why the house is important.

c. **Explain** what makes New Zealand a special place regarding women's rights.

Doc 2 — Video

▲ Dame Whina Cooper and her granddaughter Irenee marching to Parliament, 1975.

GRAMMAR SPOT

When they **came** across the Auckland bridge, it **was swaying** with the amount of people...

Observe les deux formes du prétérit. Analyse leur formation. Quelle forme utilise-t-on pour commenter une action ?

TEAM WORK

Team A

a. **Look** at the picture (**doc 2**), **watch** the video and **give** the reason for the march.

Team B

a. **Read** the text (**doc 3**) and **identify** the objective of the march.

b. **Share** with the other team and **say** what shows the march was a success.

Doc 3

On 14 September 1975, fifty marchers left Te Hāpua[1] in the far north of Aotearoa[2] New Zealand for the 1,000 km walk to Parliament Buildings in Wellington. The hīkoi (march) was organised to raise awareness about the catastrophic loss of Māori land rights since colonisation. Led by 79-year-old Dame Whina Cooper, the hīkoi grew in strength as local people joined in along the way. About 5,000 marchers arrived at Parliament on 13 October, where they presented a petition signed by 60,000 people to Prime Minister Bill Rowling.

Rachel Sayers, *corpus.nz*, 2018

1. Māori community 2. Māori name for "New Zealand"

YOUR SNAP MISSION — STEP 1

You are a member of the team organising Purple Power Week in your school. Choose a picture of an inspiring New Zealand woman and introduce her to the class.

1. **Describe** the picture and **explain** what it says about the woman you have chosen.
2. **Find out** about the great things she did and **tell** the class about it.

WB → p. 32

Build your skills! **Décrire une scène passée**

- Utilise le prétérit en *be* + V-*ing* pour commenter ce qui se passait : *That bridge* ***was swaying*** *with the amount of people who* ***were crossing*** *it.* • *They* ***were*** *all* ***being led*** *by this old woman.*
- Exprime un point de vue personnel en insistant sur l'effet produit : *It was* ***the most emotional*** *experience …* • *What* ***I remember most*** *about it …*

BUILD YOUR ENGLISH → p. 36

3 Getting there

WB → p. 33

Doc 1 — Video

1. Māori word for "woman"

a. **Explain** why Angela Swann-Cronin is on the magazine cover.
b. **Watch** the video and **give** information about her career.
c. **Pick out** words and sentences showing the difficulties she encountered.
d. **Explain** why she can be considered a role model.

CULTURE SPOT

Jacinda Ardern, who was born in 1980 in New Zealand, was elected **Prime Minister** in 2017. She became the world's youngest female **head of government** at age 37.

a. **Read** the article and **explain** who Jacinda Ardern is.
b. **Comment** on the impact her choices will have on future generations.

GRAMMAR SPOT

- I know women **who** thought of Ardern...
- There were some gentlemen **that** didn't like me there...

À quoi servent les mots en gras ? Comment sont-ils appelés ?

Doc 2

The important legacy of Prime Minister Jacinda Ardern having a baby while in office

Michelle Duff · 12:43, Jun 21 2019

In having a baby while holding the top job in the country, Ardern has not only shown us it can be done but also that there's no reason why it shouldn't be. I know women who thought of Ardern and asked themselves: "Why can't I apply for[1] that promotion now, even if I am pregnant[2]?" Men who have looked to Gayford and thought: "If he can stay home and look after a baby, so can I."

Prime Minister Jacinda Ardern speaks at the 2018 United Nations General Assembly, while her partner Clarke Gayford looks after their daughter Neve.

1. *postuler à* 2. expecting a baby

4 Lord – with an 'e'

WB DIFFÉRENCIATION → p. 34

Doc 1

AUDIO VERSION

Once there was a girl who didn't plan to be a singer. Her name was Ella, and she lived in Auckland. She loved drama[1] lessons and reading.

Ella read so many books that she was chosen for Kids' Lit Quiz, and her team came runner-up[2] in the world finals. By now Ella was sure she'd be a writer.

But things don't always turn out how you think.

At intermediate school, Ella and a friend sang and played in the talent quest. They won. Then they were asked to sing on afternoon radio. Next thing, Ella was signed up for development with Universal Music Group.

For development? thought Ella. *Okay I guess it means singing lessons.*

She listened to jazz and soul music.

She played CDs of Fleetwood Mac, and far too many other great groups and musicians to say in a hundred breaths. She co-wrote songs with her friend Joel. She tried writing her own songs, too, but somehow[3] they didn't make her feel satisfied.

At last it was time to record an EP, and Ella had to find a stage name[4]. Lord – with an 'e' – she decided. Lorde.

On free download, Lorde released *The Love Club*, four songs she co-wrote with Joel. One of them was called 'Royals'. It was about being happy and ordinary, not envious of the super-rich and super-famous, about loving just being with your friends. The EP had 60,000 hits[5].

Then Universal Music Group released it for sale.

Three months later, Universal released 'Royals' on its own. Sales went crazy.

Lorde, only 16 years old, had a number-one hit. The song expressed something in the hearts of young people all over the world.

Ella kept trying to write her own songs. They still didn't work for her. Then she read some short stories and something clicked. Finally, she understood how to make words say what she wanted.

Lyrics and music began pouring out of[6] her. She wrote about being young with her friends, how it felt and what it meant. Her words, her voice and her music came together.

Things didn't turn out how Ella expected. They turned out better. She's a singer and writer – a writer of songs.

Barbara ELSE, *Go Girl: A storybook of epic NZ women*, 2018

1. theatre 2. second 3. for a reason that is not clear 4. pseudonym 5. clicks 6. coming from in great quantity

a. Read the text (doc 1) and **give** information about Lorde's career.

b. Watch the video (doc 2) and **comment** on her stage name.

PHONOLOGY SPOT

hated • loved • sounded • liked

AUDIO

Écoute ces mots. Comment se prononce la terminaison *-ed* dans chaque cas ?

Doc 2 — Video

YOUR SNAP MISSION — STEP 2

Write the life story of an inspiring woman for the school newspaper.

1. **Gather** all the information you found about the celebrity you selected in step 1, p. 33.
2. **Write** an article about her life and achievements.

Build your skills! **Rédiger une biographie**

- Utilise le prétérit simple pour évoquer des actions passées : *At intermediate school, Ella and a friend **sang** and **played** in the talent quest. They **won**.*
- Emploie des propositions relatives pour éviter les répétitions : *Once there was a girl **who** didn't plan…* • *There were some gentlemen **that** didn't like…*

WB → p. 36 HOW TO SHINE IN WRITING → p. 140 BUILD YOUR ENGLISH → p. 36

QUIZ Test college.nathan.fr/3sb35

GRAMMAR

+ EXERCISES → p. 167

A Évoquer des faits du passé à l'aide du prétérit simple ou du prétérit en *be* + V-*ing*

Grammar tuto

Prétérit simple
Évoquer des faits passés sans les commenter.

1975

50 marchers **left** Te Hāpua on 14 September 1975.

People **joined** them along the way.

They **arrived** at Parliament on 13 October 1975.

Prétérit en *be* + V-*ing*
Décrire une situation en cours dans le passé.

The bridge **was swaying** with the amount of people who **were crossing** it.

Alternance des 2 prétérits
Évoquer une action en cours interrompue par une action plus ponctuelle.

Dame Whina Cooper **was leading** the march when they **arrived** in Wellington.

1 **Mets les verbes entre parenthèses au prétérit simple ou au prétérit en *be* + V-*ing*.**

a. This (be) incredible: so many people (demonstrate) in the streets.

b. As they (fight) for their rights, they (come) upon obstacles.

c. First they (decide) to take action; then they (launch) a movement; finally they (go) to Parliament.

d. Some people (criticise) Jacinda Arden because she (have) a baby while she (hold) a high position.

2 **Utilise ces éléments pour écrire des phrases au prétérit simple ou au prétérit en *be* + V-*ing*.**

Sujets : Jacinda Arden • Lorde • Dame Whina Cooper • Women

Verbes : fight for their rights • defend a cause • meet opponents • get criticism • walk to Wellington • help a cause • take action • raise awareness

Marqueurs de temps : As... • While... • When... • Then... After... Finally...

HOW TO SHINE IN GRAMMAR → p. 150

B Relier deux phrases avec les pronoms relatifs

→ Le pronom relatif dépend de l'antécédent et de la fonction qu'il occupe dans la subordonnée relative : sujet ou complément.

Antécédent	Pronom relatif sujet	Pronom relatif complément
Humain	*The person **who spoke** was Dame Whina Cooper.*	*The woman **(that) I met** was Dame Whina Cooper.*
Objet	*The speech **that / which triggered** the movement was very powerful.*	*The speech **(that) she delivered** was so touching.*
Lieu		*The parliament **where we met** was impressive.*
Moment		*The moment **when she appeared** was decisive.*
Phrase entière	*They signed a petition, **which is** courageous.*	*They signed a petition, **which I find** courageous.*

3 **Complète les phrases avec le relatif qui convient.**

a. Women are powerful in New Zealand, ... is unusual in other parts of the world.

b. Lorde is a singer ... is a feminist.

c. Purple Power Week is a project ... is supported by Wellington students

d. This is the Parliament ... Dame Whina Cooper arrived.

e. The bridge ... they crossed was swaying.

HOW TO SHINE IN GRAMMAR → p. 154

VOCABULARY

EXERCISES ➜ p. 167

Fighting for equality

AUDIO

- **fe**male /ˈfiːmeɪl/ vote
- **fe**minism
- glass **cei**ling
- pio**neer** /ˌpaɪəˈnɪə/
- **suf**frage
- em**pow**ering
- in**spi**ring /ɪnˈspaɪərɪŋ/
- break through /θruː/
- en**cou**rage
- fight for
- pro**mote**
- sup**port**

Getting involved

AUDIO

- **le**gacy = **her**itage
- **so**vereignty /ˈsɒvrɪnti/
- **or**dinary ≠ ex**traor**dinary
- **sa**tisfied ≠ dis**sa**tisfied
- do **some**thing for **some**body
- express **some**thing in one's heart
- lend a **help**ing hand: *donner un coup de main*
- raise a**ware**ness
- show **some**thing can be done

Inspiring life stories

AUDIO

- at**tempt**
- role **mo**del
- **preg**nant
- a**chieve**
- be born
- be **bu**ried /ˈberid/
- fail
- fight hard
- grow up
- **qua**lify
- re**tire** /rɪˈtaɪə/
- suc**ceed** in V-ing

Careers and jobs

AUDIO

- ca**reer**
- flight at**ten**dant
- **pi**lot
- poli**ti**cian /ˌpɒləˈtɪʃən/
- Prime **Mi**nister
- pro**mo**tion
- **bril**liant
- suc**cess**ful
- ap**ply** for
- plan to be
- stay home

Get into pairs!
Partner A **Name a historical figure.**
Partner B **Tell his or her life story using as many words or expressions from the wordmap as possible. Then, swap roles.**

● NOUN ● ADJECTIVE ● VERB

HOW TO SHINE IN VOCABULARY ➜ p. 160

PHONOLOGY

La prononciation de la terminaison *-ed*

- La **terminaison *-ed*** du **prétérit**, ainsi que du **participe passé** des verbes réguliers, peut se prononcer soit /t/, soit /d/, soit /ɪd/.

Son précédant *-ed*	/p/, /k/, /f/, /s/, /tʃ/ ou /ʃ/	/t/ ou /d/	Tous les autres sons !
Prononciation de *-ed*	/t/	/ɪd/	/d/
Exemples	*stopped • blocked • laughed • missed • marched • washed*	*invited • decided • started*	*signed • lived • claimed*

1 **Écoute et répète ces verbes, puis classe-les selon la prononciation de la terminaison *-ed*.** AUDIO

worked • decided • organised • swayed • watched • waited • started • stayed

2 **Anticipe la prononciation de ces verbes au prétérit, puis écoute et vérifie.** AUDIO

They **needed** help because they **wanted** change, that is why many people **supported** them as they **reached** Parliament and **signed** the petition.

HOW TO SHINE IN PHONOLOGY ➜ p. 156

FILE 4 Teen entrepreneurs

How do US teens feel encouraged to create?

More on SPEAKEASY NEWS
speakeasy-news.com

> "I believe age is just a number. If you have an idea, no matter how old you are, you have the power to change the world."

Samaira Mehta (13 years old)
Tech entrepreneur, founder of Coder Bunnyz and Boss Bizz Entrepreneurship Academy

YOUR FINAL MISSION

Act out an interview between a journalist and a teen entrepreneur for *Entrepreneur* magazine.

Video

"Inspiring teen business ideas", *TRUiC*, 2021.

TEAM WORK

WB → p. 37

Team A
Look at the drawings and **guess** what the girl is thinking about.

Team B
Read the quote and **explain** what it means in your own words.

Team C
Watch the video and **find out** what is encouraged.

- Now **share** what you studied with the class. What does it inspire in you?

EXPLORE The USA: a nation of young entrepreneurs

1 The lemonade stand tradition

WB DIFFÉRENCIATION → p. 38

Doc 1 Video

1. dollars 2. *offre*

a. Look at the cartoon. **Identify** and **describe** the situation. **Explain** Calvin's state of mind.

b. Watch the video and **pick out** what makes a successful lemonade stand.

c. Comment on the result of the lemonade stand (money earned, donation).

GRAMMAR SPOT

What do you do with the money you make? • Do you want to run your own business as an adult?

De quel type de phrases s'agit-il ? Rappelle l'ordre des mots.

a. Read the text and **explain** what "Lemonade Day" is.

b. Compare Avery's lemonade stand to the girl's in the video (**doc 1**).

c. Present the "Triple S Method" and give your opinion.

Doc 2 AUDIO VERSION

Kids who rock Lemonade Day

An estimated 10,000 children will participate this year in ***Lemonade Day Indianapolis*** *on May 21. We wanted to know: who are the young minds behind some of the successful stands in the city?*

Avery Huggins, 9, Carmel

What's the name of your stand and its location?

Lemons, Limes and Bow Ties. I will be located in front of the Carmel Arts Council Children's Gallery on Main Street in Carmel.

What's the coolest thing about Lemonade Day?

I get to choose what to do with my profits using the Triple S Method — spend, share and save.

What do you do with the money you make?

This year, I will be sharing most of my profits with two local charities[1], the Woodland Christmas Club and Camp Saturday. The money I save will go toward buying parts to build a new computer. And I was thinking of spending some money on taking my mom out to lunch for all of the hard work she puts into helping me, but I'm still deciding on that one. [...]

Do you want to run your own business as an adult? If so, what kind?

Yes! I want to have a video game-making business. I would love to design video games and even card games. My friends and I talk about this at lunch. I will be the CEO[2]!

Maureen C. Gilmer, *indystar.com*, 18 May 2016

1. *associations caritatives*
2. Chief Executive Officer = *PDG*

2 The entrepreneurial spirit

WB → p. 40

Have you always hoped to have enough money to buy what you want? Open a business and you can! You'll earn more money in business than you'll make in allowance[1] over the next fifty years! In a free country, anyone can open a business—even you. You may believe you can't do anything to make money except deliver newspapers or flip[2] burgers. Change your thinking. Become a part of the free-enterprise system!

Daryl BERNSTEIN (15 years old),
Better than a Lemonade Stand, 2012

a. **Read** the extract from the book and **identify** who the author is and who the readers are.

b. **Rephrase** the author's message.

c. **Comment** on the use of *you* and the imperative forms (*change*, *become*) and **explain** its effect on the readers.

1. pocket money 2. cook

3 United States of Teenpreneurs

WB → p. 40

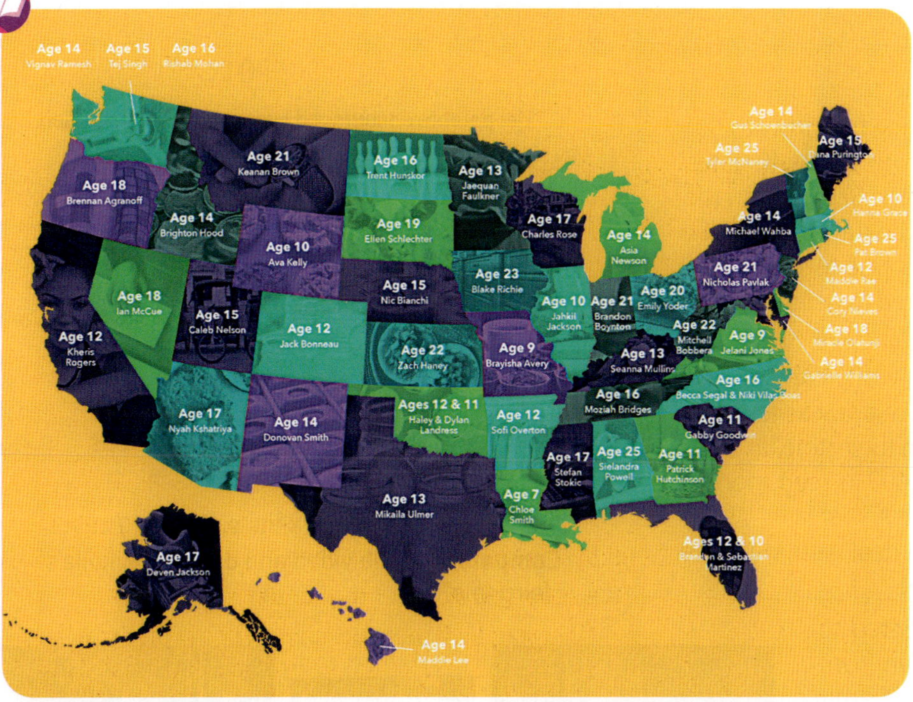

◀ "The 50 youngest kid entrepreneurs in the US", *business.org*, 2019.

a. **Observe** the document and **explain** what it is about.

b. **Read** the ages on the map and **justify** the expression "United States of Teenpreneurs."

YOUR MISSION

Act out a conversation with your best friend about opening a lemonade stand this weekend.

Partner A **Try** to convince your partner to open a lemonade stand. **Make** a list of arguments. **Think** of what you can learn, earn, etc.

Partner B **Listen** to the arguments and **ask** questions to make your own decision.

Build your skills! **Convaincre quelqu'un**

- Pose des questions pour interpeller et faire réfléchir : *Have you always hoped to have enough money to buy what you want?*
- Utilise le modal ***will*** pour évoquer les perspectives : *I **will** be sharing most of my profits with two local charities… • The money I save **will** go toward buying parts to build a new computer.*

WB → p. 40 HOW TO SHINE IN INTERACTING → p. 142 BUILD YOUR ENGLISH → p. 47

QUIZ Test college.nathan.fr/3sb41

EXPLORE Good enough, old enough

1 Becoming a bees-ness girl

WB DIFFÉRENCIATION → p. 41

Doc 1 — Video

a. **Watch** the video and **pick out** information about Mikaila.

b. **Explain** what makes her lemonade stand special.

c. **Focus** on the way the story is told and **say** what type of story it reminds you of.

Doc 2

"It's rare for a beverage company to start with $50 and grow to being sold in 2,500 stores across 40 states," says Mikaila Ulmer, CEO[1] of Me & the Bees Lemonade. It's rarer still for that company to be run by a 15-year-old. "Age didn't faze[2] me when it came to starting my business," she says. "I was just excited to get started." [...]

She got the attention of Whole Foods[3] when she began teaching free pollination workshops for kids there. "They said if I could figure out[4] a way to bottle my product, they could carry it in their store." In 2015, at age nine, Ulmer secured $60,000 in seed money[5] on ABC's reality show *Shark Tank*. A year later, Whole Foods announced a distribution deal with Me & the Bees for $11 million.

"When I started, I never expected to appear on *Shark Tank* or speak in front of 20,000 people or meet Barack Obama, but I did!" says Ulmer. Her future goals are as lofty[6] ("I want to see my product in all 50 states!"), but her focus is clear: "I want my business to always be more than just lemonade—I want to have an even bigger impact on saving the bees."

Christina Izzo, *rachaelraymag.com*, 2020

1. Chief Executive Officer = *PDG*
2. worry
3. a large American chain of supermarkets
4. find
5. *capital de départ*
6. ambitious

GRAMMAR SPOT

- Her parents **encouraged her to enter** a competition.
- I **want my business to always be** more than just lemonade—I **want to have** an even bigger impact on saving the bees.

Observe comment sont construites les expressions en gras. Que permettent d'exprimer ces structures ?

a. **Read** the text and **pick out** different steps in the evolution of Mikaila's business.

b. **Comment** on her feelings.

c. **Compare** with the video and **discuss** Mikaila's "fairy tale".

▲ Mikaila presenting her business during the TV show *Shark Tank*.

2 Helping the community

WB → p. 44

Doc 1 Video

▲ Mahsa Riar, founder of Limitless Limb.

Team A

a. **Watch** the video (**doc 1**) and **pick out** information about Mahsa Riar's business.

b. **Explain** the advantages of 3D-printed limbs compared to traditional prosthetics.

Team B

a. **Read** the article (**doc 2**) and **pick out** information about Adom Appiah's nonprofit organisation.

b. **Explain** what Adom Appiah's plans are for his organisation.

c. **Share** your information with the other team. **Explain** how the teenagers help their communities.

Doc 2

Adom Appiah, 17, a Spartanburg[1] philanthropist[2], traveled to New York City where he was honored by ESPN[3] for his work as creator of the sports-centered nonprofit[4], Ball4Good, at the ESPN Humanitarian Awards ceremony. [...]

Appiah started Ball4Good during a seventh-grade project assigned by teacher Kelsea Turner, that challenged students to spend 20 percent of their time in class on a project to give back to their communities. Since then, Ball4Good has raised thousands

of dollars for local charities[5] including The Boys and Girls Club of the Upstate, HALTER, Children's Cancer Partners and Project Hope. [...]

The next Ball4Good effort will be a charity soccer tournament to benefit Sidewalk Hope, Children's Cancer Partners, Tyger River Children's Center and Criminal Justice Youth Institute on Aug. 29. The next Ball4Good basketball tournament is currently set for April 2022. Appiah is confident it will not be the last.

Samantha Swann, *Spartanburg Herald Journal*, 2021

1. city in North Carolina 2. someone who helps people in need 3. sports cable TV company 4. *organisme à but non lucratif* 5. *associations caritatives*

YOUR MISSION

On social media, write a message to a teen entrepreneur to say how inspiring he or she is and what you admire in his or her career and ideas.

1 **Choose** one of the teen entrepreneurs from p. 42-43 and **make** a list of his or her actions.

2 **Write** your message using infinitives to describe the impact of the young entrepreneur's business on your life or on society.

WB → p. 45

Build your skills! **Mettre en avant les caractéristiques d'un projet**

→ Donne des détails grâce aux pronoms relatifs : *Prosthetics* ***that*** *are a lot cheaper…* • *A tournament* ***that*** *would benefit…*

→ Utilise des structures infinitives pour montrer l'impact créé : *We* ***encouraged*** *her* ***to overcome*** *her fears…* • *I* ***want*** *my business* ***to*** *always* ***be*** *more than just lemonade.*

BUILD YOUR ENGLISH → p. 47

QUIZ Test college.nathan.fr/3sb43

EXPLORE Teenspiration

1 Meet an idea girl

WB DIFFÉRENCIATION → p. 46

Doc 1 — Video

◀ Alina Morse, CEO and founder of Zolli Candy.

a. Observe the picture and **guess** who Alina Morse is (age, business).

b. Watch the video and **explain** how she got her business idea.

c. Identify her friends' reactions. **Discuss** her relationship with her friends.

> **PHONOLOGY SPOT** — AUDIO
>
> How <u>did</u> you start a business? • <u>Do</u> they admire you for this?
>
> Écoute ces phrases interrogatives. Que remarques-tu concernant leur intonation ? Comment se prononce *How* ?

Doc 2 — Video

a. Watch the video and **comment** on Alina Morse's daily routine.

b. Pick out the advice given by Alina to other young entrepreneurs.

c. Say what her projects are for the future.

d. Discuss Alina Morse's inspiring role for young entrepreneurs.

2 Keys to success

WB → p. 48

Doc 1

Video

▲ The Yummy Brothers, 2022.

a. **Look** at the picture and **say** all you can about these boys.

b. **Watch** the video and **explain** their secret to success.

c. **Compare** them with Alina Morse (p. 44) and **discuss** their common point.

Doc 2

8 TIPS FOR SUCCESS FROM a Teen Entrepreneur

1 **Action Over Words:** Take action and stop spending months perfecting every little detail on your business plan. Jump in and learn as you go.

2 **Set Realistic Goals:** Your goals need to be challenging but still accomplishable.

3 **Don't Start a Business to Make Money:** Start a business doing what you love and are passionate about.

4 **Connections are Key[1]:** Build a network of people for everything so that way you have a person for everything.

5 **Social Media is Everything.**

6 **Don't Be Afraid to Fail[2]:** Use your failures to motivate you to succeed more.

7 **You Don't Know It All:** Education is a life-long process, nobody knows everything. You should always be willing to take advice and listen to others.

8 **Believe in Yourself:** You can do it, so stop telling yourself you can't.

Adapted from Mary Juetten, *forbes.com*, 2020.

1. very important 2. not succeed

a. **Read** the document and **identify** its target.

b. **Say** which tips were important to the young entrepreneurs from p. 40-45.

c. **Discuss** with the class which tip is the most useful to succeed as a young entrepreneur.

YOUR MISSION

DIFFÉRENCIATION

As a journalist for *Entrepreneur* magazine, record a podcast on how to become a successful teen entrepreneur.

WAY 1

Give five tips to a young entrepreneur who wants to start a cookie company.

WAY 2

Explain the different steps to become a successful young entrepreneur.

WB → p. 49

Build your skills! **Guider et encourager quelqu'un**

→ Exprime des hypothèses avec des subordonnées en *if* : ***If*** *you work hard, you can do anything.* • ***If*** *I have a good attitude, we sell out…*

→ Utilise l'impératif : ***Believe*** *in yourself.* • ***Don't be*** *afraid to fail.* • ***Take*** *action and* ***stop*** *spending months perfecting every little detail…*

BUILD YOUR ENGLISH → p. 47

QUIZ Test
college.nathan.fr/3sb45

GAME ON!

EXO Interactive game
college.nathan.fr/3sb46

THE TEEN ENTREPRENEURS CHARITY CHALLENGE

How to play

- **Play in pairs.**
- You want to start your charity to help your community but you need money!
- **Answer** questions from potential investors so they give you money.
- You have **three minutes** to answer as many questions as you can and raise money for your charity.

1. Give a definition of a charity. — $750
2. Explain what "philanthropist" means? — $750
3. Give 3 expressions using the word "money". — $500
4. You have 30 seconds to give as many tips as possible to succeed as an entrepreneur. — $1,000
5. What can you do to raise money? Give 3 ideas. — $750
6. It is often viewed as a way for children to start their first business in which they make and sell a sweet fizzy drink. What is it? — $250
7. Find 3 questions you could ask a successful entrepreneur. — $500
8. What does "CEO" mean? — $500
9. Complete the Triple S Method: SPEND, _____ and SAVE. — $250
10. What does K.A.S.H. stand for? — $500

+ EXERCISES → p. 168

A Poser des questions (1)

Grammar tuto

Il existe **deux types de questions** en anglais.

LES QUESTIONS FERMÉES

= *Yes/No questions*

On peut y **répondre par oui ou non**.

Auxiliaire + Sujet + Verbe

Did they start a business? → Yes, they did.

Don't you sell cookies? → Yes, we do.

Does he have a stand? → No, he doesn't.

LES QUESTIONS OUVERTES

= *WH- questions*

Elles commencent par un **mot interrogatif** indiquant le **type d'information attendue**.

Mot interrogatif + Auxiliaire + Sujet + Verbe

What do you sell? → We sell cookies.

When did they start a business?
→ They started a business last year.

How often does he go to his office?
→ He goes to his office every day.

***Be* est à la fois verbe et auxiliaire.**

Where is Mikaila? → She's at Whole Foods for a meeting.

Are you a basketball fan? → Yes, I **am**.

Quand le mot interrogatif est sujet de la question, il n'y a pas d'auxiliaire.

Who launched the business? → Alina did.

Which book inspired her? → *Better than a Lemonade Stand* did.

1 Remets les mots dans l'ordre pour former des questions.

a. did | why | start | you | a business | ?

b. the TV show | was | a good experience | ?

c. Mikaila | like | did | bees | she | a child | when | was | ?

d. who | you | launch | a business | helped | ?

2 Pose la question sur l'élément en bleu.

a. He had a lemonade stand **in Indiana**.

b. **Mahsa Riar** invented 3-D prosthetics for children who lost a limb.

c. She sells **healthy lollipops**.

d. He launched a business **when he was five**.

HOW TO SHINE IN GRAMMAR → p. 149

B Exprimer la pression, l'attente ou la permission grâce aux propositions infinitives

Pour exprimer **l'influence d'une ou de plusieurs personnes sur autrui,** on peut utiliser des verbes comme ***want*** ou ***make*** suivis de **propositions infinitives**. Certains sont suivis de ***to***, d'autres ne le sont pas.

They want him to write a book about his success. Sujet: They – personne sur laquelle s'exerce la pression: him – BV: write		**They made her promote** her idea on TV. Sujet: They – personne sur laquelle s'exerce la pression: her – BV: promote	
Verbes suivis de ***to*** :	**expect** (*s'attendre à*) • **encourage** • **want** • **order** • **force** • **allow** (*autoriser*) • **enable** (*permettre*)	Verbes non suivis de ***to*** :	**make** • **let** (*laisser*)

3 Remets les mots dans l'ordre pour exprimer la pression ou l'autorisation/la permission.

a. launch her business • made • bees • Mikaila

b. teen entrepreneurs' parents • their children • encourage • think differently • to

c. school teachers • Adom Appiah's • let • start a project • him

d. this book • me • enabled • open • a lemonade stand • to

4 Termine les phrases suivantes de façon logique.

a. Having a lemonade stand encourages teens...

b. This book made Mahsa Riar...

c. Many teen entrepreneurs want...

d. Respecting the eight tips enables you...

HOW TO SHINE IN GRAMMAR → p. 148

VOCABULARY

EXERCISES → p. 168

1 Name it!

a. Somebody who gives money in order to help other people : ...

b. The action of starting and running a business : ...

c. Money used to launch a business : ...

d. A piece of advice : ...

2 Put the letters in the right order to find the words.

3 Complete with the right verb.

a. When you are a CEO, you ... a business.

b. When you compete, you ... a competition.

c. When you are successful, you ... .

d. When you make money thanks to your work, you ... money.

4 Find the opposite of the following verbs.

a. give up ≠ ...

b. succeed ≠ ...

c. spend ≠ ...

d. donate ≠ ...

HOW TO SHINE IN VOCABULARY → p. 160

PHONOLOGY

A La prononciation du <wh> et du <h> dans les mots interrogatifs

- Contrairement au français, le <h> se prononce en anglais, sauf dans quelques mots comme *hour* et *honest* et *honour*, où il est muet.
- Le mot interrogatif ***how*** se prononce donc /haʊ/. Le <h> se prononce également dans *who* /huː/.
- En revanche, il ne se prononce pas dans les autres mots interrogatifs en ***wh-*** comme *when* /wen/ ou *where* /weə/.

1 Anticipe la prononciation des mots suivants, puis écoute et répète.

who • how • what • where • when • why

2 Répète ces questions en te concentrant sur la prononciation du <wh> et <h> en début de question.

a. Who helped you with your business?

b. When did you start your company?

c. How did you get the idea?

HOW TO SHINE IN PHONOLOGY → p. 156

B L'intonation des questions

En anglais, **l'intonation des questions varie** selon le type de question : ouverte ou fermée.

- L'intonation **descend** en fin de question **ouverte**.
  - When did you launch your business? ↘
- L'intonation **monte** en fin de question **fermée**.
  - Is he a teen entrepreneur? ↗

3 Écoute, repère l'intonation de ces questions, puis répète-les.

a. Who is the girl who launched this business?

b. Did she raise funds?

c. Why did you want to start a business?

d. What helped you launch your business?

4 Prononce ces questions, puis écoute et vérifie ton intonation.

a. Who are these brothers?

b. Did anyone help you with your business?

c. What's your next idea?

d. Do you have any other plans for your business?

HOW TO SHINE IN PHONOLOGY → p. 159

WORDMAP

WB → p. 37

TEEN ENTREPRENEURS

Business

- CEO /ˌsiːiːˈəʊ/
- entrepre**neur**ship /ɒntrəprəˈnɜːʃɪp/ = entrepre**neur**ial **spi**rit
- **pro**fits
- sup**ply** and de**mand**
- make / earn **mo**ney
- **o**pen / start / launch a **bus**iness
- run a **com**pany
- spend ≠ save

Personality

- com**pe**titor
- **will**power = determi**na**tion
- ad**ven**turous
- com**pe**titive
- de**ter**mined /dɪˈtɜːmɪnd/
- enthusi**as**tic /ɪnˌθjuːziˈæstɪk/
- in**spi**ring
- strong-**willed**

Achievements

- **a**wards **ce**remony
- suc**cess** ≠ **fail**ure /ˈfeɪljə/
- **chal**lenging
- suc**cess**ful
- be a**war**ded a prize
- be **ho**noured
- de**ve**lop a skill
- dream of + V-ing
- **en**ter a compe**ti**tion
- make a **di**fference
- over**come** one's fears
- suc**ceed** ≠ fail

Helping the community

- **cha**rity = non-**pro**fit organi**sa**tion
- **fund**raiser
- phi**lan**thropist /fɪˈlænθrəpɪst/
- **so**cial goal **com**pany
- **be**nefit
- do**nate**
- help **peo**ple out
- raise **mo**ney / funds
- reach out to **peo**ple
- share
- sup**port**

Motivations

- goal = aim = ob**jec**tive
- tip = piece of ad**vice**
- in**spired**
- **pa**ssionate a**bout**
- **will**ing to + BV
- **de**dicate one's time to **some**thing
- en**cou**rage **some**one to do **some**thing
- give up ≠ be**lieve** in one**self**
- jump in
- split one's time **in**to
- take ad**vice**

● NOUN ● ADJECTIVE ● VERB ● ADVERB OR PREPOSITION

YOUR FINAL MISSION

Act out an interview between a journalist and a teen entrepreneur for *Entrepreneur* magazine.

WB → p. 50

→ Teen entrepreneur : you are a young entrepreneur who launched a successful business. You have won the Teenpreneur of the Year award. Answer the journalist's questions.

→ Journalist : you are a journalist for *Entrepreneur* magazine. Ask questions to the young entrepreneur who won the Teenpreneur of the Year award.

STEP 1 ▶ **Choose** your partner and **define** your roles.

STEP 2 ▶ **Gather** your ideas, focusing on:

As a journalist

– what you want to learn about the teen entrepreneur and his or her business;

– the questions you may ask about his or her career, projects, advice for others.

As a teen entrepreneur

– the type of business you launched (charity, service, products), a name for it and a goal;

– the advice you could give young entrepreneurs to be.

STEP 3 ▶ **Practise** your interview. **Make sure** you respect the intonation and make it lively.

YES YOU CAN!

Conduct and give an interview.

Introduction

Accueille ton invité(e) et remercie-le/la d'accepter de répondre à tes questions. Tu peux exposer brièvement le sujet.

Alina Morse was just 7 years old when she launched the idea that revolutionised the candy industry. She's now 13 years old and the CEO of Zollipops and a millionaire. Alina good to see you. ***Thank you*** *so much* ***for*** *joining us.*

▶ Video

Salutations

Remercie l'animateur/trice ou le/la journaliste pour son accueil.

Thank you for *having me.*

Animation

Pose des questions courtes et ciblées sur le sujet.

How did you start your business?

Relance ton invité(e) pour obtenir plus de détails.

So, that's how you got the idea but how did you get the funding?

Attitude

Écoute attentivement les propos de ton invité(e) et réagis à ses propos.

Tu peux exprimer ta surprise ou ton adhésion à ses propos, ou les utiliser pour rebondir.

Wow! That's so great!
It's a ***pretty incredible*** *story. You're a millionaire and running a company and you're not even 15 yet.*

Posture

Regarde ton interlocuteur/trice dans les yeux et sois souriant(e).

Parle haut et fort, adapte ton débit et fais des pauses quand tu passes d'une idée à une autre.

Veille à être le/la plus naturel(le) possible. Pour cela, tu peux utiliser des *gap fillers* qui rendent le discours plus authentique.

Well*, when I was 7 years old…* ***You know*** *they're…* ***I mean*** *the fact that…*

Argumentation

Réponds de façon claire, sans oublier les mots de liaison.

My dad told me I shouldn't have a candy ***because*** *sugar is terrible for your teeth,* ***so*** *I asked him…*

Argumente ton discours à l'aide de verbes de point de vue, d'adjectifs et d'adverbes.

They ***think*** *it's* ***really cool****…*

HOW TO SHINE IN INTERACTING
→ p. 142

Test your skills!

Compréhension de l'oral

B1 OBJECTIF Comprendre un témoignage

Video

▲ Lacrosse is a very popular team sport in North America, played with a crosse, a ball and a net.

A2 **1** **Listen** and **identify** the type of document.

2 **Find** information about Rachel Zietz and her business.

A2+ **3** **Identify** if her business is successful. **Give** some elements showing it.

B1 **4** **Explain** Rachel's future plans.

Compréhension de l'écrit

B1 OBJECTIF Comprendre un article de presse en ligne

What Is It Like Being a CEO at 17?

As you may already be aware I am part of the World Youth Organization, however, I am not just 'part' of it- but one of the CEOs. My partner Maliha Reza is also a CEO of the organisation. [...]

WYO was founded in October 2014 after we both wanted to make a change and provide[1] teenagers our age and beyond with opportunities to help better them in life. [...]

Setting up a charity is not as simple as 1, 2, and 3, in fact it is far from that. [...] It is not always easy juggling school work alongside WYO work and sometimes we have been guilty of prioritising WYO over school but we try our best to keep things balanced. [...]

We believe in hard work, and this has been our ethos[2] since the very start. You cannot achieve anything great without the blood, sweat and tears. [...]

Teenagers need a voice, they need opportunities and most of all a strong platform to build this on, which is what we hope WYO can offer. Life is full of opportunities but they are not always clear until you are shown them. Then it is your duty to show others these opportunities until it is made clear. And this is what WYO wishes to demonstrate to the youth and adults across the world.

Kieran Goodwin, *huffingtonpost.co.uk*, 2016

A2 **1** **Read** the document and **identify** its nature and source.

2 **Say** what WYO is and **find** information about Kieran Goodwin.

A2+ **3** **Explain** what WYO believes in.

B1 **4** **Identify** WYO's objectives.

1. give
2. *philosophie*

QUIZ Test de positionnement
college.nathan.fr/3sb51

SNAPFILE 5 A winning formula

▶ How is Formula One adapting to the challenges of the 21st century?

YOUR SNAP MISSION

Write a speech for a campaign to make F1 more attractive to teens.

1 So British!

WB DIFFÉRENCIATION ➜ p. 51

a. Look at the photo and **guess** what the situation is.

b. Watch the video and **find** information about the event.

c. Explain how popular Formula One is in Britain.

PHONOLOGY SPOT AUDIO

What a win!

De quel type de phrase s'agit-il ? Quelle émotion véhicule-t-elle ?

Doc 1

Video

▲ Lewis Hamilton, Silverstone Circuit, England, 18 July 2021.

Doc 2

Here's why we love going racing at Silverstone...

1. It's an awesome test of an F1 car

The circuit is a high-speed test of an F1 car's aerodynamics, and the rapid changes of direction make it stand out[1].

2. The venue is steeped in history

The first Formula 1 World Championship race was held at Silverstone back in 1950, and since then it has gone on to host the British Grand Prix on 52 occasions. The track has evolved a lot in that time, but has been the location for some iconic moments.

3. Incredible fans

Silverstone has the space for numerous big grandstands[2] and that has led to recent attendance figures exceeding 140,000 on race day.

4. The British weather

The good old British weather can make for some exciting races.

5. It's the home race for many

Of the 10 Formula 1 teams, seven have their headquarters[3] in England.

Chris Medland, *formula1.com*, 2019

a. Read the article and **pick out** elements showing that Silverstone is a fantastic location.

b. Explain why Silverstone symbolises British pride.

1. be remarkable
2. *tribunes*
3. *quartier général*

2 Going green

WB → p. 53

Doc 1 — Video

Audio

TEAM WORK

Team A

a. **Watch** the video and **explain** who the people are.

b. **Identify** the elements you see. **Explain** what the purpose of the video is.

Team B

a. **Listen** to the audio and **identify** the topic.

b. **Note down** the numbers and what they refer to. What is the impact of Formula One on the environment?

c. Now **share** what you have learnt and **discuss** the challenge Formula One has to meet.

GRAMMAR SPOT

- a winning formula
- Ø Formula One

Quel article introduit *formula* dans chaque exemple ? Pourquoi ?

Doc 2 — AUDIO VERSION

Over its 70-year history, F1 has pioneered numerous technologies and innovations that have positively contributed to society and helped to combat carbon emissions.

From ground-breaking[1] aerodynamics to improved brake[2] designs, the progress led by F1 teams has benefitted millions of cars on the road today. Few people know that the current hybrid power unit is the most efficient in the world, delivering more power using less fuel, and hence CO_2, than any other road car.

We believe that F1 can continue to be a pioneer for the auto industry, working with the energy and automotive sectors to deliver the world's first net-zero carbon power unit, driving down carbon emissions across the globe.

In launching F1's first-ever sustainability strategy, with an ambitious target to be a net zero carbon sport by 2030, we recognise the critical role that all organisations must play in tackling[3] this global issue.

Leveraging[4] the immense talent, passion and drive for innovation held by all members of the F1 community, we hope to make a significant positive impact on the environment and communities in which we operate.

Chase Carey, CEO[5] of Formula 1®

formula1.com, 2019

a. **Read** the text and **pick out** expressions showing that Chase Carey wants to deliver a positive speech.

b. **Explain** how Formula One has changed the automobile industry.

1. revolutionary 2. *frein* 3. working on
4. thanks to 5. Chief Executive Officer = *PDG*

YOUR SNAP MISSION — STEP 1

Start writing your speech. Introduce British Formula One.

1. **Say** how important this sport is for Britain and how it unites British people.
2. **Explain** how and why Formula One must continue taking up today's ecological challenges.

WB → p. 54

Build your skills! Présenter des enjeux

- Introduis des faits avec les bons articles :
  - *We hope to make **a** positive impact on **the** environment.*
- Utilise des modaux et des verbes exprimant un défi :
  - *We **can't** do it without you.* • *We **have to** keep innovating.*
  - *We **believe** that F1 can continue to be a pioneer…*

BUILD YOUR ENGLISH → p. 56

3 Women on track

WB → p. 55

Doc 1 — Video

▲ Bernadette Collins, British engineer for the Aston Martin Formula One team.

a. Look at the picture and **watch** the video. **Say** who the three women are.

b. List all the positive aspects of their job.

PHONOLOGY SPOT — AUDIO

explore • university • fruits • realise • important • limit

Écoute et prononce ces mots transparents. Que remarques-tu ?

Doc 2

The FIA[1] set up a Women in Motorsport Commission 10 years ago—that's right, it's been 10 years since efforts began to increase female involvement[2] in the sport. [...]

There are and have been for many years a lot of women involved in all aspects of the sport—except the driving. [...] There are a lot more woman engineers and mechanics than there used to be, but still no drivers. [...] Since the F1 World Championship began in 1950, only two women have qualified for Grands Prix. [...]

There are many initiatives going on, notably the W Series—the championship for female race drivers—and Ferrari's ongoing[3] search for a young woman to join its Academy, but will these make a difference?

Joe Saward, *autoweek.com*, 2021

1. *Fédération Internationale de l'Automobile*
2. participation 3. unfinished

a. Read the text and **say** what it is about.

b. Explain the role of the Women & Motor Sport Commission and **say** what it has achieved so far.

c. Name the remaining problem. **Think** of an explanation.

GRAMMAR SPOT

That's right, it's been 10 years since efforts began…

Remplace **'s** par la forme verbale complète. Pourquoi emploie-t-on le *present perfect* ici ?

▲ Jamie Chadwick won the W Series championship in 2019 and 2021, and her dream is to race in Formula One.

4 There is only one race

WB DIFFÉRENCIATION → p. 57

▲ A young Lewis Hamilton at the beginning of his karting career in the mid-90s.

Doc 1 — Video

a. Watch the report and **say** who it is about.
b. Explain why the young racer felt hurt at first.
c. Pick out the verbs that define the attitude he and his family have adopted since those early days.

Doc 2

The recent events that have been taking place around the world concerning discrimination and racism have led various companies and large-scale[1] organisations to implement certain measures to combat these aspects that affect society. [...] Formula 1 has announced the creation of the initiative called "We Race as One". [...]

"*We fully recognise that Formula 1 needs to be more inclusive and diverse. That is why we will establish a Task Force*[2] *to listen and ensure the right initiatives are identified to increase diversity in Formula 1. We want to ensure we give people from all backgrounds the best chances to work in Formula 1 regardless of*[3] *their gender, ethnicity, sexual orientation, or physical abilities,*" commented F1's CEO, Chase Carey.

motorlat.com, 2020

1. big, important 2. group of professionals 3. whatever

a. Look at the poster and **say** how you understand it.
b. Read the text and **explain** what "We Race as One" is.
c. Give your opinion about this initiative.

YOUR SNAP MISSION — STEP 2

Write the second part of your speech. Show how Formula One has developed its inclusion strategy.

1. **List** the efforts the FIA and F1's CEO have made to welcome people from all backgrounds. **Give** your opinion about each one of them.
2. **Add** three suggestions that could help make F1 even more inclusive.
3. **Make** your speech stand out: **start** and **end** it with impactful sentences.

Build your skills! — Faire le bilan d'une action

- Utilise le *present perfect* associé à ***for*** pour insister sur la durée : *There **have been** a lot of women involved in all aspects of the sport **for** many years—except the driving.*
- Utilise le *present perfect* associé à ***since*** pour attirer l'attention sur le point de départ : ***I've been** into F1 **since** I was very little.*

WB → p. 58 HOW TO SHINE IN WRITING → p. 140 BUILD YOUR ENGLISH → p. 56

QUIZ Test college.nathan.fr/3sb55

Build your English! GRAMMAR

EXERCISES ➜ p. 168

A Évoquer le lien entre le passé et le présent avec le *present perfect*

Grammar tuto

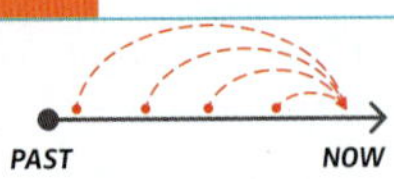

On utilise le ***present perfect*** pour établir un **lien entre le passé et le présent** : des actions du passé ont encore un impact sur le présent.

Formula One **has improved** its technology **since** the 1980s.

- **has** : *auxiliaire* ***have*** *au présent*
- **improved** : *verbe* ***improve*** *au participe passé*
- **since** : *= point de départ de l'action dans le passé*

Women **have competed for** 10 years.

- **have** : *auxiliaire* ***have*** *au présent*
- **competed** : *verbe* ***compete*** *au participe passé*
- **for** : *= durée de l'action jusqu'à aujourd'hui*

Have the drivers **finished** the race **yet**?
= déjà, jusqu'à maintenant

Lewis Hamilton **has already crossed** the finish line.
= déjà

George Russell **hasn't crossed** the finish line **yet**.
= pas encore

8 Si l'événement est **rattaché à une date précise**, on utilise le **prétérit** : *He* ***won*** *the race last week.*

1 Utilise les éléments suivants pour rédiger des phrases avec *for* ou *since*. N'oublie pas de conjuguer le verbe !

a. Engineers • work to make F1 engines more ecological • the early 2000s
b. Formula One • be a popular sport • 60 years
c. F1 engineers • take the environment into consideration • about 10 years
d. Lewis Hamilton • compete • he was a teenager

2 Reformule les phrases suivantes à l'aide de *not… yet* ou *already*.

Ex : *She has won many titles.* ➜ *She has* ***already*** *won many titles.*

a. He has never won a race.
b. Engineers have worked on better engines.
c. I have never met Lewis Hamilton but I plan to!
d. Lewis Hamilton has competed for McLaren.

HOW TO SHINE IN GRAMMAR ➜ p. 150

B Désigner des éléments en utilisant les articles

Selon comment l'on veut présenter un fait ou un objet, on n'utilise pas le même **article**.

➜ Si l'on parle d'une **généralité**, on utilise **l'article *Ø***.

• ***Ø F1*** *has pioneered numerous technologies.*

➜ Si l'on parle d'un **cas singulier**, sans préciser, on emploie **l'article *a*** (ou ***an*** devant un son voyelle).

• *We hope to make* ***a positive impact****.*

➜ Si l'on parle d'un élément **précis** et repéré, on utilise l'article ***the***.

• *It had a positive consequence on* ***the environment****.*

3 Complète avec *the*, *a* (ou *an*) ou *Ø*.

a. … race has already started and all … spectators are cheering … drivers!
b. I think … pollution is … real problem and we should try to find … solutions.
c. … engines they designed are very efficient, we can hope they will design … electric one soon.
d. … special committee was appointed to handle … issues of racism in this sport.

4 Tu es pilote et viens de gagner une course. Remercie l'équipe et évoque les améliorations techniques. Veille à utiliser les articles appropriés.

HOW TO SHINE IN GRAMMAR ➜ p. 146

VOCABULARY

EXERCISES → p. 169

FORMULA ONE

Car racing (AUDIO)

- aerody**na**mics
- brakes /breɪks/
- **dri**ver
- **en**gine
- engi**neer** /ˌendʒɪ'nɪə/
- me**cha**nic /mə'kænɪk/
- race
- **stee**ring wheel
- tyres /taɪəz/
- e**lec**tric
- **hy**brid

Talking business (AUDIO)

- ca**reer** /kə'rɪə/
- CEO = Chief **Exe**cutive **O**fficer
- **in**dustry
- inno**va**tion /ˌɪnə'veɪʃən/
- organi**sa**tion /ˌɔːgənaɪ'zeɪʃən/
- **stra**tegy
- **tar**get
- tech**no**logy
- suc**cess**ful
- de**ve**lop /dɪ'veləp/
- im**pact**

Setting goals (AUDIO)

- i**ni**tiative /ɪ'nɪʃətɪv/
- in**vol**vement
- e**ffi**cient /ɪ'fɪʃənt/
- de**li**ver
- **im**plement: *mettre en place*
- in**crease**
- launch (a cam**paign**)
- push the **li**mits
- set up
- dra**ma**tically
- **gra**dually = **slow**ly

Environment (AUDIO)

- **car**bon e**mi**ssions /ɪ'mɪʃənz/
- sustaina**bi**lity
- **glo**bal (**iss**ue)
- cam**paign** for
- drive down = re**duce**

Inclusion (AUDIO)

- eth**ni**city
- **gen**der
- di**verse** /daɪ'vɜːs/
- in**clu**sive
- take a step

- NOUN
- ADJECTIVE
- VERB
- ADVERB

→ **Imagine and draw the F1 car of the future. Name the different innovations with a caption.**

HOW TO SHINE IN VOCABULARY → p. 160

PHONOLOGY

→ La prononciation des mots transparents

- De nombreux mots de la langue anglaise **ressemblent** à leur équivalent **français** et ont la **même signification**. On dit qu'ils sont **transparents**.
- Mais leur **prononciation** est très **différente** ! Assure-toi que tu sais placer **l'accent de mot** et prononcer tous les **phonèmes** du mot anglais.

• organi**sa**tion /ˌɔːgənaɪ'zeɪʃənz/
• e**mi**ssions /ɪ'mɪʃənz/ • ca**reer** /kə'rɪə/

1 Écoute ces mots et identifie la syllabe accentuée. (AUDIO)

a. diverse • inclusive • campaign • aerodynamics • engineer • electric

b. emissions • career • innovation • initiative • mechanic • strategy

2 Écoute et répète ces phrases en veillant à bien prononcer les mots transparents. (AUDIO)

"We fully recognise that Formula One needs to be more inclusive and diverse. That is why we will establish a Task Force to listen and ensure the right initiatives are identified to increase diversity in Formula One."

HOW TO SHINE IN PHONOLOGY → p. 156

FILE 6 Move on up

"If it hadn't been for music, the Civil Rights Movement would've been like a bird without wings."

John Lewis (1940-2020)

Civil rights leader and Democrat representative for Georgia, USA

How have African Americans used music to empower themselves?

More on SPEAKEASY NEWS speakeasy-news.com

YOUR FINAL MISSION

Select and present a song for a playlist of essential African-American classics.

Kendrick Lamar performing on stage during the 58th GRAMMY Awards in 2016.

Video

National Museum of African American Music, Nashville, 2021.

TEAM WORK

WB → p. 59

Team A

Look at the main picture and **say** everything you know about the artist. **Comment** on his performance.

Team B

Read the quote by John Lewis and **explain** the comparison.

Team C

Watch the video and **find out** information about the museum.

- Now **share** what you know about African-American music with the class.

EXPLORE Music to express feelings

1 A long journey

WB DIFFÉRENCIATION → p. 60

Doc 1 Video

CULTURE SPOT

Slavery was legal in the USA between the 17th and the 19th centuries. Many slaves were taken from Africa and sold to plantation owners, mostly in the southern states. Slavery was abolished in **1865**.

Doc 2 AUDIO VERSION

1738. Amari is a 15-year-old African girl who was captured and dragged onto a slave ship.

The ship of death was surprisingly very much alive. It inhaled and exhaled the foul[1] air of where they lay chained, and it rolled with the rhythm of the water. Loud noises echoed down to them—pounding[2], clanging[3], and screeching[4]. And it seemed the white men were always shouting. She also heard laughter above. No one in the hidden, dark area beneath the ship laughed. All were silent with fear.

Eventually, the activity above seemed to slow down. Amari felt a sense of anticipation, as if something was about to happen. Perhaps it was night. She could not tell. Afi, still chained next to her, quietly began to hum[5] an old Ewe[6] song. It was the lament sung at a funeral—a death song. She sang to the ancestors and to the other slaves. Gradually, even those not of that tribe joined in. Close to a hundred women softly sang with her. It was the saddest sound Amari had ever heard.

Sharon M. Draper, *Copper Sun*, 2006

1. disgusting 2. hitting
3. metallic sounds 4. *cri strident*
5. *fredonner (les lèvres fermées)*
6. West African language

GRAMMAR SPOT

Afi, who **was chained**, **began** to hum.

Quelle forme verbale montre Afi dans une position active ? Passive ? Comment s'appellent ces formes ?

a. **Watch** the video (**doc 1**) and **pick out** information about African-American spirituals.

b. **Read** the text (**doc 2**) and **say** all you know about Amari.

c. **Guess** why the women started singing.

d. **Think** about **doc 1**. **Explain** how Nicole Taylor's words echo or contrast with Amari's situation.

2 The birth of protest songs

WB → p. 62

No more auction block for me
No more, no more
No more auction block for me
Many thousand gone

No more hundred lash[1] for me
No more, no more
No more hundred lash for me
Many thousand gone

No more mistress[2] call for me
No more, no more
No more mistress call for me
Many thousand gone

No more children stole[3] from me
No more, no more
No more children stole from me
Many thousand gone

No more slavery chains for me
No more, no more
No more slavery chains for me
Many thousand gone

Slave Songs of the United States, 1867

1. *coup de fouet*
2. feminine of "master"
3. stolen

▲ Slaves on the auction block, 18th century.

a. **Look** at the pictures and **describe** the situation illustrated by each one of them.

b. **Read** the lyrics and **connect** them to the pictures.

c. **Say** what feelings or hopes are expressed here.

AT HOME **Listen** to Odetta singing this song and **get ready** to talk about the feelings expressed by her interpretation.

Video
college.nathan.fr/**3sb61a**

A LITTLE EXTRA
Listen to Kendrick Lamar and **say** what was going on "*four hundred years ago*". **Explain** why Kendrick Lamar says "*we need music to heal*".

Audio

YOUR MISSION

DIFFÉRENCIATION

Show the power of slave protest songs.

WAY 1

You are Amari's descendant, talking about his/her ancestor's voyage at a conference about slavery. **Say** how slaves were treated, what music meant to her.

WAY 2

You are an African-American music fan. **Choose** and **explain** two verses of the song "No More Auction Block For Me" for a YouTube video.

WB → p. 63

Build your skills! **Décrire une prise de conscience**

- Utilise le passif pour décrire une situation subie : *The slaves* ***were given*** *physical punishment.* • *They* ***were chained*** *at the bottom of the ship.*
- Exprime l'intention avec la préposition ***to*** : *Music was used (as a way)* ***to*** *express devotion.* • *It was a way* ***to*** *support the Civil Rights Movement.*

BUILD YOUR ENGLISH → p. 67

QUIZ Test
college.nathan.fr/**3sb61b**

EXPLORE A call for change

1 "It's been a long time coming"

WB DIFFÉRENCIATION → p. 64

Doc 1

I was born by the river, in a little tent
Oh, and just like the river
I've been running ever since

CHORUS
It's been a long
A long time coming[1]
But I know a change is gonna[2] come
Oh, yes it will [...]

I go to the movie
And I go downtown[3]
Somebody keep telling me
Don't hang around[4]

CHORUS
It's been a long
A long time coming
But I know a change is gonna come
Oh, yes it will [...]

Oh, there been times that I thought[5]
I couldn't last for long
But now I think I'm able to carry on[6]

CHORUS
It's been a long
A long time coming
But I know a change is gonna come
Oh, yes it will

Sam Cooke,
"A Change is Gonna Come", 1964

a. Read the lyrics and **list** the places mentioned.

b. Draw a picture for each verse and **explain** the chorus.

AT HOME Listen to Sam Cooke singing and **get ready** to **comment** on his interpretation.

Video college.nathan.fr/3sb62

▲ Sam Cooke (1931-1964).

GRAMMAR SPOT

- I **was** born by the river...
- I**'ve been** running ever since.

Quel énoncé appartient au passé ?
Quel énoncé fait un lien entre le passé et le présent ?

1. *Cela a pris du temps* 2. going to 3. to the city centre
4. Don't stay here 5. there have been times when I thought
6. continue

Doc 2 Audio

▲ A segregated movie theatre in Mississippi, 1939.

a. Explain what you can see in the picture.

b. Listen to Sam Cooke's brother. **Name** the period he describes.

c. List what people could or could not do in those days.

A LITTLE EXTRA Watch and **note down** what inspired Sam Cooke to write his song. **Explain** the expression "a civil rights anthem".

Video

2 "One of the most iconic moments"

WB → p. 66

Video

◀ The March on Washington, 28 August 1963.

CULTURE SPOT

- After the USA abolished slavery, African Americans continued to be marginalised through **segregation**.
- The **civil rights movement** was a struggle for social justice that took place mainly during the 1950s and 1960s for African Americans to gain equal **rights**.

history.com

a. **Say** what you know about the man in the picture. **Guess** what cause the crowd was marching for.

b. **Watch** the video and check your hypotheses.

c. **Recap** what happened in 1963, 1964, 1965 and 1968.

3 "Tonight, change has finally come"

WB → p. 66

a. **Name** the people in the picture and **imagine** the occasion.

b. **Watch** the video and **explain** the situation.

c. **Explain** who Barack Obama pays tribute to.

Video

▲ Chicago, 4 November 2008.

PHONOLOGY SPOT — AUDIO

Change has come to America.

Écoute cette phrase. Quels mots sont accentués ? Que peux-tu en déduire ?

YOUR MISSION

You are a music journalist. You have one minute to explain why Sam Cooke's song is a classic.

1 **Describe** the context in which it was written.

2 **Explain** why this song is still famous today.

WB → p. 67

Build your skills! **Décrire un changement**

- *Because of what we did, change has come to America.*
- *The song Sam Cooke wrote when a motel employee turned him away so many years ago has become an American classic.*

→ Utilise le prétérit pour évoquer des faits passés : *did • wrote • turned away*

→ Utilise le *present perfect* pour décrire un résultat ou une évolution qui a un impact sur le présent : *has come • has become*

BUILD YOUR ENGLISH → p. 67

QUIZ Test
college.nathan.fr/**3sb63**

EXPLORE Black Voices Matter

1 #BLM

WB DIFFÉRENCIATION → p. 68

Doc 1 — Video

▲ Demonstration in Portland, 2014.

CULTURE SPOT

George Zimmerman, a neighbourhood watch volunteer, was acquitted on charges resulting from his **fatal shooting** of Trayvon Martin, an unarmed black teenager, in Florida, in February 2012.

Doc 2

Inspired by the Black Lives Matter movement, singers use music to make their voices heard.

The role of popular musicians and other celebrities in the promotion of BLM has become more prominent[1] of late. [...]

[Janelle] Monáe aligned herself with BLM fairly early on. She took part in one of the movement's marches in Philadelphia in August last year, and led fellow artists from her Wondaland Records label on the protest single "Hell You Talmbout" that same month.

"We recorded it to challenge the indifference, disregard and negligence of all who remain quiet about this issue," Monáe wrote in an Instagram post.

"Silence is our enemy. Sound is our weapon[2]."

James McNair, *thenationalnews.com*, July 2016

1. important. 2. *arme*

a. **Look** at the picture (**doc 1**) and **comment** on the message and the situation.

b. **Watch** the video and **explain** the impact of social media in the BLM movement.

c. **Read** the article (**doc 2**) and **explain** Janelle Monáe's role in the BLM movement.

d. **Discuss** Janelle Monáe's quote (l. 10). How can music make a difference?

PHONOLOGY SPOT AUDIO

black • labour • call • shared • lives • exist

Écoute, puis répète ces mots. Comment se prononcent les lettres <a> et <i>?

2 Black pride

WB → p. 70

Doc 1 — Video

I'm a young black man
Doing all that I can
To stand
Oh, but when I look around
And I see what's being done
To my kind
Every day
I'm being hunted as prey
My people don't want no trouble
We've had enough struggle

Keedron Bryant,
"I just wanna live", 2020

TEAMWORK

Team A

a. **Look** at the picture (doc 1) and **imagine** the boy's goal.

b. **Read** the song and **say** what it is about.

c. **Watch** the video and **explain** the impact of the song.

Team B

a. **Read** the Instagram post (doc 2). **Identify** its author and its goal.

b. Using the culture spot, **explain** the purpose of the "Black Parade" single.

c. **Pick out** the repeated words and **name** Beyoncé's feelings.

d. Now **share** what you know on both singers' commitment to Black Pride. **Show** how they use social media to convey their message and fight racism.

AT HOME **Listen** to Keedron singing and **explain** why he has become a symbol of protest.

Video college.nathan.fr/3sb65a

Doc 2

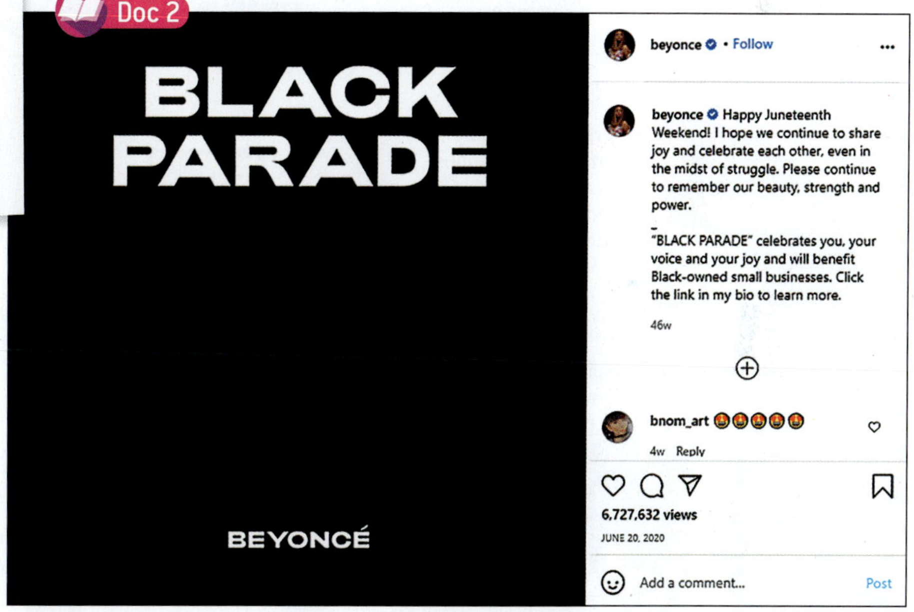

CULTURE SPOT

Juneteenth is a holiday celebrating the **emancipation** of those who were **enslaved** in the USA.

YOUR MISSION

DIFFÉRENCIATION

You have just listened to one of these three artists' songs. Write a post on your favourite social network.

WAY 1

Share your feelings in your post.

WAY 2

Express your feelings and **say** how these singers use music to make their voices heard.

WB → p. 71

Build your skills! **Exprimer des émotions**

- Utilise des verbes de perception, de goût ou d'espoir : *It* ***touched*** *me in a way I wasn't prepared for.* • *I* ***love*** *you.* • *I* ***hope*** *we continue…*
- Ajoute des adverbes : *It is* ***so*** *good to see your faces.*
- Choisis des adjectifs appréciatifs : *It was an* ***incredible*** *thing to see.*

BUILD YOUR ENGLISH → p. 67

QUIZ Test college.nathan.fr/3sb65

GAME ON!

SOUL Train

EXO Interactive game
college.nathan.fr/**3sb66a**

How to play

- **Join your team** and **get on board** the Soul Train.
- **Write down** your answers as you go from question 1 to question 10.
- The first team to meet the train driver with all the correct answers wins.

1

Complete the lyrics.

No more a..... b..... for me
No more, no more

2

Who is the girl travelling on a slave ship in the novel *Copper Sun*?

3

BEAT THE CLOCK!

You have 30 seconds to write the longest possible list of **African-American musicians**.

4

WORDMIX

Find the four **African-American musical genres**:

AZJZ SUEBL
PIH-OPH PELGOS

5

Where, **when** and **by whom** was the famous "I Have A Dream" speech given?

6

Which historical periods inspired each one of these classic album covers?

7

What does **#BLM** stand for?

8

BEAT THE CLOCK!

You have 30 seconds to write the longest possible list of **artists who support the BLM movement**.

9

Match the names and the portraits in this Musical Hall of Fame.

Kendrick Lamar
James Brown
Janelle Monáe
Beyoncé

10

Name the train driver:
He was born by the Mississippi river. He endured segregation and denounced it in a classic song. He was nicknamed the King of Soul.

You have reached your destination and you are welcome to join the party at the Soul Station!

Video
college.nathan.fr/**3sb66b**

EXERCISES → p. 169

A Évoquer le passé avec le prétérit et lier passé et présent avec le *present perfect*

Grammar tuto

On utilise le **prétérit** pour évoquer des actions ou des faits **passés, datés et achevés**.

On utilise le ***present perfect*** pour évoquer des actions ou des faits qui ont **commencé dans le passé** et **continuent dans le présent ou** pour évoquer les **conséquences d'une action passée** sur le présent.

Segregation **was** unfair.
In the 1950s, black children **didn't go** to school with white children, they **went** to segregated schools.
Black people **wanted** the same rights.

Black people **have fought** for their rights **for years.**
auxiliaire au présent — *verbe au participe passé* — *= durée*
They **have voiced** their discontent **since the end of segregation.**
= point de départ

Society **has begun** to change but we **haven't forgotten** the past.

1 Mets les verbes en bleu au prétérit ou au *present perfect*.

a. Segregation (start) in the 1890s.
b. During Segregation, black people (not / have) the same rights as white people.
c. Segregation (last) 70 years and since then, black people (keep) on fighting for equality.

2 Termine chaque phrase en utilisant les éléments proposés.

a. Since the 17th century, … African-American singers sing for Black people's rights
b. In 1963, … Martin Luther King deliver a speech
c. For a very long time, … Black people fight for their rights in the USA.

HOW TO SHINE IN GRAMMAR → p. 150

B Attirer l'attention sur le résultat d'une action avec la voix passive

→ Pour mettre en avant le **résultat** d'une action plutôt que son auteur, on utilise la voix passive (***be*** + participe passé du verbe). L'auteur de l'action peut être introduit par ***by***.

- *Slave traders **took** African slaves to America.*
  *→ African slaves **were** taken to America **by** slave traders.*

→ On peut utiliser la voix passive même si on ne connaît pas l'auteur, notamment dans les phrases avec deux compléments (C).

- *They **gave** him his freedom. → He **was** given his freedom.*
  (C1) (C2)

3 Exprime ces faits passés à l'aide de la voix passive.

a. slavery • abolish • President Lincoln
b. R.E.S.P.E.C.T. • sing • Aretha Franklin
c. rap music • create • in the Bronx
d. segregation • denounce • many soul singers

4 Utilise ces éléments pour exprimer des émotions à l'aide de la voix passive.

touched | impressed | surprised | discouraged

a. the journalist • Keedron Bryant • song
b. people • MLK Jr • speech • Washington, D.C.
c. you • Kendrick Lamar • lyrics?
d. spiritual songs • slaves • not • thanks to

HOW TO SHINE IN GRAMMAR → p. 149

Build your English!

VOCABULARY

EXERCISES → p. 169

1 Let's talk music! How many words can you build? You can only use each box once.

PRO	RE	CER	GEN	DU	GER	SIN
	SONG	TER	RI	LY	WRI	
		CHO	CS	RUS		

2 Spot the correct explanation.

a. If a picture goes viral it:

1. makes you feel sick. 2. is shared many times.

b. A hashtag is:

1. a symbol in front of a word or group of words.
2. what is left when you have burnt many price tags.

c. Social media are:

1. TV channels that talk about social problems.
2. websites and apps to create and share content.

3 Name it!

a. A system in which people were owned by other people and had to work without getting paid: ...

b. The practice of officially keeping apart people of different sexes, racial or religious groups: ...

c. A person who campaigns for political or social change: ...

4 Write five sentences about this picture using words from the wordmap.

HOW TO SHINE IN VOCABULARY → p. 160

PHONOLOGY

A La prononciation des graphies <a> et <i>

- Les graphies **<a>** et **<i>** ne se prononcent pas toujours de la même manière en anglais.

<a>
- black /æ/ • call /ɔː/ • above /ə/
- slave /eɪ/ • past /ɑː/ • care /eə/
- watch /ɒ/ • image /ɪ/

<i>
- girl /ɜː/ • music /ɪ/ • alive /aɪ/

1 Écoute et répète ces mots, puis classe-les selon leur prononciation de la lettre <a>. AUDIO

message • artist • walk • ago • change • carry • share • disregard • matter • create • equality

2 Écoute et répète ces mots, puis classe-les selon leur prononciation de la lettre <i>. AUDIO

history • final • first • online • river • singer • issue • lyrics • viral • children • birth

HOW TO SHINE IN PHONOLOGY → p. 156

B Rendre un discours dynamique

- Pour rendre un discours **dynamique** et passionnant, **accentue** bien les mots qui véhiculent le **message** que tu veux faire passer.
- Parle **lentement** et **distinctement** sans regarder tes notes, en **t'adressant** directement à ton auditoire.
- **Fluidifie** ton discours en pensant à bien faire les **liaisons** entre les mots.

3 Écoute et répète ces extraits de discours. AUDIO

a. Black Lives Matter is our call to action. It is a tool to reimagine a world where Black people are free to exist, free to live.

b. It's been a long time coming, but tonight, because of what we did on this day, in this election, at this defining moment, change has come to America.

4 Prononce ces phrases en faisant les liaisons. AUDIO

a. These African-American spirituals are the music of my ancestors.

b. We all felt a sense of anticipation when the boat arrived.

HOW TO SHINE IN PHONOLOGY → p. 159

WORDMAP

WB → p. 59

AFRICAN-AMERICAN MUSIC

Feelings and emotions

AUDIO

- **goose**bumps
- a**ma**zing
- **joy**ful
- up**lif**ting
- feel
- hear ≠ **lis**ten
- strike
- touch **some**one

Civil rights movement

AUDIO

- discrimi**na**tion
- segre**ga**tion
- **e**qual
- de**se**gregate
- fight
- march
- pro**test**

Social media

AUDIO

- **com**ment
- **hash**tag
- on**line**
- **com**ment on
- go **vi**ral
- post = write a post
- share

Slavery

AUDIO

- abo**li**tion
- **an**cestors
- **cen**tury
- plan**ta**tion
- **sla**very
- slave ship
- chain
- en**slave**

Music and musicians

AUDIO

- **cho**rus /ˈkɔːrəs/
- genre /ˈʒɑnrə/
- **ly**rics
- **mes**sage /ˈmesɪdʒ/
- pro**du**cer
- **re**cord
- **rhy**thm /ˈrɪðəm/
- **sin**ger
- **song**writer
- verse
- per**form**
- re**lease** (a song)

Taking action

AUDIO

- **ac**tivist
- **al**ly /ˈælaɪ/ ≠ **en**emy
- pro**mo**tion
- call to **ac**tion
- re**cord** a **pro**test song
- **strug**gle
- take part in a march

● NOUN ● ADJECTIVE ● VERB

YOUR FINAL MISSION

Select and present a song for a playlist of essential African-American classics.

WB → p. 72

→ The National Museum of African American Music is creating its official "Most Influential Songs" playlist, a playlist of essential African-American classics that the visitors will hear during their tour.

→ **Convince** the panel the song you have picked is an absolute classic.

STEP 1 ▶ **Pick** a track remembered for its message. You can use some of the songs you discovered in the unit. Here are some other suggestions.

STEP 2 ▶ **Find out** about the artist, where she/he was born, when she/he started playing music…

STEP 3 ▶ **Find out** about the historical context. What was happening in the USA when this song was written?

STEP 4 ▶ **Prepare** your notes for the presentation, **don't forget** to **be convincing** when you explain why this song is important!

YES YOU CAN!

Present a work of art.

▶ Video

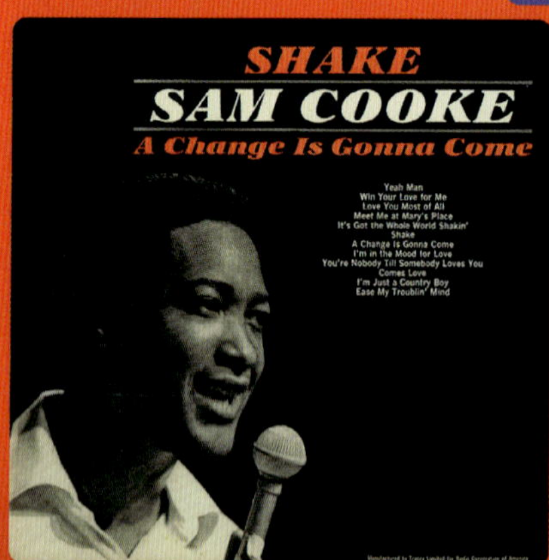

1 L'œuvre

Choisis une œuvre qui reflète son époque :
Sam Cooke "A Change is Gonna Come" (les années 60), *Prince "Purple Rain"* (les années 80), *Beyoncé "Halo"* (les années 2000)…

2 L'introduction

Présente l'artiste et l'ensemble de son œuvre :
With hits like "You Send Me" Sam Cooke became one of the most popular artists in the country.

3 Le contexte

Explique ce qui se passait dans le pays ou dans le monde et qui a peut-être influencé l'artiste :
But by 1964 with the civil rights movement spreading, the singer wanted to send a different message.

4 L'importance de l'œuvre

Explique ce qui fait que l'on parle encore de cette œuvre de nos jours.
"A Change is Gonna Come" quickly became a civil rights anthem…

5 Des éléments de biographie

Donne des éléments permettant d'en savoir plus sur l'artiste.
Cooke did not live to see it. He was shot two weeks before its release.

HOW TO SHINE IN SPEAKING → p. 144

Test your skills!

Compréhension de l'oral

B1 OBJECTIF Découvrir un mouvement artistique

▲ Archibald J. Motley Jr., *The Jazz Singers*, 1934

A1 1 **Watch** the video and **say** where and when the Harlem Renaissance took place.

A2 2 **Identify** the artistic fields which this movement involved.

3 **Give** details about Harlem: which community lives there, since when and what it represents culturally.

4 **Explain** what impact the Harlem Renaissance had on African-American music.

B1 5 **Say** which stereotypes about African Americans changed thanks to this movement.

Compréhension de l'écrit

B1 OBJECTIF Comprendre un article de presse

By the early 1960s, Nina Simone was well known to the world as a singer, songwriter and classically trained pianist. But around 1963, as race relations in America hit a boiling point, she made a sharp turn in her music — toward activism.

First, there was the murder of Medgar Evers that summer. The civil-rights leader was killed by a Klansman[1], shot in the back in his own driveway in Mississippi. Three months later, in Birmingham, Ala., four black girls were killed in a church bombing. In response to the grief and outrage, Simone wrote a powerful song with unsparing[2] lyrics and a provocative title: "Mississippi Goddam".

Then, in 1968, she identified a different side of the struggle. The Black Power movement was rising. Pride in being black and beautiful was expressed in big afros and raised fists[3]. She aimed to capture that moment of joy in black identity — and though the song she wrote was addressed to children, it became an anthem for adults, too.

"To Be Young, Gifted and Black" was a dedication to Nina Simone's friend, the playwright Lorraine Hansberry, who wrote *A Raisin in the Sun*. Hansberry was the first black woman to have a play performed on Broadway; she and Simone bonded[4] over civil rights and radical politics.

Noel King and Walter Ray Watson, *npr.org*[5], January 2019

1. member of a racist group 2. brutally honest 3. *poings*
4. became friends 5. NPR: National Public Radio

A2 1 **Read** the text, **say** what type of document this is.

2 **Identify** the person in the text (name, activities, time period).

3 **Pick out** historical events that had an impact on her life.

B1 4 **Give examples** of what she did in reaction to these events.

5 **Explain** how music and history can be related.

QUIZ Test de positionnement
college.nathan.fr/3sb71

SNAPFILE 7 Dive into Barbados

▶ How are Barbadians trying to preserve their marine treasures?

YOUR SNAP MISSION

Make a video to encourage tourists to protect the marine environment in Barbados.

1 Diving into paradise

WB → p. 73

Video

TEAM WORK

Team A	Team B
a. **Look** at the map and **gather** information about it.	a. **Watch** part 1 of the video and **pick out** elements about Barbados.

b. Now **share** what you have learnt with the other team. What makes Barbados a *"world class holiday destination"*?

c. **Watch** part 2 of the video and **explain** why *"Barbados really does have it all."*

PHONOLOGY SPOT AUDIO

major → majority • equal → equally

Écoute et répète ces mots. Quel suffixe entraîne un changement d'accentuation entre le mot d'origine et le mot dérivé ?

2 Paradise lost?

WB DIFFÉRENCIATION → p. 75

Doc 1 — Video

▲ "Plastic containers" by Barbados Sea Turtle Project, 2019.

a. **Look** at the picture and **react** to it.

b. **Watch** the video and **say** what will happen if Barbadians do not play their part in keeping their island clean.

GRAMMAR SPOT

The Earth **will not continue** to offer its beautiful gifts **if** mankind keeps destroying it.

Qu'expriment les mots en gras ?

Doc 2

AUDIO VERSION

Jaimmie-Lee is a 23-year-old HEY (Healthy and Environment-friendly Youth) Campaign Ambassador.

My island is surrounded by crystal clear seas and on the island you can often see green monkeys playing in the trees. I would like to protect our sea and beaches and the green monkeys who are treated as pests when humans are the ones building on their territories. [...]

Some acts that frustrate me are: people burning their garbage instead of recycling and the dumping[1] of home appliances (fridges, stoves, etc.) on the side of the road. I believe educating the public about the dangers of burning can be one solution. For roadside dumping the government should supply[2] a number for a collection service that would collect these items[3] at a reasonable price.

Jaimmie-Lee Jordan, *childrenvironment.org*, 2020

1. getting rid of something unwanted or useless 2. give 3. objects

◀ Alexia Daniel's message for the HEY campaign, 2020.

a. **Focus** on the picture and **comment** on Alexia's message.

b. **Read** the text and **identify** human activities that can be dangerous for the environment.

c. **Explain** Jaimmie-Lee's solutions to environmental problems.

YOUR SNAP MISSION — STEP 1

As a volunteer for Barbados Sea Turtle Project, prepare the first part of your video to raise awareness about environmental issues.

1. **Recap** what you have learnt about Barbados and **show** why it is a paradise.
2. **Talk** about the ecological problems and **explain** what will happen if we do not react. WB → p. 76

Build your skills! **Décrire une situation future hypothétique**

- Introduis tes phrases par ***if*** pour exprimer la condition : *If we don't play our part, Barbados **won't be** a paradise anymore.*
- Utilise le futur en ***will*** pour décrire la situation future : *The Earth **will lose** its beauty **if** mankind keeps destroying it.*

BUILD YOUR ENGLISH → p. 76

3 Environmental policies

WB DIFFÉRENCIATION → p. 77

Doc 1

Why are sea turtles threatened?

Natural predators like crabs and birds may prey on hatchlings[1], but more significantly, turtles are threatened[2] by human action. In the past, sea turtles were harvested[3] for their shell, meat and eggs. Some turtles are accidentally caught and drowned[4] by fishing nets or hit by motorboats. Nesting[5] beaches are also under threat. Eroding beaches, beachfront properties without proper planning permission or lighting can affect a mother's ability to lay eggs or hatchling ability to make it to the ocean.

What can we do to help?

- ▶ Avoid any harsh lighting on the beach that may confuse baby turtles as they make their journey from their nest to the ocean. At Craggy Nook we use turtle-friendly lighting and turn off all lights at night when possible.
- ▶ Do not disturb nesting females (do not use flash photography).
- ▶ Keep the waters and beaches clean and litter[6] free. Sea turtles can mistake plastic bags at sea for jellyfish and choke on them. [...]
- ▶ Attend an educational hatchling release hosted by the BSTP where you can ask your questions and find out how you can volunteer with the project on your vacation.

craggynook.com

a. Read the text and **pick out** information about marine life and human activities.

b. Explain why sea turtles are endangered. If nothing is done to protect them, what will happen?

c. Identify possible solutions to protect sea turtles.

1. baby turtles
2. endangered
3. collected for food
4. *noyées*
5. where turtles lay eggs
6. garbage, trash

Doc 2

Video

GRAMMAR SPOT

We **have to** protect our marine life.

Quels mots expriment l'obligation ?

a. Look at the poster and **identify** its goal.

b. Watch the video and **say** who is speaking.

c. Explain what Barbadians have to do to protect the environment.

4 Take action!

WB → p. 79

Doc 1 — Video

▲ Volunteers doing a beach cleanup in Barbados, 2020.

a. **Watch** the video and **pick out** information about Anjelica Catling.
b. **Describe** the role of volunteers.
c. **Give** arguments to recruit volunteers for the next Barbados International Coastal Cleanup.

a. **Read** the text and **say** to whom it is directed.
b. **List** the skills and abilities the volunteers must have to be selected.
c. **Explain** what they will do if they work for the Barbados Sea Turtle Project.

Doc 2

THE BARBADOS SEA TURTLE PROJECT

VOLUNTEER INFORMATION PACKAGE 2021

GET INVOLVED AND VOLUNTEER!

All volunteers must understand the importance of accurate[1] and thorough data collection, and be able to work and live closely with others, as equally contributing members of a team. As the Barbados Sea Turtle Project is also a public outreach[2] organization, candidates must have good interpersonal skills and the ability to relate to people of different nationalities and socio-economic backgrounds.

Candidates must be physically fit (potentially walking up to 20 km per shift in soft sand at night, in the heat of the day or in the rain) without health problems that could prevent sustained high levels of activity.

VOLUNTEER REQUIREMENTS

Candidates who can drive should hold a valid, clean driving licence. They should also be able to drive both manual and automatic transmission and drive comfortably and safely on the left side of the road.

barbadosseaturtles.org

1. precise 2. *sensibilisation*

YOUR SNAP MISSION — STEP 2

Prepare the second part of your video encouraging tourists to protect the marine environment.

1. **Explain** to tourists what they have to do and what they should do to protect sea turtles and their environment.
2. **Encourage** them to volunteer for beach cleanups and associations like the Barbados Sea Turtle Project.

WB → p. 80

Build your skills! Dire ce qu'il faut faire

- Utilise ***must***, ***have to*** et ***need to*** pour exprimer l'obligation et la nécessité : *Candidates **must** be physically fit.* • *We **have to** protect our marine life.*
- Emploie ***should*** pour faire une recommandation : *They **should** also be able to drive.*

BUILD YOUR ENGLISH → p. 76
HOW TO SHINE IN SPEAKING → p. 144

QUIZ Test
college.nathan.fr/3sb75

+ EXERCISES → p. 170

A Exprimer le conseil et l'obligation grâce à *should*, *must*, *have to* et *need to*

Grammar tuto

Should exprime le **conseil** et ***must*** une **obligation** qui **vient de la personne** qui parle.

Have to et ***need to*** expriment une **obligation**, une **contrainte** qui vient de **l'extérieur**.

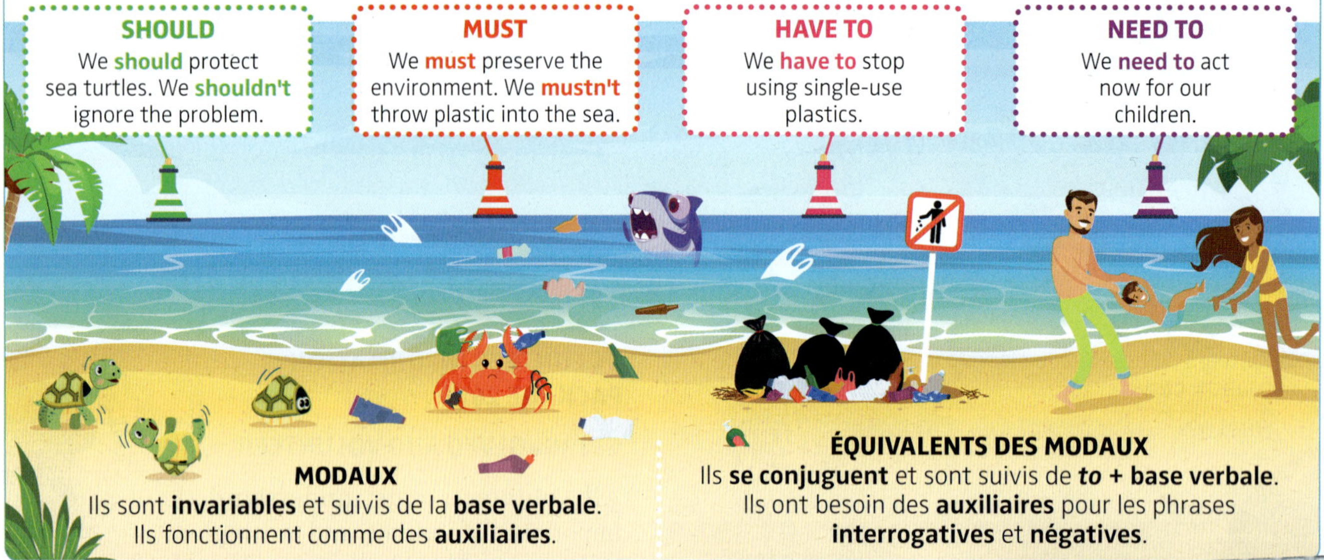

SHOULD
We **should** protect sea turtles. We **shouldn't** ignore the problem.

MUST
We **must** preserve the environment. We **mustn't** throw plastic into the sea.

HAVE TO
We **have to** stop using single-use plastics.

NEED TO
We **need to** act now for our children.

MODAUX
Ils sont **invariables** et suivis de la **base verbale**.
Ils fonctionnent comme des **auxiliaires**.

ÉQUIVALENTS DES MODAUX
Ils **se conjuguent** et sont suivis de ***to* + base verbale**.
Ils ont besoin des **auxiliaires** pour les phrases **interrogatives** et **négatives**.

1 Reconstitue ces phrases d'un ambassadeur de la campagne HEY.

a. take / everyone / action / must

b. people / more / get / to / have / involved

c. need / we / to / planet / our / protect / beautiful

d. laws / the government / propose / should / more

2 Écris au moins cinq phrases exprimant le conseil et l'obligation que pourraient dire ces manifestants.

HOW TO SHINE IN GRAMMAR → p. 152

B Exprimer une situation future hypothétique à l'aide de *if* et *will*

Pour exprimer la **condition**, l'**hypothèse**, on utilise une subordonnée introduite par la conjonction ***if*** et une proposition principale au futur avec ***will***.

Subordonnée en *if* = la condition, l'hypothèse	Proposition principale avec *will* = la conséquence, le résultat probable
If + Sujet + Verbe au présent	Sujet + *will* + Base verbale
If we don't stop polluting,	*the turtles will disappear.*

On peut inverser l'ordre des propositions et commencer par la proposition principale.

- *The Earth will lose its beauty* (principale) *if mankind keeps destroying it* (subordonnée).

3 Reconstitue ces phrases exprimant des risques écologiques à la Barbade.

a. you • If • into the ocean, • throw plastic • will • probably die. • the turtles

b. don't act • There • be clean oceans • won't • if • now. • we

c. seriously endanger • We • using plastic. • we • will • some species • if • don't stop

4 Termine ces phrases hypothétiques.

a. We will get involved in a beach cleanup programme if …

b. If I have enough time in Barbados, …

c. Sea turtles will lay their eggs safely if …

HOW TO SHINE IN GRAMMAR → p. 151-154

VOCABULARY

EXERCISES → p. 170

ECOLOGY IN BARBADOS

Tourism
AUDIO

- diving /'daɪvɪŋ/
- paradise
- snorkelling
- surfing
- water-based activities
- spectacular = stunning
- worth exploring

Ecological problems
AUDIO

- climate change
- dumping
- litter (GB) = trash (US) = garbage /'gɑːrbɪdʒ/ (US)
- (single-use) plastic
- threatened = endangered /ɪn'deɪndʒəd/

Nature
AUDIO

- bay
- coast = coastline
- coral reef
- dry land
- hatchling
- island /'aɪlənd/
- jellyfish
- landscape
- marine /mə'riːn/ park
- nest
- (sea) turtle
- species /'spiːʃiːz/
- unspoilt = preserved
- untamed = wild
- lay an egg
- release

Volunteering and getting involved
AUDIO

- ability = skill
- beach cleanup = coastal cleanup
- candidate /'kændɪdeɪt/
- membership /'membəʃɪp/
- volunteer /ˌvɒlən'tɪə/
- contribute to + V-ing
- prevent /prɪ'vent/ from + V-ing
- stand up for

Environmental policies
AUDIO

- ban on
- campaign
- outreach /'aʊtˌriːtʃ/
- educate somebody about something
- raise awareness
- recycle /ˌriː'saɪkəl/, reuse, repurpose, regenerate /rɪ'dʒenəreɪt/ = the 4 Rs

→ **Using words from the wordmap, encourage your friends to do green tourism in Barbados.**

- NOUN
- ADJECTIVE
- VERB

HOW TO SHINE IN VOCABULARY → p. 160

PHONOLOGY

→ L'accentuation des mots possédant un suffixe

- Quand on ajoute un **suffixe** à un mot, la **syllabe accentuée** de ce nouveau mot peut **rester la même** que dans le mot d'origine.
  - **e**qual /'iːkwəl/ → **e**qually /'iːkwəli/

  C'est le cas avec les suffixes ***-ly***, ***-al***, ***-er***, ***-ed***, ***-ist***, ***-ing***, ***-ous***, ***-ment***, ***-ness***, ***-ship*** par exemple.
- Mais certains suffixes font **varier la place de l'accent tonique**.
  - **ma**jor /'meɪdʒə/ → ma**jo**rity /mə'dʒɒrəti/

  Les suffixes ***-ity***, ***-ion***, ***-ual***, ***-ial***, ***-ient***, ***-ious***, ***-ic***, ***-ian*** sont dans ce cas. L'accent tonique se place sur la **syllabe précédant le suffixe**.

1 Souligne les suffixes et classe les mots selon le type de suffixe concerné. Écoute et répète les mots et entoure la syllabe accentuée. AUDIO

ability • coastal • education • ecological • surfing • economic • environmental

2 Repère les suffixes et anticipe l'accentuation du mot, puis écoute et répète. AUDIO

active / activity • member / membership • organise / organisation • snorkel / snorkelling • aware / awareness • contribute / contribution

HOW TO SHINE IN PHONOLOGY → p. 158

FILE 8 America's most wanted

"Al Capone is one of those rare figures in American history who has, through the strange machinery of celebrity culture, arrived at the status of a synonym. His name means gangster. Or vice versa."

Oisin Curran
history.howstuffworks.com, 2020

Who were the American gangsters behind the myths?

More on
SPEAKEASY NEWS
speakeasy-news.com

YOUR FINAL MISSION

As a crime reporter, write and publish an interview with a reformed gangster.

Mural of the famous bank robber John Dillinger, painted in 2020 by local artist Gabriel Moskolis, in Lincoln Park Alley in Chicago, where Dillinger was killed by FBI agents 86 years before.

Video

The Making of the Mob, AMC, 2016.

TEAM WORK

WB → p. 81

Team A

Look at the main picture. **Say** what kind of artwork it is and what it tells us about the person represented.

Team B

Read the quote and **say** what you understand about Al Capone and his status.

Team C

Watch the video. **Describe** the actions and the context.

- Now **share** with the other teams what you know about the way gangsters are represented.

EXPLORE Gangsters' paradise

1 The "Noble Experiment"

WB DIFFÉRENCIATION → p. 82

Doc 1 Video

▲ Police destroying illegal alcohol, New York City, 1921.

a. **Look** at the picture and **describe** the scene.
b. **Watch** the video and **identify** the events, places and people mentioned.
c. **Explain** the link between Prohibition and the Mafia.

VOCABULARY SPOT

Prohibition-era words

- **Prohibition:** period when the production, transportation and sale of alcohol was illegal.
- **bootleggers:** people who manufactured, transported or sold alcohol illegally.
- **Mob** *(informal)* = **Mafia:** large criminal organisation.
- **speakeasies:** bars where people drank illegal alcohol.

Doc 2

a. **Identify** the periods when life was difficult for many Americans.
b. **Find** the events in the 1920s that show society was changing.
c. **Compare** the 1920s to the decades that came before and after.

AT HOME Investigate the reasons behind Prohibition.

Video college.nathan.fr/3sb80

2 Meet Scarface

WB → p. 83

Doc 1 · Video

▲ *Spot Magazine*, 1930.

TEAM WORK

Team A

a. **Look** at the magazine cover and **watch** the video (**doc 1**).

b. **Identify** the people, period and places and **explain** why Al Capone became so famous.

Team B

a. **Observe** the newspaper (**doc 2**) and **read** the text (**doc 3**).

b. **Describe** Al Capone's ambiguous relationship with society.

c. Now **share** your information with the other team and **comment** on Al Capone's relationship with the press.

PHONOLOGY SPOT · AUDIO

celebrity • media • series

Écoute ces mots. Que remarques-tu concernant la prononciation des lettres en rouge ?

Doc 2

DAILY TIMES, CHICAGO, TUESDAY, FEBRUARY 10, 1931

CAPONE PUBLIC ENEMY NO. 1.

How Much Longer Can He Get Away with It?

Lone Gorilla of Gangland Whines on Tottering Throne as He Sees Writing on Wall

By EDWARD DOHERTY

FOR 10 years and more Alphonse Capone, Scarface Al, has been building up his kingdom. For 10 years he has been fortifying himself against the day of wrath. He has built well. He has amassed millions and millions of dollars. He has intrenched himself politically. He has powerful friends in high places. He has an army of men who will kill anyone at his nod.

He has reached his goal. He is public enemy No. 1 in Chicago. And the day of wrath has arrived, and he turns uneasily and sees the writing on the wall, and whines.

PUBLIC ENEMY NO. 1

This is Al Capone, dubbed by the Chicago Crime Commission as "Public Enemy No. 1." Capone is better advertised than most American statesmen in many foreign countries, where people think he rules Chicago. Mr. Doherty's story tells how Capone got started as

The TIMES in Brief

Doc 3

From 1925 through 1929, Capone was the most visible mobster in America. Capone worked with local media and friendly politicians to cultivate an image of a businessman concerned with the welfare[1] of his fellow Chicagoans. But Capone's tenure[2] was also a period of rising rivalries with other Chicago gangsters, conflicts that frequently turned violent.

themobmuseum.org

1. *bien-être* 2. period of power

YOUR MISSION

Write a short presentation about 1920s America for the Mob Museum website.

1 **Describe** the historical context of the 1920s.

2 **Explain** how the American mafia became very powerful at that time.

WB → p. 85

Build your skills! **Présenter une chronologie**

→ Utilise le prétérit avec des marqueurs de temps pour situer les actions dans le passé :

- *In the twenties, celebrities **were** in demand.*
- *One hundred years ago, the 18th Amendment **came** into force.*
- *The American mafia crime syndicate **was born** during the 1920s and 1930s.*

BUILD YOUR ENGLISH → p. 87

QUIZ **Test**
college.nathan.fr/3sb81

EXPLORE Gangsters in the spotlight

1 The Great Depression

WB → p. 86

Doc 1 — Video

◀ Bank robbery scene from the miniseries *Bonnie & Clyde*, 2013.

CULTURE SPOT

The Great Depression
The period in the 1930s when there were serious economic problems in the United States and Europe, and many people had no work and were very poor.
dictionary.cambridge.org

Doc 2

Journalist: Dillinger really captured the imagination of the people and became a folk[1] hero. Why was that?

Johnny Depp: Well, I think if you look back at the time, the Great Depression, 1933 [...] the banks were the enemy at that point. The banks were foreclosing on[2] people's homes, taking farms away, taking businesses and livelihoods[3] away and the Government was not much better... So John Dillinger went out there and did what everybody wished to do, you know... Take it back!

Promotional interview of lead actor Johnny Depp for *Public Enemies*, 2009.

TEAM WORK

Team A

a. **Look** at the picture (**doc 1**) and **explain** what is happening.

b. **Watch** the video, **identify** the period and **pick out** the words describing how the American people felt.

Team B

a. **Look** at the film poster (**doc 2**), **read** the interview and **say** who the film is about.

b. **Identify** the period and **pick out** the words describing what was happening in the USA.

c. **Share** your information and **explain** who the villains were for many Americans.

1. popular
2. taking back
3. *moyens de subsistance*

2 Partners in crime

WB DIFFÉRENCIATION → p. 87

Doc 1

AUDIO VERSION

The guard on duty perked up[1] when 19-year-old Bonnie Parker stepped into the McLennan County jail[2] in Waco, Texas, on the evening of March 11th 1930. [...] Bonnie smiled and worked her way to the second floor of the jail, where her boyfriend Clyde Barrow waited in his cell. Once there, she slipped Clyde a revolver through the bars, headed back downstairs and walked past the guard out into the evening air. With Bonnie safely away, Clyde sprang into action. He and two other prisoners summoned[3] a guard to the second floor. Threatening[4] the guard with the smuggled revolver, they escaped from the county jail. [...]

While Clyde left Texas behind, Bonnie waited for word on what to do next. There was no separating them now. She had smuggled him the revolver just like he had asked. They were already in love and now they were partners in crime.

Infamous America Podcast – Bonnie and Clyde episode 1: The fairytale, Black Barrel Media, 2021

1. became interested 2. prison 3. called 4. intimidating

Doc 2

Audio

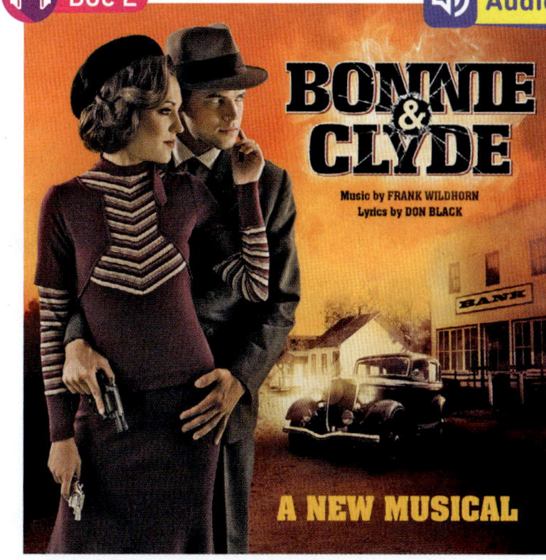

▲ *Bonnie & Clyde* musical, Broadway, New York City, 2011.

PAIR WORK

Partner A

a. **Read** the text (doc 1) and **say** where the scene takes place.

b. **Define** Bonnie's role in the scene and her relationship with Clyde.

Partner B

a. **Listen** (doc 2) and **take** notes about Bonnie and Clyde.

b. **Name** the items that turned them into celebrities.

c. **Share** your information and **look** at the poster. Why has the couple inspired a musical?

GRAMMAR SPOT

- She **had smuggled** him the revolver.
- Now they **were** partners in crime.

Quelle action a eu lieu en premier ?
Quel temps est utilisé pour ce verbe ?

YOUR MISSION

DIFFÉRENCIATION

Bonnie and Clyde have just escaped from jail. Imagine a newspaper's front page.

1 **Imagine** a catchy headline.

2 **Write** a short article explaining when and how it happened and **illustrate** it with a picture.

WB → p. 89

Build your skills! Raconter une scène

→ Utilise le *past perfect* pour rappeler des faits antérieurs : *She **had smuggled** him the revolver just like he **had asked**.* • *Bonnie and Clyde **had been** on a two-year crime spree.*

→ Emploie le prétérit pour décrire des événements simultanés : *The guard on duty **perked** up when 19-year-old Bonnie Parker **stepped** into the McLennan County jail in Waco.*

BUILD YOUR ENGLISH → p. 87

QUIZ Test
college.nathan.fr/3sb83

EXPLORE The harder they fall

1 The hunt is on

WB DIFFÉRENCIATION → p. 90

Doc 1 — Video

a. **Study** the poster and **find** what Dillinger was wanted for.

b. **Watch** the video and **find** information about John Dillinger's arrest.

PHONOLOGY SPOT — AUDIO

FBI Director J. Edgar Hoover wanted him captured dead or alive.

Écoute cette même phrase prononcée avec un accent britannique puis américain. Quelles différences constates-tu ?

Doc 2

On May 20, 1933, the United States Commissioner at Dallas, Texas, issued a warrant[1] against Clyde Barrow and Bonnie Parker, charging them with the interstate transportation, from Dallas to Oklahoma, of [an] automobile stolen in Illinois. The FBI[2] then started its hunt for this elusive[3] pair. [...] In addition to the automobile theft charge, Bonnie and Clyde were suspects in other crimes. At the time they were killed in 1934, they were believed to have committed 13 murders and several robberies and burglaries. [...]

Before dawn on May 23, 1934, a posse[4] composed of police officers from Louisiana and Texas, including Texas Ranger Frank Hamer, concealed[5] themselves in bushes along the highway near Sailes, Louisiana. In the early daylight, Bonnie and Clyde appeared in an automobile and when they attempted to drive away, the officers opened fire. Bonnie and Clyde were killed instantly.

fbi.gov

a. **Study** the film poster and **guess** who the two men are.

b. **Read** the text and **name** one of them.

c. **Explain** what happened to Bonnie and Clyde.

1. official document 2. Federal Bureau of Investigation 3. difficult to find 4. a group 5. hid

2 Life behind bars

WB → p. 92

AUDIO VERSION

Toughest Convict on the Rock

Robert Luke, Alcatraz convict[1] #1118, was on the island from 1954 to 1959.

Interviewed by Gennifer Choldenko in Cotati, California, on February 23, 2013.

While on Alcatraz, did you dream of being free?

All the time. [...]

What question do you get asked the most?

Did you know Al Capone?

Capone died before your time on Alcatraz, of course.

Yes. But if I had been in prison with him, I would have kept my distance. I stayed away from connected criminals because they often have influence over the police or the guards.

But you knew Machine Gun Kelly, right?

Yes, he played bridge on the recreation yard.

Did you have visits on Alcatraz?

Only one. I didn't like visits because they reminded me too much of what it was like outside. [...]

Why do you think you ended up on Alcatraz?

I made the wrong choices. We are all born with the ability to make our own choices. But once you make the wrong choice, other people make your decisions for you. [...]

What would you tell a kid growing up today?

Go to school. Learn to read. The illiteracy[2] rate of cons[3] is so high. Make the right choices.

Gennifer Choldenko, *Al Capone Does My Shirts*, 2014

1. prisoner 2. people who can't read or write 3. convicts

GRAMMAR SPOT

Why do you think you ended up in Alcatraz?

Simplifie cette question. Que deviennent *do* et *ended* si l'on supprime *you think* ?

▲ The Alcatraz Federal Penitentiary in San Francisco Bay.

a. **Look** at the picture and **say** everything you can about the place.

b. **Read** the interview and **explain** who Robert Luke was.

c. **Explain** the advice he gives in the interview.

YOUR MISSION

Prepare and act out an interview between a journalist and a guard about Al Capone's life in Alcatraz.

Journalist **Imagine** and **ask** five questions to the guard in charge of Al Capone's surveillance.

Guard **Decide** what you can or cannot say about the famous convict and **answer** the journalist's questions.

WB → p. 93

Build your skills! **Conduire un entretien journalistique**

- Emploie des questions ouvertes qui demandent une réponse étoffée : ***Why** do you think you ended up on Alcatraz?*
- Si tu poses une question fermée, enchaîne sur une autre question : ***Did** you have visits on Alcatraz? **Can** you tell us more about them?*

BUILD YOUR ENGLISH → p. 87

QUIZ Test
college.nathan.fr/3sb85

EXO Interactive game college.nathan.fr/3sb86

GANGSTER QUIZ

How to play

- **Split** the class into two groups and **name** a referee.
  Group A **answers** "Parker", "Capone" or "Both!" to its 1st statement.
  Group B **does** the same with its 1st statement.
- The groups **take turns** to answer their 2nd statement, then their 3rd statement, etc.
- The referee **counts** the points: 1 point per correct answer.
- If the game ends in a draw, each group has to **invent** another statement for the other group.

CAPONE

PARKER

OR BOTH?

GROUP A

1. This gangster ended up shot.
2. This gangster ended up in jail.
3. This gangster made a fortune during Prohibition.
4. This gangster was active in the early 1930s.
5. This gangster was turned into a celebrity by the media.
6. There are many famous photos of this gangster.
7. This gangster robbed banks.
8. This gangster helped Mr Barrow escape from jail.
9. This gangster was active in Texas.
10. This gangster had Italian origins.

GROUP B

1. This gangster attacked a prison.
2. This gangster was active in the Chicago area.
3. This gangster was sent to prison for tax evasion.
4. This gangster was armed and dangerous.
5. This gangster was nicknamed "Scarface".
6. This gangster's criminal activity ended in 1934.
7. This gangster had a long criminal career.
8. This gangster had a short criminal career.
9. This gangster was active in the 1920s.
10. Films have been made about this gangster.

+ EXERCISES → p. 170

A Situer les événements passés grâce au prétérit et au *past perfect*

▷ Grammar tuto

Le *past perfect* permet d'évoquer un événement antérieur à un autre au prétérit.

They **had robbed** many banks *when* / *by the time* / *before* the FBI **arrested** them.

auxiliaire **have** au passé — verbe **rob** au participe passé — marqueur de temps — verbe **arrest** au prétérit

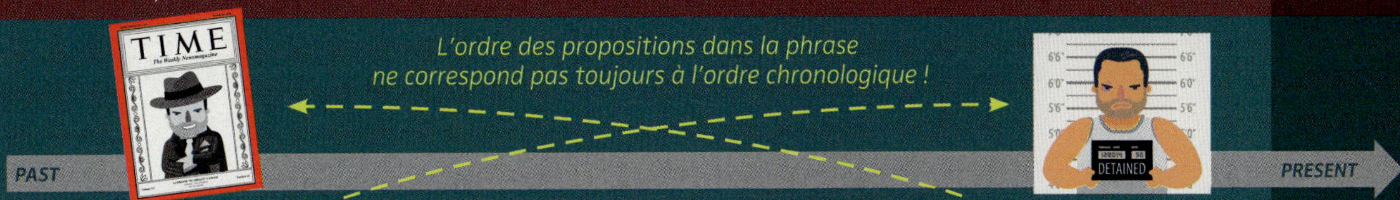

When / *By the time* / *Before* he **went** to Alcatraz, Al Capone **had become** a folk hero.

1 Complète les phrases avec les verbes conjugués. Attention à la chronologie des événements !

had started • ended • had committed • had become • found • happened • had been • became

a. Bonnie and Clyde ... many crimes when the FBI finally ... them.

b. By the time Prohibition ..., many mobsters ... rich.

c. Al Capone ... a minor criminal before he ... public enemy number 1.

d. Prohibition ... before the Great Depression ... .

2 Conjugue les verbes en bleu au prétérit ou au *past perfect* selon la logique des événements.

a. The media (turn) Bonnie and Clyde into romantic runaways before they (show) them as criminals.

b. Before the Great Depression (hit), Americans (experience) restrictions due to WW1 and Prohibition.

c. Capone (help) other criminals before he (become) a Mafia boss.

d. Before I (watch) *The Godfather* I (hear) about famous gangsters like Capone and Dillinger.

HOW TO SHINE IN GRAMMAR → p. 151

B Poser des questions (2)

→ Si l'on veut obtenir une **confirmation** d'une information ou d'une supposition, on utilise un *question tag*.

• *You knew Machine Gun Kelly, didn't you?*
forme affirmative — forme négative

• *You didn't know Machine Gun Kelly, did you?*
forme négative — forme affirmative

→ Attention aux **questions complexes** ! Dans cet exemple, le mot interrogatif *why* porte sur *ended up in Alcatraz*. Mais comme on intercale la proposition *do you think*, c'est elle qui porte l'inversion auxiliaire/sujet.

• *Why do you think you ended up in Alcatraz?*
= *In your opinion, why did you end up in Alcatraz?*

3 Reconstitue ces phrases contenant des *question tags*.

a. was • before • famous • Al Capone • the Great Depression, • he • wasn't • ?

b. Baby Face Nelson • hadn't • heard • you • about • you • had • ?

c. she • Bonnie • had • a revolver, • smuggled • hadn't • ?

4 Reformule comme dans l'exemple.

Ex : *What do you think the FBI did after they caught him? → In your opinion, what did the FBI do after they caught him?*

a. Who do you think arrested Al Capone?

b. Where do you guess Al Capone hid?

c. How do you think he became so famous?

HOW TO SHINE IN GRAMMAR → p. 149

Build your English!

VOCABULARY

EXERCISE → p. 171

1 Name it!

a. The years between 1920 and 1930: ...

b. The period during which no alcohol could be produced or sold in the USA: ...

c. A period of ten years: ...

d. A dramatic period of economic downturn in the USA: ...

2 A notorious gangster in Chicago has just been arrested. Imagine his criminal record.

3 Build as many expressions as you can.

root • hold • break • track • open • capture • do

up • for someone • down • fire • out of jail • time • the imagination

4 Say what happened on that December morning in Chicago, 1933.

HOW TO SHINE IN VOCABULARY → p. 160

PHONOLOGY

A La prononciation des graphies <e> et <u>

- Les graphies **<e>** et **<u>** ne se prononcent pas toujours de la même manière en anglais.

<e>
- enemy /e/ • perfect /ɜː/ • Depression /ɪ/
- listen /ə/ • there /eə/ • hero /ɪə/
- illegal /iː/

<u>
- public /ʌ/ • murder /ɜː/ • blue /uː/
- survive /ə/ • push /ʊ/ • united /juː/
- Bureau /jʊə/

1 Écoute et répète ces mots. AUDIO

era • gangster • pull • where • uniform • escape • status • legalise • were • statue • gun • decade

2 Écoute ces phrases et répète-les. Classe les mots selon la prononciation des lettres <e> et <u>. AUDIO

a. Al Capone was a thug who was considered a folk hero but was convicted for tax evasion.

b. During the Great Depression, Federal Agents and mobsters captured the imagination and even a century later, we still celebrate them in movies!

HOW TO SHINE IN PHONOLOGY → p. 156

B L'accent américain

- La prononciation de nombreuses lettres est différente en anglais **américain** et en anglais **britannique**.
  - gangster /ə/ (GB) → /ɚ/ (US)
  - committed /t/ (GB) → /t̬/ (US)
  - robbery /ɒ/ (GB) → /ɑː/ (US)
  - poor /ɔː/ (GB) → /ʊ/ (US)
  - criminal /ɪ/ (GB) → /ə/ (US)

⚠ L'orthographe de certains mots diffère entre anglais britannique et américain !

- neighbour (GB) → neighbor (US)
- organise (GB) → organize (US)
- theatre (GB) → theater (US)

3 Écoute ces mots prononcés avec l'accent britannique, puis américain et répète-les. AUDIO

murder • inspector • reporter • gangsters • investigate • bottle of water • tomato

4 Écoute ces mêmes mots dans des phrases puis répète-les dans les deux accents. AUDIO

a. The inspector arrested the gangsters who had committed different murders.

b. Twenty years later, the FBI investigated and the criminals were finally identified.

5 Prononce quelques mots avec l'accent de ton choix. Fais deviner quel accent tu as choisi !

WORDMAP

WB → p. 81

AMERICAN GANGSTERS

History

AUDIO

- century
- decade
- eighteenth amendment
- era /'ɪərə/
- Great Depression = economic downturn
- immigration
- Prohibition
- the Thirties = 1930s = 30s
- the (roaring) Twenties = 1920s = 20s
- poor /pɔː/

Crime

AUDIO

- gang
- hold up
- murder
- tax evasion /ɪ'veɪʒən/
- (bank) robbery
- thug
- weapon /'wepən/
- reformed: *repenti(e)*
- break out (of jail)
- escape
- rob somebody or a bank
- smuggle: *faire passer clandestinement*
- steal /stiːl/ something
- threaten

Media

AUDIO

- article /'ɑːtɪkəl/
- headline
- newspaper /'njuːzˌpeɪpə/
- press
- public opinion
- readers
- reporter
- tabloid /'tæblɔɪd/
- investigate
- publish
- write

Celebrity

AUDIO

- fame /feɪm/
- folk hero /'hɪərəʊ/
- status /'steɪtəs/
- celebrated
- famous
- notorious
- capture the imagination
- root for someone

Law and order

AUDIO

- (prison) cell
- federal agent
- (prison) guard
- inspector
- jail = prison /'prɪzən/
- policeman
- ranger
- sheriff
- arrest
- open fire
- track down

Street talk

AUDIO

- booze *(informal)* = alcohol
- cop *(informal)* = policeman
- dough /dəʊ/ *(informal)* = money
- job *(informal)* = criminal operation
- Mob *(informal)* = Mafia
- mobster *(informal)* = gangster
- do time *(informal)* = serve a prison sentence
- inside *(informal)* = in prison

NOUN ADJECTIVE VERB ADVERB OR PREPOSITION

YOUR FINAL MISSION

As a crime reporter, write and publish an interview with a reformed gangster.

WB → p. 94

→ You are a 1920s American crime reporter who managed to interview a famous Federal Prison inmate.

→ **Write** and **publish** a front-page story so the public discovers the facts behind the myth.

STEP 1 ▸ **Choose** the reformed prisoner you want to interview. You can invent a fictional gangster: **imagine** a name, a nickname and a criminal record.

STEP 2 ▸ **Write** a short introduction to your interview.

STEP 3 ▸ **Imagine** relevant questions you can ask about his or her real story.

STEP 4 ▸ **Invent** his or her answers. **Explain** why he or she is full of regrets.

YES YOU CAN! Write a great newspaper interview.

2 DAILY TIMES, CHICAGO, TUESDAY, FEBRUARY 10, 1931

CAPONE PUBLIC ENEMY NO. 1.
How Much Longer Can He Get Away with It?

Lone Gorilla of Gangland Whines on Tottering Throne as He Sees Writing on Wall

By EDWARD DOHERTY

FOR 10 years and more Alphonse Capone, Scarface Al, has been building up his kingdom.

For 10 years he has been fortifying himself against the day of wrath. He has built well. He has amassed millions and millions of dollars. He has intrenched himself politically. He has powerful friends in high places. He has an army of men who will kill anyone at his nod.

He has reached his goal. He is public enemy No. 1 in Chicago.

And the day of wrath has arrived, and he turns uneasily and sees the writing on the wall, and whines.

He built his power on the bodies of women and the lusts and the blood of men. He built it with brothels, with crooked gambling devices, with cut booze and young beer, with machine guns and armored cars. He built it with gunmen and crooked policemen and judges and shady lawyers and politicians. Incidentally, you and I and every man and woman who drinks, helped him to build it.

And now that he shows weakness, now that his troubles are multiplied, now that his throne shakes, we ask, "How much longer can he get away with it?" —and grudge him none of his fate.

Like Job of Uz, Capone has become a song and a byword and a thing of horror, and his enemies "spare not to spit at the sight" of him.

Something new has happened in the land.

"The Boss of Chicago's Red Decade"

A little while ago Capone was doing a $100,000,000 business a year. His friends were legion. His name was ...

... ing of machine guns, the weeping of women, men dying in the streets of Chicago, autos roaring through the Loop (autos filled with murderers shooting at policemen), bodies found on sidewalks, in apartment courts, in ditches, in the drainage canal. His name has meant trucks and trains of beer and booze rumbling into Chicago and out of it. It has meant graft, corruption, fear. But nothing was done about it.

Perhaps there was something dramatic in the spectacle of this one man pitted against all the others in the jungles of gangland, this lone gorilla emerging out of the jungles, bloody and triumphant and smiling, to march on the cities of law-abiding people.

Perhaps there was something that appealed to the popular sympathy in the thought that here was a boy who ...

PUBLIC ENEMY NO. 1

This is Al Capone, dubbed by the Chicago Crime Commission as "Public Enemy No. 1." Capone is better advertised than most American statesmen in many foreign countries, where people think he rules Chicago. Mr. Doherty's story tells how Capone ...

The TIMES in Brief

UNITED STATES

Washington (AP)—Drought loan agreement on relief legislation attacked in senate by Sen. La Follette as "unconditional surrender" by senate coalition.

Wells, Nev. (AP)—Louis Notar, field manager of Boeing Airport at Elko, Nev., killed and Burr Winslow, pilot, injured seriously when Boeing eastbound airmail plane crashes into beacon during heavy fog.

Washington (AP)—President Hoover signs Wagner bill providing advance planning of public works as means of combating unemployment.

Washington (AP)—Venezuela protests proposed restriction on oil imports.

Brownwood, Tex. (AP)—Two small boys dead and other members of family of seven in serious condition here as result of eating poison food.

St. Louis (AP)—Two women shot to death as three gunmen shoot up saloon.

Washington Courthouse, O. (AP)—Tentative jury is chosen to try Mal S. Daugherty on charges growing from Ohio State bank failure.

Miami, Fla. (AP)—Crew of 25 from steamer British Chancellor aground at Callinas Point, Colombia, picked up from small boats by steamer Tekoa.

Indio, Cal. (AP)—Mob drives 25 Filipino vegetable farm workers out of Coachella valley district.

Lawrence, Kas. (AP)—University of Kansas fraternities officially swear off use of liquor.

CHICAGO AND SUBURBS

Leo V. Brothers wins three points in legal tiffs with prosecution, chief of which is right to examine seized records of Riviera hotel, where he lived at time of Lingle killing.

1 Le titre

Choisis un titre court et percutant.

2 Le sous-titre

Annonce le contenu de l'article en une phrase courte qui présente le sujet et éveille la curiosité.

3 La photo

Joins une photo du prisonnier, de la prison ou d'un document compromettant.

4 L'introduction

Présente rapidement le prisonnier.
Sépare l'introduction du corps de texte et utilise une police plus grande.
Donne envie au lecteur de lire la suite !

5 L'interview

Varie tes questions, qui peuvent porter sur la vie avant et pendant l'emprisonnement. Pense à poser des questions qui montrent la « VRAIE » personne derrière le mythe ! N'hésite pas à inventer des réponses surprenantes !

Why do you think you ended up in Alcatraz?
What did you do to pass the time?

HOW TO SHINE IN WRITING → p. 140

Test your skills!

Compréhension de l'oral

B1 OBJECTIF Comprendre une biographie

Audio

▲ Robert de Niro as Al Capone (with glasses) in the film *The Untouchables*, 1987.

A2 **1 Listen** and **say** when Al Capone was born.

2 Identify the different places mentioned.

A2+ **3 Give** the important events of Capone's life and how old he was at the time.

4 Explain why Capone went to prison.

B1 **5 Describe** Capone's attitude to the police.

Compréhension de l'écrit

B1 OBJECTIF Comprendre un extrait de biographie

Each bank robbery by John Dillinger was different. Yet all were alike in certain ways. A fast, shiny, new car with four or five men crowded inside would park near a bank. The time was usually near noon or at closing time. A driver stayed with the car, one of the robbers stood watch at the front door, and the other men entered the bank. The bandits were well dressed in suits and hats and had Thompson submachine guns inside their long overcoats. Once inside the robbers ordered the bank customers to line up along a wall or lay down on the floor. [...]

People still rob banks in the twenty-first century and yet their names are not remembered. No bank robber has been both as celebrated and notorious as John Dillinger from Indiana. Dillinger went about his work during the worst economic times America has ever experienced. These were very hard years of the 1930s, known as the Great Depression. Over a period of fourteen months during 1933 and 1934 Dillinger became the most famous bandit in American history.

John A. Beineke, *Hoosier Public Enemy: A Life of John Dillinger*, 2014

A2 **1 Identify** the author and the name of the book.

2 Say where John Dillinger came from and **find** the dates when he and his gang were active.

A2+ **3 Say** how Dillinger and his gang travelled, and how they dressed.

4 Explain how the robbers entered the bank with their weapons.

B1 **5 Describe** and **explain** the general public's opinion of Dillinger.

QUIZ Test de positionnement
college.nathan.fr/3sb91

SNAPFILE 9

Captain America: born in the USA

▶ How has the superhero been shaped by American history?

YOUR SNAP MISSION

Write and record a portrait of Captain America for the next Marvel exhibition.

1 This is the Captain

WB → p. 95

CAPTAIN AMERICA

HIS SHIELD & ABILITIES

Steve Rogers is Captain America. He has no superpowers but he has exceptional abilities and skills.

MASTER MARTIAL ARTIST

MASTER TACTICIAN & STRATEGIST

MASTER ACROBAT

PROFESSIONAL SKETCH ARTIST
He worked as a freelance illustrator and sketch artist, even loaning[1] his skills to the NYPD[2] at one time.

EXPERT SWORDSMAN

EXPERT MARKSMAN[5]

ADVANCED MILITARY OPERATOR
He is well-versed in intelligence gathering, escape arts, survival tactics, hunting and other skills.

MASTER SHIELDMANSHIP
Aside from bashing and blocking attacks, he is able to throw his shield[3] with perfect aim. He can hit multiple targets with the same throw and achieve a boomerang-like effect allowing him to strike enemies from behind.

INDOMITABLE[4] WILL
He is capable of resisting all forms of mind control.

MULTI-LINGUAL
Fluent in English, German, Russian, Spanish and Japanese. Some French and Italian.

Adapted from *visme.co*

a. **Read** the document and **say** what Captain America can do.
b. **Identify** the patriotic symbols on his equipment.
c. **Imagine** the authors' intention when building such a character.

AT HOME Watch the trailer for *Captain America: The First Avenger* to understand how Steve Rogers became the first Captain America.

Video
college.nathan.fr/3sb92

GRAMMAR SPOT

He is capable of **resisting** all forms of mind control.

Le mot en gras est-il un nom ou un verbe? Comment est-il formé ?

1. lending 2. New York Police Department 3. large piece of metal used as a protection 4. invincible 5. person skilled in shooting

2 A superhero for the real world

WB DIFFÉRENCIATION → p. 96

Doc 1 Audio

▲ Cover of the first *Captain America* comics, 1941.

a. **Look** at the cover and **identify** the characters.

b. **Listen** to Professor David Onyon and **explain** the political influence of Captain America during World War II.

c. **Explain** why he says Captain America is "*propaganda*".

PHONOLOGY SPOT AUDIO

fighting • supporting • going

Écoute ces mots. Entends-tu toutes les lettres de leur terminaison ?

Doc 2

THE MAN WHO PUNCHED HITLER

The America of the 1930s was staunchly isolationist[1] and satisfied to let the rest of the world handle their own problems. [...]

By mid-1940, Germany had invaded Poland, Denmark, Norway and France; over half a million Jews had been ghettoized. Still, public opinion was split[2]. And it's in that tempestuous mess[3] that two Jewish artists, born Hymie Simon and Jacob Kurtzberg, took matters into their own hands. [...]

Captain America, the creation of Joe Simon and Jack Kirby, flew across the page to sock[4] Hitler in the face. [...] Cap launched himself into the dictator with vicious fury. *Captain America Comics* #1 was an instant success, selling approximately a million copies.

John R. Parker, *comicsalliance.com*, 2016

1. avoiding relationships with other countries 2. divided 3. very complicated situation 4. hit

a. **Read** the text and **say** what "*the 1930s*" and "*mid-1940*" refer to.

b. **Explain** why Simon and Kirby created such a superhero.

YOUR SNAP MISSION STEP 1

DIFFÉRENCIATION

Write and record the first part of your audio guide presentation. Explain Captain America's birth and say what he represents.

WAY 1

1 **Describe** how Steve Rogers became Captain America.

2 **Explain** what makes him patriotic.

WAY 2

1 **Detail** the historical context of Captain America's birth.

2 **Explain** the authors' intentions.

WB → p. 99

Build your skills! **Décrire un personnage**

- Transforme les verbes en noms pour lister des caractéristiques : *Aside from **bashing** and **blocking** attacks… • He is capable of **resisting** all forms of mind control.*
- Explique ce que le personnage représente en commençant tes phrases par un gérondif : ***Fighting** for the United States was viewed as heroic.*

BUILD YOUR ENGLISH → p. 96

3 Reinventing the Patriot

WB DIFFÉRENCIATION → p. 99

GRAMMAR SPOT

- Serving his country gets **more complicated**.
- His attitude is **less patriotic**.

Observe les formes en gras. Que t'apprennent-elles sur l'évolution de Captain America ?

Audio

Captain America: The First Avenger (2011)

Steve Rogers becomes Captain America, not because he is stronger than other people, but because he is a good man. His costume and his shield symbolise his loyalty to his country.

Captain America: The Winter Soldier (2014)

Captain America learns the terrible truth that the SHIELD (led by the US government) has been infiltrated by HYDRA (the villains). That doesn't stop him being just as righteous as he appeared in *The First Avenger* but his attitude is less patriotic.

Avengers: Infinity War (2018)

Steve Rogers, as a human, not a superhero, joins the Avengers in fighting Thanos, who is more powerful than ever. After an epic battle, Steve is left psychologically weaker and less confident, facing an uncertain future.

speakeasy-news.com

a. **Look** at the pictures and **list** the similarities and differences in Captain America's successive appearances.
b. **Read** the texts and **comment** on Captain America's evolution.
c. **Listen** to the audio and **list** Captain America's qualities. **Say** why Steve Rogers was chosen.
d. **Pick out** information about Captain America's values.
e. **Explain** why Captain America's behaviour has changed over time.

4 Meet the new Captain

WB → p. 101

Doc 1 Audio

▲ Anthony Mackie is Sam Wilson, chosen by Steve Rogers to be the new Captain America (2021).

Doc 2 AUDIO VERSION

SAM WILSON (CAPTAIN AMERICA): I'm a black man, carrying the Stars and Stripes[1]. What don't I understand? Every time I pick this thing up, I know there are millions of people out there who are going to hate me for it. Even now, here. I feel it. The stares[2], the judgement, and there's nothing I can do to change it. And I'm still here. No super serum. No blonde hair or blue eyes. The only power I have is that I believe we can do better.

Last episode of the series *The Falcon and the Winter Soldier*, 2021

1. the American flag 2. *regards*

TEAM WORK

a. **Observe** and **comment** on the poster.

Team A

b. **Listen** to Anthony Mackie's interview. **Compare** Sam Wilson to Steve Rogers.

c. **Explain** why it is difficult for him to be a black Captain America.

Team B

b. **Read** the text and **list** the differences between Sam Wilson and Steve Rogers.

c. **Say** how people reacted when Sam became Captain America.

d. **Share** what you have learnt with the other team. **Discuss** how different the new Captain America is.

YOUR SNAP MISSION STEP 2

DIFFÉRENCIATION

Write and record the second part of your audio guide. Explain how Captain America has evolved over time.

WAY 1

1. **Describe** Captain America's physical evolution.
2. **Say** what his values are.

WAY 2

1. **Say** how Captain America has changed over time.
2. **Explain** the influence that American society has had on his evolution.

Build your skills! Décrire une évolution

→ Utilise le comparatif de supériorité, d'égalité ou d'infériorité pour faire part d'un changement : *His inner moral compass is **stronger than** his allegiance to any law.* • *He is just **as righteous as** he appeared in* The First Avenger *but his attitude is **less patriotic**.*

→ Utilise des noms en ***-ity*** pour mettre en avant des valeurs : *The core of the American **identity** should also be our **morality**.* • *What sets Cap apart are his **qualities**…*

WB → p. 102 HOW TO SHINE IN WRITING → p. 140 BUILD YOUR ENGLISH → p. 96

QUIZ Test
college.nathan.fr/3sb95

GRAMMAR

EXERCISES → p. 171

A Transformer les verbes en noms grâce au gérondif

Grammar tuto

On utilise le **gérondif** pour désigner une **activité**. Il fonctionne comme un **nom**. On l'utilise :

1 Termine ces phrases sur les superhéros en utilisant le gérondif.

a. Marvel started…
b. Captain America is capable of…
c. Superheroes manage to fight evil without…
d. I read some comics before…

2 Mets les verbes entre parenthèses au gérondif si nécessaire.

a. I started (read) comics when I was 8.
b. (Choose) an actor to embody Captain America is not easy.
c. Captain America fights evil in order to (protect) civilians.
d. Marvel is famous for (invent) superheroes.

HOW TO SHINE IN GRAMMAR → p. 148

B Comparer en utilisant le comparatif de supériorité, d'égalité et d'infériorité

Pour comparer des éléments, tu peux utiliser le comparatif **de supériorité** (plus ... que ...), **d'égalité** (aussi ... que ...) ou **d'infériorité** (moins ... que ...).

comparatif de supériorité	**adjectif court + *-er* (+ *than*)** *Captain America is **taller than** many superheroes.*	***more* + adjectif long (+ *than*)** *Captain America is **more courageous than** the villains.*
comparatif d'égalité	***as* + adjectif + *as*** *Captain America is **as famous as** all the other superheroes.*	
comparatif d'infériorité	***less* + adjectif + *than*** *Captain America is **less powerful than** many other superheroes.*	

⚠ Attention aux modifications orthographiques au comparatif de supériorité !

big → bigger • fit → fitter • funny → funnier

3 Mets les adjectifs entre parenthèses au comparatif demandé : supériorité (>), égalité (=) ou infériorité (<).

a. Superheroes are (> strong) human beings.
b. Marvel movies are (= popular) Marvel comic books.
c. His shield is (> heavy) his helmet.
d. Fighting evil (< difficult) preserving peace.

4 Compare Captain America et Iron Man à l'aide de ces adjectifs et d'autres de ton choix.

strong • courageous • tall • patriotic • fast • sporty

HOW TO SHINE IN GRAMMAR → p. 147

VOCABULARY

EXERCISES → p. 171

CAPTAIN AMERICA

Patriotism
AUDIO

- flag
- re**solve** = determi**na**tion
- Stars and Stripes = A**me**rican flag
- he**ro**ic
- patri**o**tic
- serve one's **coun**try
- sup**port**

Abilities
AUDIO

- **mas**ter
- **stra**tegist /'strætədʒɪst/
- **swords**man /'sɔːdzmən/
- tac**ti**cian /tæk'tɪʃən/
- **ca**pable of
- **ex**pert (at)
- in**do**mitable /ɪn'dɒmɪtəbəl/ = in**vin**cible
- well-**versed** = **know**ledgeable
- throw

World War II
AUDIO

- **al**ly /'ælaɪ/
- **con**flict
- dic**ta**tor
- **go**vernment
- law
- **mi**litary **ser**vice
- propa**gan**da
- war bonds: *emprunts de guerre*
- war **ef**fort
- dicta**to**rial
- iso**la**tionist
- in**vade**

Equipment
AUDIO

- **cos**tume /'kɒstjuːm/ = **out**fit
- **se**rum /'sɪərəm/
- shield
- **su**per **sol**dier /'səʊldʒə/
- **wea**pon /'wepən/
- **bul**letproof

Identity
AUDIO

- al**le**giance /ə'liːdʒəns/ = **lo**yalty
- **cou**rage
- **free**dom
- mo**ra**lity
- **qua**lity
- shift = change
- **wil**lingness = **rea**diness
- de**fen**sive ≠ of**fen**sive
- disi**llu**sioned
- groomed: *soigné*
- right ≠ wrong

- NOUN
- ADJECTIVE
- VERB

In pairs:
Partner A has 30 seconds to define a word from the wordmap.
Partner B has to guess the word. Swap roles.

HOW TO SHINE IN VOCABULARY → p. 160

PHONOLOGY

La prononciation du suffixe *-ing*

- Le **suffixe *-ing*** n'est pas prononcé comme en français : on ne prononce pas le <g> final. C'est le cas par exemple pour les adjectifs comme ***interesting*** /'ɪntrəstɪŋ/, mais aussi pour les gérondifs :
  - **Reinventing** /ˌriːɪn'ventɪŋ/ Captain America was a challenge.
  - Marvel superheroes are famous for **fighting** /'faɪtɪŋ/ evil.

1 Écoute et répète ces mots en faisant attention au *-ing* final. AUDIO

fascinating • surprising • thrilling • choosing • fighting • creating • watching • resisting

2 Prononce ces phrases en veillant aux gérondifs, puis vérifie et répète. AUDIO

a. Captain America is famous for **fighting** evil and **defending** his country.

b. All over the world, people enjoy **watching** Marvel movies and buying goodies.

HOW TO SHINE IN PHONOLOGY → p. 156

FILE 10 All dressed up!

“Fashion should be a form of escapism, and not a form of imprisonment.”

Alexander McQueen (1969-2010)
British fashion designer

How do British people assert their identities through their clothes?

More on **SPEAKEASY NEWS**
speakeasy-news.com

A man with a Mohican hairstyle, standing out from the crowd in London's business district.

YOUR FINAL MISSION

Take part in a talk show about fashion: "Should we wear whatever we want?"

Video

The Duchess and Duke of Cambridge with their children Louis, Charlotte and George.

TEAM WORK

WB → p. 103

Team A

Describe the main picture and **say** in what way the man is "standing out from the crowd".

Team B

Read the quote and **say** what sort of clothes can make you feel free or not.

Team C

Watch the video and **make** a list of what the Royals are allowed to wear.

- **Share** with the other teams and **discuss** what dress codes can mean in the UK.

EXPLORE Norms and uniforms

1 The smart choice

WB → p. 104

Doc 1 Video

Doc 2

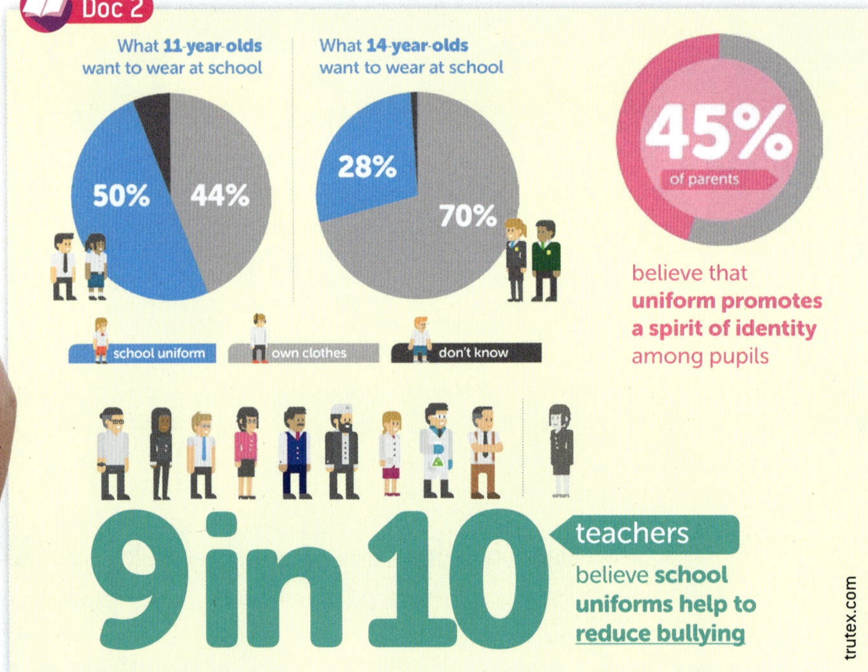

Doc 3

We asked for your opinions on whether uniforms should be scrapped[1] and were inundated with responses.

Finda Hughes said: "No, there are so many other ways for kids to show their individuality, without fear of being picked on[2] for not conforming to a 'designer' norm. I wore a uniform at school and have for most of my working life and it didn't suppress my individuality."

Susan Dunne said: "No definitely not. School is not a place for a fashion parade and uniform means that no child is viewed as better or worse than another. It also prepares them for life after school where many jobs have a uniform."

Richard Hughes said: "No, because school becomes a fashion show where poor children and poor families are put under more pressure. School should be about education."

Alan Weston, *liverpoolecho.co.uk*, 2021

1. abandoned 2. bullied

a. **Watch** the video (doc 1) and **say** what the students think of their uniform.
b. **Read** the infographic (doc 2) and **explain** what it reveals about uniforms.
c. **Read** the article (doc 3) and **identify** the parents' arguments in favour of school uniforms.
d. **List** the pros and cons of wearing a uniform. (docs 1, 2 and 3)

A LITTLE EXTRA Watch this debate about school uniforms in the USA and **identify** the arguments in favour or against them. Video

GRAMMAR SPOT

- I don't have **any** pictures of me in Year 7 but I sent **some** pictures of me in Year 11.
- **Many** jobs have a uniform.

Qu'expriment les mots en gras ?

2 Flirting with the rules

WB → p. 106

Victory for Exeter's boys in skirts as heatwave strikes again.

On June 22 2017, boys at the school decided to wear skirts to school as part of a protest against rules forcing them to wear trousers in the heat[1]. Since then, the school has changed its uniform policy[2], meaning boys are now allowed to wear shorts during the summer term. [...] The boys and their parents campaigned to be allowed to wear shorts in hot weather. [...]

Claire Reeves, 30, was one of the first mums to criticise the school policy. She said: "I have called the school several times and they have told me that if I send my son to school in shorts then he will be sent to the isolation room all day, and if I keep him off school then it'll be an unauthorised absence." One mother said: "My 14-year-old son wanted to wear shorts. Children also don't like injustice. The boys see the women teachers in sandals and nice cool skirts and tops while they are wearing long trousers and shoes and the older boys have to wear blazers. [...] The girls are allowed to wear skirts all year round so I think it's completely unfair[3] that the boys can't wear shorts."

Jamie Hawkins, *devonlive.com*, 2018

a. Guess what the boys are doing in the picture.

b. Read the text and **explain** their uniform.

c. Explain why the parents criticise the school policy.

d. Discuss: should boys be allowed to wear shorts?

GRAMMAR SPOT

- The girls are allowed to wear skirts **so** it's unfair that the boys can't wear shorts.
- If I send my son to school in shorts **then** he will be sent to the isolation room.

Explique le sens des mots en gras.

1. hot weather
2. rules
3. *injuste*

3 Gender-neutral uniforms

WB DIFFÉRENCIATION → p. 107

Video

a. Watch the video and **identify** the topic.

b. Pick out details of these school uniforms and **say** what makes them different.

c. Give the reasons why these school uniforms are better for parents and students.

YOUR MISSION

With your team, choose a dress code for your school and be ready to justify your choices.

1. **Discuss** with your team and **introduce** your dress code to the class.
2. **Explain** your choice to your classmates.

WB → p. 108

Build your skills! **Exprimer un point de vue**

- Utilise des verbes d'opinion et des adverbes : *I **think** I'd **actually rather** have … • I **find** it **really** difficult …*
- Emploie ***so*** et ***then*** pour expliquer ton avis : *The girls are allowed to wear skirts **so** it's unfair that the boys can't wear shorts.*
- Utilise des quantifieurs pour illustrer ton point de vue : *There are so **many** other ways for kids to show their individuality.*

BUILD YOUR ENGLISH → p. 107

QUIZ Test college.nathan.fr/3sb101

EXPLORE Me and my clique

1 British youth cultures

WB → p. 108

Mods (1960s)

Short for modernists, Mods emerged in the early 1960s as a distinct social group that wore bold[1] new clothing. [...] Mods were renowned for riding scooters — usually Vespas or Lambrettas — that were fitted[2] with as many mirrors as possible.

Although they were bitter rivals of the Mods, the Rockers also took much of their inspiration from the Teddy Boys[3] of the 1950s, but with less attention to detail and a far more casual[4] overall style. The fact that most Rockers rode motorbikes led them to choose clothing that was suitable[5] for such transportation.

Rockers (1960s)

TEAM WORK

Team A

a. **Comment** on the pictures of the Mods and the Rockers.

b. **Read** the texts and **compare** the two cultures. **Explain** how they influenced each other.

Team B

a. **Comment** on the pictures of the Punks and the New Romantics.

b. **Read** the texts and **say** how these cultures were influenced by society.

c. **Share** with the other team and **discuss** the relationship between group identity and fashion.

1. *audacieux* 2. equipped 3. British youth culture (Teddy Boys dressed like Dandies and listened to rock'n'roll.) 4. relaxed 5. appropriate

2 A generation without an identity?

WB DIFFÉRENCIATION → p. 110

Video

▲ Nick, 19, explains his views on British youth identity.

a. **Watch** the video and **pick out** all the aspects that help define someone's identity.

b. **Explain** where young people take inspiration from.

c. **Say** why there is more than one British youth identity.

PHONOLOGY SPOT AUDIO

- Wow! Um, what a big question!
- This generation is able to, **you know**, to create their own identity…

Écoute ces phrases. À quoi servent les mots en gras ci-dessus ?

Punks (1970s)

The Punk movement spawned[6] a DIY[7] fashion revolution that saw a new generation of youths cutting and dying[8] their own hair, adapting their old clothes to suit the new trend and buying garments from charity shops and jumble sales[9].

New Romantics (1980s)

The New Romantics boomed in the 1980s, setting off a generation of eccentric and bold[1] fashionistas that was dubbed the 'New Dandies' by the press. The New Romantics played with the idea of gender and period costume dress[10]; think oversized blouses, glamorous frills[11] and luxurious satins and silks[12] with colourful, glam make-up looks.

simplychicblogboutique.com and *arts.ac.uk*, 2021

6. created 7. Do It Yourself 8. colouring
9. *ventes de charité* 10. *costumes historiques*
11. decorations 12. *soies*

GRAMMAR SPOT

Although they were rivals of the Mods, the Rockers also took their inspiration from the Teddy Boys of the 1950s, **but** with less attention to detail.

À quoi servent les mots en gras dans l'organisation de cette phrase ?

YOUR MISSION

Present a youth culture on your fashion YouTube channel.

WAY 1

Speak about the Mods, the Rockers, the Punks or the New Romantics.

WAY 2

Choose another British culture from the past and **describe** its style.

Website
college.nathan.fr/**3sb103a**

WB → p. 112

Build your skills! Comparer des styles vestimentaires

- Exprime la concession avec ***although*** et l'opposition avec **but** : ***Although*** *they were rivals of the Mods, the Rockers …* • *The youth are able to mix and match their identity influences.* ***But*** *is this a true identity?*
- Fais des descriptions précises en utilisant des adjectifs et des adverbes : *a* ***far more casual*** *overall style* • ***glamorous*** *frills and* ***luxurious*** *satins and silks*

BUILD YOUR ENGLISH → p. 107

QUIZ Test
college.nathan.fr/**3sb103b**

EXPLORE Style as a statement

1 Wearing the national flag

WB → p. 112

Doc 1

▲ BRIT Awards: the British flag as a fashion statement, 24 years apart — Dua Lipa (2021) and Geri Halliwell of the Spice Girls (1997).

therealgerihalliwell • Follow

therealgerihalliwell Trust yourself. ... this dress is a reminder to follow your instincts and be yourself.

24 years ago I had an idea- to wear a Union Jack to celebrate The Brit Awards.
Despite the doubts, I trusted my instincts and wore it anyway. All these years later to see it worn by a fellow sister is so special. GB ✌#girlpower
P.S. it was £5 tea towel on a Gucci dress.
#followyourdreams

37w

signesunshine_ 🔥🔥🔥

5d Reply

98,885 likes

MAY 12, 2021

Add a comment... Post

TEAMWORK

Team A

a. Look at the pictures (**doc 1**) and **imagine** what the "BRIT Awards" are.

b. Read the Instagram post. **Say** what Geri Halliwell did and why.

Team B

a. Read the article (**doc 2**) and **identify** the reasons why the Union Jack is such a popular symbol.

b. Explain how the British flag unites people around the world.

c. Now **share** what you have learned about the Union Jack as a style statement.

Doc 2

How has the Union Jack Become a Fashion Symbol?

The distinctive colours of the Union Jack make a bold[1] statement[2]. What was once an explicit symbol of British patriotism has now become a well-loved fashion icon. [...]

From the punk-rock fashion era right through to the likes of bands such as Blur, Oasis and Geri Halliwell of the Spice Girls in the 1990s, the Union Jack has lost its nationalistic stigma[3] and become a popular fashion icon that everyone can enjoy, either to show their love for the UK, to celebrate their British heritage or simply because it's an awesome-looking design to have on your clothes. [...]

This symbol of British identity is so widespread[4] it is now uniting people around the world through popular culture and fashion.

"Why Do We Love Union Jack Clothing?", *londonhut.com*

1. *audacieux* 2. declaration 3. negative image 4. common

2 Dressing like a dandy

WB DIFFÉRENCIATION → p. 113

a. Look at the picture and **comment** on Zack Pinsent's style.
b. Watch the video and **say** how people react to his style.
c. Explain his choices and **give** your opinion.

PHONOLOGY SPOT AUDIO

Clothes are social history.

Écoute cette phrase. Comment est prononcée la lettre <o> ? Dans quel mot l'entend-on moins ?

3 Using fashion to fight for change

WB → p. 114

a. Read the text and **say** who Vivienne Westwood is and what she is famous for.
b. Describe what she wants clothes-buyers to do.
c. Explain how her slogan could impact the fashion market.

Ethical Fashion series: the legendary Vivienne Westwood

A grande dame of the fashion world, famous for her designs that play with the codes of punk and Britishness, Vivienne Westwood is also renowned as a pioneer of sustainable[1] clothing. [...]

Westwood has ceaselessly worked for the protection of the planet and its ecosystems, seeking to raise awareness. [...] Over time, her commitment[2] has intensified, to the point where today she is just as well known for her historically inspired collections as for her ecological militancy. One of her best-known slogans, "*Buy less, choose well, make it last*[3]," calls for balanced[4] consumption, whether of fashion or any other resources.

Lea Zetlaoui, *numero.com*, 2019

1. eco-friendly
2. *engagement*
3. *durer*
4. *équilibrée*

YOUR MISSION

Prepare an article on fashion and identity for your school magazine.

"If I enjoy what I'm wearing, why change?" Zack Pinsent

"Buy less, choose well, make it last." Vivienne Westwood

"Follow your (fashion) instincts and be yourself." Geri Halliwell

1 **Choose** one of the quotes above.
2 **Write** four arguments for and four arguments against the statement. **Give** examples.

WB → p. 115

Build your skills! **Argumenter pour convaincre**

- Introduis ton argument avec une prise de position claire : ***I don't think*** *this is the identity-less generation at all.*
- Justifie tes arguments avec des exemples : ***From*** *punk* ***right through to*** *bands like Blur…* • ***One of*** *her best-known slogans…*
- Utilise des questions rhétoriques pour renforcer tes arguments : *If I enjoy what I'm doing then* ***why change?*** • ***What's the point*** *of returning once evolved?*

BUILD YOUR ENGLISH → p. 107

QUIZ Test college.nathan.fr/3sb105

GAME ON!

EXO Interactive game
college.nathan.fr/3sb106

The "dressing challenge"

1 Name a rule from the British Royal family dress code.

2 Give one argument for and one argument against wearing a uniform.

3 What did the Mods ride?

4 Identify the clothing style and define it.

5 Say why Punks started a fashion revolution in the 1970s.

6 Give five adjectives to characterise the New Romantics' style.

7 "The new generation is identity-less." Give two arguments to refute this statement.

9 Which fashion designer is renowned as a pioneer of sustainable clothing?

8 "I'm twenty-five years old and I don't own or wear any modern clothing." What is my clothing style?

a. Rocker
b. Dandy
c. Punk

10 Explain why the Union Jack is such a popular symbol.

How to play

- **Take part** in a jumble sale to raise money for a charity!
- **Join your team** and **choose** the clothes you want to sell. If you answer the question correctly, you can sell the piece of clothing.
- The team with the fewest clothes left wins! **Be quick**: you only have three minutes!

+ EXERCISES → p. 172

A Exprimer la quantité grâce aux quantifieurs

Grammar tuto

Les **quantifieurs** sont des déterminants exprimant **un nombre ou une quantité**.

Noms dénombrables		Noms indénombrables
He designs **a lot of** historical clothes.	**a lot of**	We had **a lot of** fun at the show.
Many designers are British.	**many / much**	I don't have **much** energy today.
Some schools impose uniforms.	**some**	You need to have **some** flexibility.
A few people attended the fashion week.	**a few / a little**	It brings **a little** fantasy…
Few pupils like their uniform.	**few / little**	We have **little** information.
French pupils **don't** wear **any** uniforms.	**not … any**	I **don't** have **any** space for clothes!
I see **no** sign of discrimination.	**no**	There is **no** need for this.

⚠ Certains mots **dénombrables en français** sont **indénombrables en anglais** : les conseils : *advice* — les informations : *information* — les nouvelles : *news*

1 Choisis le quantifieur adéquat et justifie ton choix.

a. In England, a lot of / no schools have uniforms and only a few / a little students are against them.

b. I really don't know: I don't have any / no opinion on the subject.

c. I think people pay too many / much attention to what others wear.

2 Complète les phrases avec le bon quantifieur.

a. There are so … items in my wardrobe!

b. Only … people are against uniforms at school.

c. There aren't … bright colours in these suits, they're all black: at work, … fantasy is allowed!

HOW TO SHINE IN GRAMMAR → p. 147

B Exprimer l'opposition et la concession, la cause et la conséquence

opposition	concession	cause	conséquence
but • while • whereas	**although** **despite** + nom	**because • as • since** **because of** + nom	**so • as a consequence • consequently • then • therefore • that's why**
*Mods rode scooters **while** Rockers rode motorbikes.*	***Although** he has a very original style, people never criticise him. **Despite** her doubts, she trusted her instincts and wore the dress.*	***As** they do not belong to a youth culture, they are called identity-less. Some people are discriminated against **because of** their style.*	*They wear uniforms at school, **therefore** there are no visible social differences.*

3 Complète ces phrases sur la mode avec le mot de liaison correspondant.

a. While / That's why teenagers are usually keen on fashion, some of them aren't interested at all.

b. They were never ostracised although / because of they were very committed.

c. They are Royals because / so they have to respect a dress code.

d. As / Despite criticisms, he chose to wear what he liked.

4 Reconstitue les phrases en ajoutant un mot de liaison entre les deux propositions. Il y a plusieurs possibilités.

a. She loves British culture

b. She never felt rejected

c. Some people refuse uniforms

d. Vivienne Westwood's fashion is unique

- she refuses to follow the rules.
- others love them!
- her original clothing style.
- she decided to wear a Union Jack dress.

HOW TO SHINE IN GRAMMAR → p. 154

VOCABULARY

EXERCISES ➜ p. 172

1 Say if the coloured word is a noun or a verb.

a. After the show, the designer started to **trend** on social media.

Social media can influence people to follow their own **trend**.

b. Vivienne Westwood is famous for her political **campaigns**.

c. Vivienne Westwood usually **campaigns** through her fashion.

2 Write 3 sentences, each using 2 words from the list. You can only use a word once!

trend · harsh · policy · smart · fashion · oversized · charity · shop · protest

3 Name it! And spot the odd one out.

CAMPAIGN · BLAZER · DRESS CODE · BRAND · INDIVIDUALITY

a. All the characteristics that make people unique and different.

b. The name of a company selling products.

c. A series of activities or events to achieve a particular objective.

d. A jacket often showing the colours or emblem of a school.

4 You are a fashion-show commentator. Choose one model and describe their outfit.

HOW TO SHINE IN VOCABULARY ➜ p. 160

PHONOLOGY

A La prononciation de la graphie <o>

- En anglais, la lettre **<o>** se prononce de façons différentes.

Son court
- socks /ɒ/
- colour /ʌ/
- look /ʊ/

Son long
- shorts /ɔː/
- world /ɜː/
- two /uː/

Son court non-accentué
- community /ə/

Diphtongue
- clothes /əʊ/

1 Écoute les mots suivants, répète-les et classe-les en fonction de la prononciation du <o>. AUDIO

shop • store • into • codes • word • Rockers • of • policy • vote • uniform • book • Mods

2 Écoute et répète ces phrases en veillant à la prononciation de la lettre <o>. AUDIO

I have no opinion on this topic: you can wear shorts with socks, or break the codes, or follow the trend... This is so personal.

HOW TO SHINE IN PHONOLOGY ➜ p. 156

B Les *gap fillers*

La langue orale n'est pas toujours fluide. On cherche parfois ses mots, on hésite, on se reprend… Comme en français, on utilise en anglais des mots ou expressions qui permettent de combler les blancs dans le discours : ce sont des ***gap fillers*** (*gap* signifie « trou » et *fill* « combler »). En voici quelques exemples : *you know*, *well*, *I mean*, *actually* (en fait), *in fact*…

3 Écoute et répète les phrases suivantes en veillant à la façon dont les *gap fillers* sont prononcés (intonation, pause). AUDIO

a. This generation is able to, **you know**, to create their own identity with such ease.

b. I would say in terms of… **yeah**, identity…

c. **And well**, he's gonna turn eight next July…

4 Repère les *gap fillers*, puis entraîne-toi à les prononcer. AUDIO

a. Uniforms are fair, I mean, they are a way to erase social differences.

b. It all depends on, you know, your style and how people look at you.

WORDMAP

WB → p. 103

FASHION AND IDENTITY

Clothes
AUDIO

- **bla**zer
- blouse /blaʊz/: *chemisier*
- **clip**-on tie
- dress
- **gar**ment
- **jum**per
- shorts
- skirt
- **trou**sers (GB) = pants (US)
- **ward**robe
- **lea**ther
- silk: *(en) soie*
- **tar**tan: *motif écossais*
- wear /weə/

Making a statement
AUDIO

- com**mit**ment: *engagement*
- **i**con /'aɪkɒn/
- i**den**tity /aɪ'dentəti/
- self-ex**pre**ssion
- as**sert** one**self**
- be**lieve**
- cam**paign**
- **cri**ticise /'krɪtɪsaɪz/
- join a **pro**test
- pro**mote**
- u**nite** /juː'naɪt/
- **ac**tually: *en fait*
- **de**finitely: *tout à fait*

Imposed clothing
AUDIO

- **bull**ying /'bʊliɪŋ/
- dress code
- individu**al**ity
- **po**licy = rules
- **pre**ssure
- fair ≠ un**fair**
- harsh = strict
- be al**lowed**
- free one**self** from
- have to = must

Styles and looks
AUDIO

- trend: *(être) tendance*
- bold: *audacieux*
- **gen**der **neu**tral
- glam(orous)
- **o**versized = too big
- **pre**tty ≠ **ug**ly
- smart ≠ **ca**sual /'kæʒjuəl/
- dye /daɪ/ = **co**lour (hair)

Fashion and business
AUDIO

- brand
- **cha**rity shop
- col**lec**tion
- con**sump**tion /kən'sʌmʃən/
- de**sign**er
- **jum**ble sale
- af**ford**able ≠ ex**pen**sive
- re**nowned** /rɪ'naʊnd/ = **fa**mous in a **po**sitive way
- boom = be**come** suc**cess**ful

NOUN ADJECTIVE VERB ADVERB

YOUR FINAL MISSION

Take part in a talk show about fashion: "Should we wear whatever we want?"

WB → p. 116

→ You and your classmates are taking part in a TV show about youth fashion.
→ The talk-show presenter starts a debate about: "Should we wear whatever we want?"
→ **Prepare** your arguments and your examples and **debate** together!

STEP 1 ▸ **Decide** which role you are playing (student, teacher, headmaster, parent...).
STEP 2 ▸ **Prepare** solid arguments and examples **FOR** and **AGAINST** wearing what you want.
STEP 3 ▸ **Present** your arguments and **justify** your opinions.
STEP 4 ▸ **Listen** to your opponents and **respond** to what they say. **Try** to **convince** others!

YES YOU CAN!

Take part in a debate.

La position prise

Annonce ta position sur la question en débat (pour ou contre), et présente tes arguments.
I think ... • I'd rather ... • I find ... • I don't think ...

L'accord et le désaccord

Exprime ton accord ou ton désaccord avec les autres participant(e)s.
I agree (with you) ... • That's exactly how I feel ...
I disagree (with you) ... • I don't think so ...

Video

Les justifications

Justifie tes arguments en citant des chiffres, des pourcentages, en utilisant des quantifieurs, en évoquant des conséquences, et en t'opposant aux autres arguments présentés.
nearly one in five • most teenagers • few people • but • although • whereas • so • then • that's why

L'attitude

Affirme-toi par ta posture, par ta voix, par ta façon de parler. Soigne ton intonation, ton accentuation, le volume et la vitesse de ta parole. Essaie de te détacher de tes notes et utilise des *gap fillers* pour parler de manière fluide.
I mean ... • You know ... • Well, first of all ... • In fact ...

L'écoute attentive

Écoute tes camarades avec attention, qu'ils soient de ton avis ou non. Anticipe ce qu'ils vont dire afin d'appuyer ou de contrer leurs arguments. Demande-leur si tu as besoin qu'ils répètent, reformulent et clarifient afin de réagir de manière pertinente.
Can you repeat that, please? • Would you mind saying it again? • What do you mean? • Could you rephrase, please?

HOW TO SHINE IN INTERACTING → p. 142

Test your skills!

Compréhension de l'oral

B1 OBJECTIF Comprendre une prise de position sur la mode et l'identité

Audio

- A1 **1** **Listen** and **identify** some of the clothes mentioned.
- A2 **2** **Say** who or what first had an influence on our clothes.
- **3** **Identify** what is a serious exercise.
- A2+ **4** **Pick out** some elements of clothes we had to make decisions about.
- **5** **Say** what the presenter thinks about some sections of the fashion industry.
- B1 **6** **Explain** what role our clothes have.

Compréhension de l'écrit

B1 OBJECTIF Comprendre un article de presse sur la mode

At the top of the stairs in Katharine Hamnett's east London studio, visitors are confronted with a rack[1] of black and white t-shirts bearing[2] slogans in enormous block lettering. 'Cancel Brexit', 'Choose Love', 'Global Green New Deal Now'. In 1984, the designer made headlines by shaking hands with Margaret Thatcher[3] during a reception at 10 Downing Street wearing a T-shirt dress that read '58% Don't Want Pershing', in reference to the stationing of US nuclear missiles across western Europe. [...]

At the end of that decade, after commissioning a report that revealed the horrifying environmental and human cost of cotton production, Hamnett dedicated herself to finding ethical, ecological alternatives and to calling out[4] ongoing[5] abuses in the fashion industry. Her A/W[6] 1989 collection was titled 'Clean Up or Die'. When she relaunched her eponymous label, to much acclaim, in 2017, it was with a small collection using only materials from sustainable sources (scrupulously detailed on her website). Yet, in the 40 years since 1989, little has changed. In fact, by many metrics[7], the situation has exponentially deteriorated. What power – or will – does the industry have to make good on her demand, as another T-shirt reads, for 'No More Fashion Victims'?

Amy Sherlock, *frieze.com*, 2019

- A2 **1** **Read** the text and **find** the name of the designer.
- **2** **Explain** what is special about her T-shirts.
- A2+ **3** **Say** what she did in 1984.
- **4** **Identify** some of the ecological problems associated with the fashion industry.
- B1 **5** **Explain** how the designer has changed her own collections.

1. selection
2. *portant*
3. British Prime Minister (1975-1990)
4. denouncing
5. continuing
6. Autumn / Winter
7. in many ways

QUIZ Test de positionnement
college.nathan.fr/3sb111

SNAPFILE 11 Twist and tell

▶ Can reality be distorted for a good cause?

YOUR SNAP MISSION

Write an article showing how images can be manipulated to raise awareness.

1 Denouncing

WB → p. 117

Doc 1

▲ *Harry Potter* film poster by Legally Black, 2018.

a. **React** to the poster (doc 1) and **give** its objective.
b. **Read** the text (doc 2) and **pick out** information about Legally Black and their campaign.
c. **Discuss** the impact of this project.

Doc 2

oh

Iconic film posters have been redesigned to feature[1] an all-black cast and put up on south London streets by a campaign group called Legally Black...

Four "advocates[2] of social justice" from southwest London have joined forces to combat the way black people are portrayed in the media by forming their project Legally Black. The aim of Legally Black is to increase awareness[3] about the lack[4] of black representation in the media and create dialogue and discussion around inaccurate and harmful[5] depictions.

Their first visual campaign replaces characters from famous white-dominant TV programmes with black people, with posters now dotted around south London. The campaign also features the tagline: "***If you're surprised, it means you don't see enough black people in major roles***," encapsulating the meaning at the heart of the project.

Alice Snape, *ohmag.co.uk*, 2018

1. present 2. defenders 3. *conscience* 4. *manque* 5. destructive

AT HOME **Watch** the video and **meet** Legally Black's team.

Video college.nathan.fr/**3sb112**

2 Defending a cause

WB → p. 118

Doc 1

Audio

a. React to the poster and **imagine** its message.

b. Listen to the audio and **explain** the campaign.

VOCABULARY SPOT

- **brandalism** = brand (*marque*) + vandalism (*destruction*)
- **subvertising** = subvert (*subvertir*) + advertising (*publicité*)

GRAMMAR SPOT

- You **may** have noticed them…
- You **must** be asking yourselves…

Remplace les deux mots en gras par une structure commençant par *It is*… Qu'expriment ces mots ?

a. Read the text and **say** what may be seen in London.

b. Define brandalism (people, origin, actions, objectives).

c. Discuss: is brandalism vandalism?

Doc 2

STREET ART FOR A CHANGE

You may have noticed them on the streets of London. [...] Noticed what? Those strange ads and billboards[1] that look like normal advertisements but with twisted[2] messages. Where do they come from? Who did them? Why do they do that? All those questions may be answered with one concept, brandalism. [...]

Brandalism is a group of artists who draws inspiration from the long history of protest art. [...] Their project sees artists from each corner of the world collaborate to challenge the authority and legitimacy of commercial images and messages present within our culture. They do so by using a form of Street Art called subvertising. What is subvertising? Subvertising consists in changing meanings in corporate[3] and political advertisements to make spoofs[4] or parodies of them. [...] After all that, you must be asking yourselves, OK that's nice, but does that change things?

Alex Courbat, *Street Art for A Change*, *blogs.buprojects.uk*, 2016

1. *panneaux publicitaires* 2. distorted 3. *des entreprises* 4. *caricatures*

YOUR SNAP MISSION — STEP 1

Start writing your article. Present an existing distorted poster and explain its goal.

1. **Find** and **describe** your poster (nature, origin, goal).
2. **Say** what brandalism is and **explain** the impact it may have on people.

WB → p. 120

Build your skills! Présenter une action

- Utilise les modaux ***may*** et ***must*** pour interpeller le lecteur sur les actions qu'il a pu voir : *You **may** have noticed them on the streets of London.* • *You **must** be asking yourselves: what is the result of all that?*
- Emploie la préposition ***by*** suivie du gérondif pour expliquer de quelle manière sont réalisées les actions : *They combat the way black people are portrayed **by forming** their project Legally Black.* • *They do so **by using** a form of Street Art…*

BUILD YOUR ENGLISH → p. 116

3 Acting positive

WB → p. 121

Doc 1

David Beckham is the face of a new campaign to try and get rid of[1] malaria, a deadly disease carried by mosquitoes which affects hundreds of millions of people every year. [...]

In the video Beckham is shown as a much older man speaking from a time in the future when the disease doesn't exist anymore. The advert by the charity[2] Malaria No More UK is designed to encourage people around the world to continue their efforts to get rid of the disease forever.

Beckham has been involved with the charity since 2009 and says it is "something he really cares about because it is a huge killer of children." He says his own kids asked him if the disease could really be ended in their lifetime and he told them, "Yes, it will be, with a lot of teamwork, with a lot of leadership and a lot of hard work and we have all of that."

BBC Newsround, *David Beckham: Star appears as old man in new malaria campaign*, 2020

1. eliminate 2. organisation fighting for a good cause

GRAMMAR SPOT

- David Beckham's kids **asked** if the disease could be ended.
- He **told** them, "Yes, it will be."

Compare les deux phrases. Comment expliques-tu la présence ou l'absence de guillemets ? Quels changements cela entraîne-t-il dans la phrase ?

Doc 2 **Video**

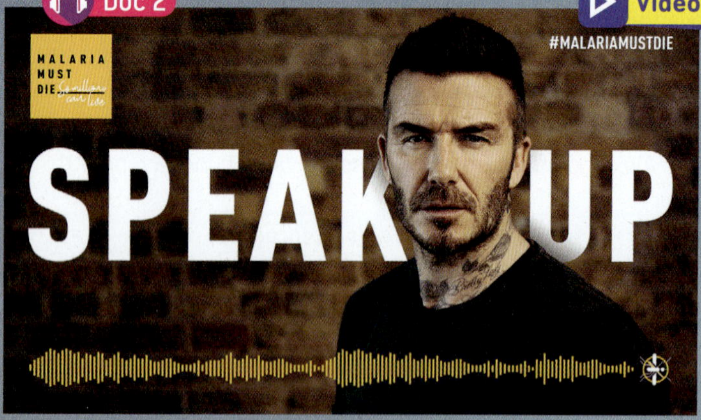

▲ David Beckham in a video against malaria using "deepfake" technology.

A LITTLE EXTRA **Watch** the video and **list** the elements you need to make a convincing deepfake video. **Video**

Team A

a. **Read** the article (doc 1) and **take** notes on the problem mentioned.
b. **Comment** on what David Beckham says and his reasons for getting involved.
c. **Explain** the special effects used in the video (l. 5-6).

Team B

a. **Watch** the video (doc 2) and **give** information about the celebrity and the issue.
b. **Explain** the objective of the video.
c. **Comment** on the special effects used.

d. **Share** your information with the other team.

4 Raising awareness

WB → p. 123

Doc 1 — Video

a. **React** to the picture (doc 1).
b. **Read** the text (doc 2) and **sum up** the project.
c. **Watch** the video (doc 1) and **explain** why Channel 4 made this deepfake.

A LITTLE EXTRA Watch the video and **design** a poster to raise awareness and give tips about fake news.

Video

PHONOLOGY SPOT — AUDIO

deepfake • like • fears • about

Écoute ces mots. Comment sont prononcées les lettres en rouge? Combien de sons entends-tu pour chaque lettre ou groupe de lettres ?

Doc 2

First Deepfake Address[1] From The Queen of England Makes Its Debut On British TV

It's "a powerful reminder that we can no longer trust our own eyes," a representative for the UK broadcaster Channel 4 told *The Guardian*. Each year, the BBC broadcasts[2] a special Christmas address to the nation from Queen Elizabeth II. [...] Channel 4 has seized the moment to broadcast its own deepfake version of the Queen's holiday message.

If you have bad eyesight[3] and limited hearing, you might, might, be fooled[4] by the fake Queen on a busy Christmas Day. But by the time she starts talking about Netflix and launches into a dance routine, you'd surely know something's up[5].

Rhett Jones, *gizmodo.com*, 25 December 2020

1. speech 2. *diffuse* 3. *vue* 4. *dupé* 5. something's wrong

YOUR SNAP MISSION — STEP 2

Write the second part of your article. Explain how deepfakes can be used to raise awareness.

1 **Choose** an example of a deepfake video from pages 114-115 and **say** which cause it defends and how deepfake technology was used.

2 **Explain** why the creators of the video decided to use a deepfake version of this celebrity.

WB → p. 124

Build your skills! **Expliquer la stratégie d'une campagne de sensibilisation**

→ Utilise le discours indirect pour rapporter les paroles de quelqu'un : *David Beckham* ***says*** *his own kids* ***asked*** *him if the disease could really be ended in their lifetime...*

→ Exprime une probabilité avec les modaux ***might*** ou ***could*** : *You* ***might*** *be fooled by the fake Queen.*

BUILD YOUR ENGLISH → p. 116
HOW TO SHINE IN WRITING → p. 140

QUIZ Test
college.nathan.fr/**3sb115**

GRAMMAR

EXERCISES → p. 172

A Exprimer la probabilité d'une action avec les modaux *must, may, could, might, can't*

Les modaux de **probabilité** indiquent les **chances de réalisation** d'un fait.

Grammar tuto

PASSÉ modal + *have* + V-*en* ou modal + *have been* + V-*ing*		PRÉSENT / FUTUR modal + BV ou modal + *be* + V-*ing*
You **must have seen** these pictures. They were everywhere!	**90% de probabilité = MUST** C'est sûr, je le déduis. (Tu as dû... Tu dois... / Il est certain que...)	You **must be wondering** what this strange picture is.
You **may have heard** about her. She was on TV last night.	**50% de probabilité = MAY** C'est possible, mais pas sûr. (Il se peut que... / Il est possible que...)	You **may see** one of these ads in the streets. There are quite a few in the city.
Some people **could have believed** this deepfake. It looked quite real.	**50% de probabilité = COULD** C'est possible si les conditions sont réunies. (Ils auraient pu... Ce pourrait...)	This **could be** fake news. It looks too good to be true.
Advertisers **might have been preparing** a new campaign.	**30% de probabilité = MIGHT** Il y a une chance, un risque pour que... (Il se pourrait que...)	Deepfakes are really well done. People **might think** they are real.
You **can't have believed** him. You never normally trust him.	**0% de probabilité = CAN'T / CANNOT** C'est impossible. (Tu ne peux pas...)	You **cannot be saying** it's true! It's obvious it is fake news.

1 Reformule les phrases suivantes à l'aide d'un modal suivi de BV ou *have* + V-*en* selon le sens de la phrase.

a. I'm not sure but I think they posted them on the net!
b. These posters are everywhere, I'm sure you saw them!
c. Twisting a film poster is a possibility for advertisers.
d. This media? Reliable? No way!

2 Termine les phrases suivantes en exprimant la probabilité au présent ou au passé. Tu peux utiliser les verbes proposés.

think – change – lie – threaten

a. When people saw these ads, they…
b. Legally Black is a powerful association, it…
c. Be careful, these ads…
d. In the end, deepfake…

HOW TO SHINE IN GRAMMAR → p. 153

B Rapporter les paroles de quelqu'un grâce aux discours direct et indirect

Pour rapporter les paroles de quelqu'un, on peut les répéter à l'identique, en utilisant des guillemets : c'est le **discours direct**.

- *He told me, "I don't trust this ad."*
- *He asked me, "Do you think it's real?"*

On peut aussi les reformuler, sans guillemets : c'est le **discours indirect**.

- *He told me (that) he didn't trust this ad.*
- *He asked me if I thought it was real.*

⚠ Pour passer du discours direct au discours indirect, veille à bien modifier les **pronoms** et le **temps des verbes** ainsi que l'ordre des mots pour les questions.

3 Rapporte ces propos au style indirect.

a. "I'm amazed when I see these ads!"
→ She says…

b. "How fast does fake news spread?"
→ They asked…

c. "We really thought it was the Queen!"
→ They explained…

4 Réécris ces phrases au discours direct.

a. They said they were fooled by the video.
b. She wondered if people often believed deepfake.
c. He explained he thought brandalism could make a difference.

HOW TO SHINE IN GRAMMAR → p. 155

VOCABULARY

EXERCISES ➜ p. 173

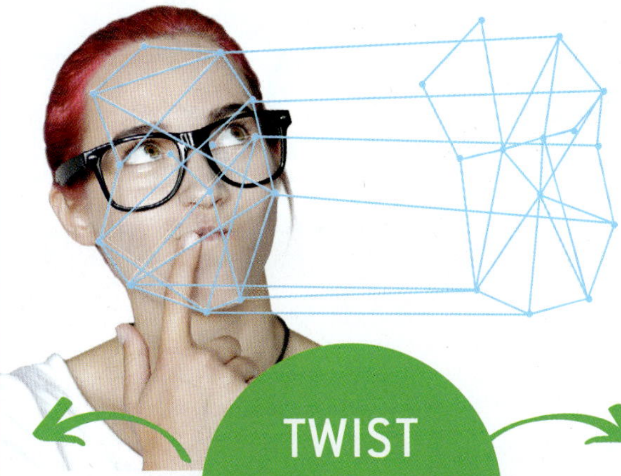

TWIST AND TELL

Media and creation

AUDIO

- depiction = illustration
- (film) poster
- TV programme = TV show
- amazing /ə'meɪzɪŋ/ = fascinating
- broadcast
- draw inspiration /ˌɪnspə'reɪʃən/
- go viral /'vaɪərəl/
- share

Goals

AUDIO

- advocate /'ædvəkeɪt/
- challenge: *remettre en question*
- empower /ɪm'paʊə/
- increase awareness
- protest
- replace
- tackle sth = deal with sth

Fakes and twists

AUDIO

- spoof = parody
- realistic ≠ unrealistic
- synthetic = artificial
- unreliable /ˌʌnrɪ'laɪəbl/: *peu fiable*
- alter = modify
- be fooled
- swap: *échanger*
- digitally /'dɪdʒɪtəli/

Campaigning

AUDIO

- advertisement /əd'vɜːtɪsmənt/ = ad
- billboard
- brand: *marque*
- campaign /kæm'peɪn/
- charity
- organisation
- subvertising
- tagline /'tæglaɪn/: *slogan*

A need for a change

AUDIO

- concern: *inquiétude*
- lack of
- prejudice
- endless /'endləs/
- harmful
- inaccurate /ɪn'ækjərət/
- be involved: *s'impliquer*
- get rid of = eliminate

➜ Get into pairs!
Partner A Choose a lexical field and roll the dice.
Partner B Give as many words as the number on the dice. Then, swap roles!

- NOUN
- ADJECTIVE
- VERB
- ADVERB

HOW TO SHINE IN VOCABULARY ➜ p. 160

PHONOLOGY

➜ La prononciation des diphtongues

- En anglais, certaines voyelles **diphtonguent**, c'est à dire que l'on entend **deux sons voyelles** rapidement prononcés l'un après l'autre.

/eɪ/ take	/aɪ/ like	/eə/ fair
/ɪə/ fear	/əʊ/ so	/ɔɪ/ join
/aʊ/ how	/ʊə/ tour	

Les diphtongues n'existent pas en français, c'est pourquoi il faut être particulièrement vigilant(e) quand tu les prononces !

1 Anticipe la prononciation des voyelles en bleu, puis écoute et vérifie. AUDIO

make • over • play • protest • voice • time

2 Observe ces mots et anticipe les voyelles qui diphtonguent, puis écoute et répète. AUDIO

replace • viral • inspiration • poster • illustration • reliable

3 Entraîne-toi à prononcer ces phrases en veillant aux lettres en bleu, puis écoute et répète. AUDIO

a. They play with videos, modify and broadcast them and finally, deepfake invades our screens.

b. I think this amazing campaign can empower minorities and raise awareness.

HOW TO SHINE IN PHONOLOGY ➜ p. 156

FILE 12

From reel to real

> "Today's science fiction is tomorrow's science fact."

Isaac Asimov (1920-1992)
American science-fiction writer

How is science fiction impacting our lives?

More on
SPEAKEASY NEWS
speakeasy-news.com

Robert John Downey Jr. in *The Avengers* (2012).

YOUR FINAL MISSION

Design and present an invention that could be inspired by science fiction for the Imagine Cup Junior!

Video

Jonathan Strickland, *Fw: Thinking*.

TEAM WORK

WB → p. 125

Team A

Look at the main picture. **Say** what you know or **imagine** what the man is doing.

Team B

Read Isaac Asimov's quote and **find** examples where science fiction became reality.

Team C

Watch the video and **explain** what cyclical relationship the presenter is talking about.

- Now **share** what you know about the connections between science fiction and reality with the other teams.

EXPLORE Changing everyday objects

1 From science fiction to science fact

WB → p. 126

a. Look at the documents and **identify** the genre of the film.

b. Imagine what Marty is doing with his glasses and Doc with his watch.

c. Explain why these images were futuristic in 1989.

Marty

Doc 1

▲ *Back to the Future: Part II* is an American film directed by Robert Zemeckis and released in 1989. It is about a young man named Marty McFly who travels into the future with Doc.

Doc 2

a. Look at the document and **identify** the gadgets used in the film. **Compare** their functions with the real-life gadgets used today.

b. Recap what you know from **doc 1** and **explain** why science fiction can become real.

AT HOME Watch the trailer for *Back to the Future: Part II* and **find** other examples of gadgets that exist today (or are still fiction).

Video college.nathan.fr/3sb120

1. gives 2. *s'attendre à* 3. *rythme cardiaque* 4. finding 5. illness

2 A sci-fi life

WB DIFFÉRENCIATION → p. 127

Doc 1

The Boston Globe

A smart watch could save your life

Dan Pfau, 70, belongs to a fairly exclusive club that few of us would want to join — people whose smart watches may have kept them alive. He was rescued by his watch about two years ago during a Martha's Vineyard cycling excursion. [...]

Pfau doesn't even recall[1] phoning 911, because he didn't. The watch did. In 2018, Apple added a feature[2] that can tell if the user has fallen down. If the user doesn't move for 60 seconds, the watch puts in a call for assistance. (The technology involved is similar to what Google highlighted this year in a TV ad about its Pixel phone detecting that a user was in a car crash.) [...] The injury[3] wasn't quite as bad as it first seemed, but Pfau believes that's because the Apple Watch was so quick to call for help. "I don't know if I would have died otherwise[4]," he said, "but it certainly would have been more serious."

Hiawatha BRAY,
bostonglobe.com, 2021

1. remember 2. characteristic 3. *blessure* 4. *autrement*

GRAMMAR SPOT

If I hadn't had my watch I would have died.

Quel mot indique une hypothèse ?

a. **Read** the text and **say** what happened to Dan Pfau.

b. **Explain** how the watch helped him.

c. **Discuss** the impact of smart watches on everyday life.

AT HOME Find other gadgets that would be useful to protect people's lives.

PHONOLOGY SPOT AUDIO

mobile phone • **science** fiction • **touch** screen

Écoute ces mots. Quelles sont les syllabes accentuées ? Quelle est la fonction des mots en gras ?

Doc 2

a. **Look** at the photo and **imagine** what Captain Kirk is using.

b. **Watch** the video and **pick out** information about *Star Trek*.

c. **Note down** as many gadgets as you can. What do they have in common?

d. **Comment** on the last sentence: *"Sci-fi inspires real-world technology."*

Video

◀ In the American sci-fi series *Star Trek* (1966-1969), Captain Kirk commands a starship whose mission is to explore space.

YOUR MISSION

Record your first science fiction podcast for the website *fictionpodcasts.com*. Imagine what gadgets you would have if you had a time machine as in *Back to the Future: Part II*!

Make a list of five gadgets you would like to have and **record** yourself!

WB → p. 129

Build your skills! Décrire un monde fictif

- Utilise des noms composés pour nommer tes gadgets : *smart watch* • *touch screen* • *smart glasses* • *mobile phone*.
- Exprime une hypothèse en utilisant ***if*** et ***would*** : ***If*** *Pfau hadn't had his watch, he* ***would*** *have died / it* ***would*** *have been more serious.*

BUILD YOUR ENGLISH → p. 127

QUIZ Test
college.nathan.fr/3sb121

EXPLORE Helping us go further

1 Space tourism: a dream

WB → p. 130

AUDIO VERSION

The passengers relaxed, enjoying the smooth, almost silent ride. Every one of them had traveled hundreds of times faster than this, on the journey to the Moon. But in space one was never conscious of speed, and this swift glide[1] across the dust was far more exciting. When Pat swung Selene into a tight turn, so that she orbited in a circle, the boat[2] almost overtook the falling veils[3] of powder her fans[4] had hurled[5] into the sky. It seemed altogether wrong that this impalpable dust should rise and fall in such clean-cut[6] curves, utterly unaffected by air resistance. On Earth it would have drifted[7] for hours—perhaps for days.

As soon as the boat had straightened out on a steady[8] course and there was nothing to look at except the empty plain, the passengers began to read the literature thoughtfully provided for them. Each had been given a folder of photographs, maps, souvenirs ("This is to certify that Mr./Mrs./Miss—has sailed the Seas of the Moon, aboard Dust-Cruiser Selene"), and informative text. They had only to read this to discover all that they wanted to know about the Sea of Thirst, and perhaps a little more.

Most of the Moon, they read, was covered by a thin layer of dust, usually no more than a few millimeters deep. Some of this was debris from the stars—the remains of meteorites that had fallen upon the Moon's unprotected face for at least five billion years. Some had flaked[9] from the lunar rocks as they expanded and contracted in the fierce temperature extremes between day and night.

Arthur C. Clarke, *A Fall of Moondust*, 1961

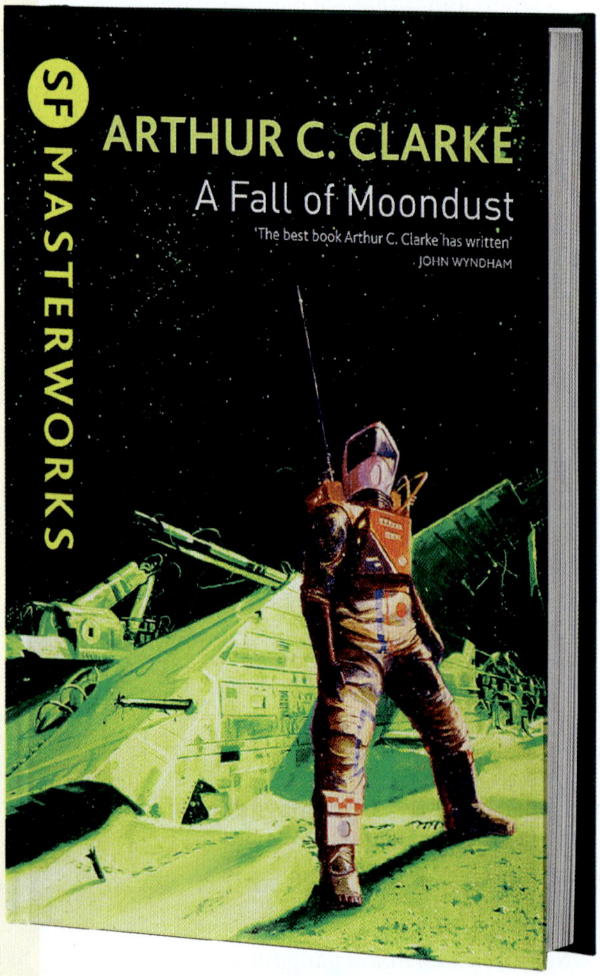

1. fast ride 2. cruiser (she) 3. *voiles (rideaux)* 4. *hélices* 5. projected 6. *bien dessinées* 7. floated 8. stable 9. fallen

a. **Read** the text and **name** the cruiser, the captain, and the destination.

b. **Describe** the tourists' experience.

c. **Say** why this trip is unusual from the reader's point of view.

CULTURE SPOT

The **Apollo Program** (1961-1975) was created by NASA to accelerate American spatial research and exploration.

The **Apollo 11** mission sent the first humans to the Moon, among whom Neil Armstrong ◀ and Buzz Aldrin, in July 1969.

A LITTLE EXTRA Read about the Apollo Program and **spot** the similarities and the differences with *A Fall of Moondust*.

Website
college.nathan.fr/3sb122

2 Space tourism: a reality

WB DIFFÉRENCIATION → p. 130

Video

▲ Billionaire Jeff Bezos and his crew going into space aboard the *New Shepard*, 2021.

TEAM WORK

Team A

a. Watch the video and **describe** the space-flight scenes and the people you can see.

b. Focus on the commentary. **Say** why these space flights are special.

Team B

a. Watch the video and **focus** on the analyst's comments. **Say** what the obstacles are for space flight today.

b. Explain what predictions they make about space flight in the near future.

c. Now **recap** with the other team. **Discuss** Richard Branson's message to the future generations.

3 Space tourism: a hope

WB → p. 132

a. Watch the video and **say** what mission it is about.

b. Focus on the beginning of the recording and **explain** what "*human spirit*" means.

c. Give the different elements that make it possible today to imagine such explorations.

GRAMMAR SPOT

We are going to do a lot of learning in this decade.

À quelle période renvoie l'expression en gras ? Comment est-elle formée ?

Video

Matt Damon in ▶ *The Martian*, 2015.

YOUR MISSION

DIFFÉRENCIATION

It's 2040, and you got a job in a space travel agency!

WAY 1

You have to **promote** a new trip to space. **Create** a poster and **write** what the tourists are going to do.

WAY 2

You are in charge of organising a seven-day trip to space. **Write down** the programme of the trip.

WB → p. 133

Build your skills! **Évoquer des événements futurs**

- Parle d'une action prévisible ou prévue avec *be going to* + BV : *We're **going to see** $50,000 tickets in the next generation of flights.*
- Utilise le modal ***may*** associé à une date future : *It **may** take a little longer.*

BUILD YOUR ENGLISH → p. 127

QUIZ Test college.nathan.fr/3sb123

EXPLORE Fuelling our imagination

1 Innovating for the big screen

WB DIFFÉRENCIATION → p. 134

For many years, the film industry has relied on green screens. With this recent technology of StageCraft, many are wondering if it's going to replace green screens. […]

Green-screen technology involves a plain static set of green walls. The actor performs in front of a solid color such as blue or green and then the background is replaced with a scene using a computer. […]

The *Mandalorian* LED wall on the other hand relies on virtual production using virtual-reality sets. The background footage[1] shifts[2] with the camera movement which makes the scene appear convincingly natural. There are also no limitations on what color should be used on the set since there's not anything to be removed. […]

With new technology like StageCraft used in the production of *The Mandalorian*, the future of the film industry looks brighter than ever. […]

Issues[3] like on-location shooting, and color limitations on the set aesthetics can be massively avoided[4]. Reshooting will also be easier than ever with this technology since instead of going on location, actors can perform the scene in front of a virtual LED display.

doitvision.com, August 2021

1. image 2. moves 3. problems 4. *évités*

GRAMMAR SPOT

- It's **going to replace** green screens.
- Reshooting **will** also **be** easier.

À quoi les formes en gras font-elles référence ?

a. **Look** at the pictures and **imagine** where *The Mandalorian* TV series is filmed.

b. **Read** the article and **identify** the technology used to film the series.

c. **Compare** the technologies mentioned in the text.

d. **Explain** what this new shooting technology will change.

▼ A virtual set used to shoot *The Mandalorian*, 2019.

2 Creating imaginary worlds

WB → p. 135

Video

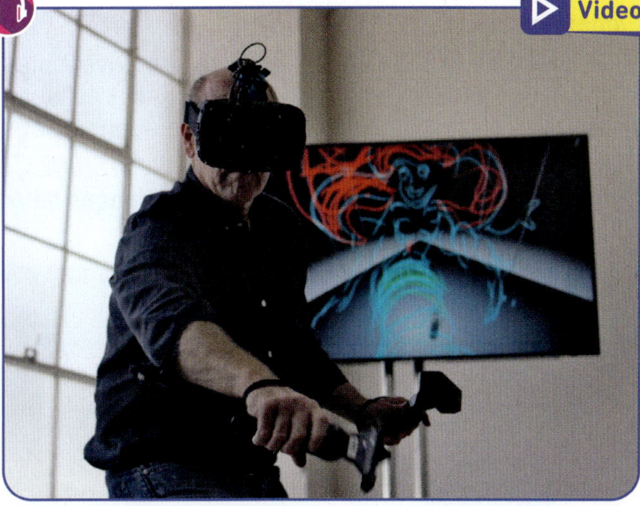

▲ Disney animator Glen Keane draws Ariel in 3D.

PHONOLOGY SPOT AUDIO

create • reality • East • real

Écoute et répète ces mots. Comment les lettres en rouge sont-elles prononcées ?

a. Look at the picture. **Imagine** the link between the man and the character in the background.

b. Watch the video and **identify** Glen Keane's job and the tools he is using.

c. Explain the changes in Glen Keane's technique.

3 Augmented human possibilities

WB → p. 136

Video

▲ *Ready Player One*, film by Steven Spielberg, 2018.

a. Look at the poster and **comment** on the catchphrase.

b. Watch the video and **identify** the new technology that is used.

c. Say what actions the players will be able to do with Omni One.

d. Discuss the impact of Omni One on reality. Can we say that "virtual" turned into "real"?

YOUR MISSION

You attend the Virtuix exhibition and you get the opportunity to try the Omni One.

List five things you will be able to do thanks to this new technology.

WB → p. 137

Build your skills! **Décrire des possibilités à venir**

- Utilise le modal ***will*** suivi d'un verbe ou d'un groupe verbal exprimant la capacité : *Omni One **will enable** people to jump...* • *I **will be able to** put the goggles on and...*
- Emploie des verbes d'action : *step into* • *crawl* • *draw* • *kneel* • *turn in space* • *dance*

BUILD YOUR ENGLISH → p. 127

QUIZ Test
college.nathan.fr/3sb125

GAME ON!

EXO Interactive game
college.nathan.fr/3sb126

MISSION SHINE ROCKET

How to play

Planet Earth, 2150

- The *SHINE* Centre (**S**pace **H**eadquarters for **I**nvention, **N**avigation and **E**xploration) has decided to accelerate research in space and build a next-generation rocket ship.
- **Join** your team! To be selected as the official *SHINE* engineering crew, you must **beat the challenges** before the other teams! You only have 15 minutes!

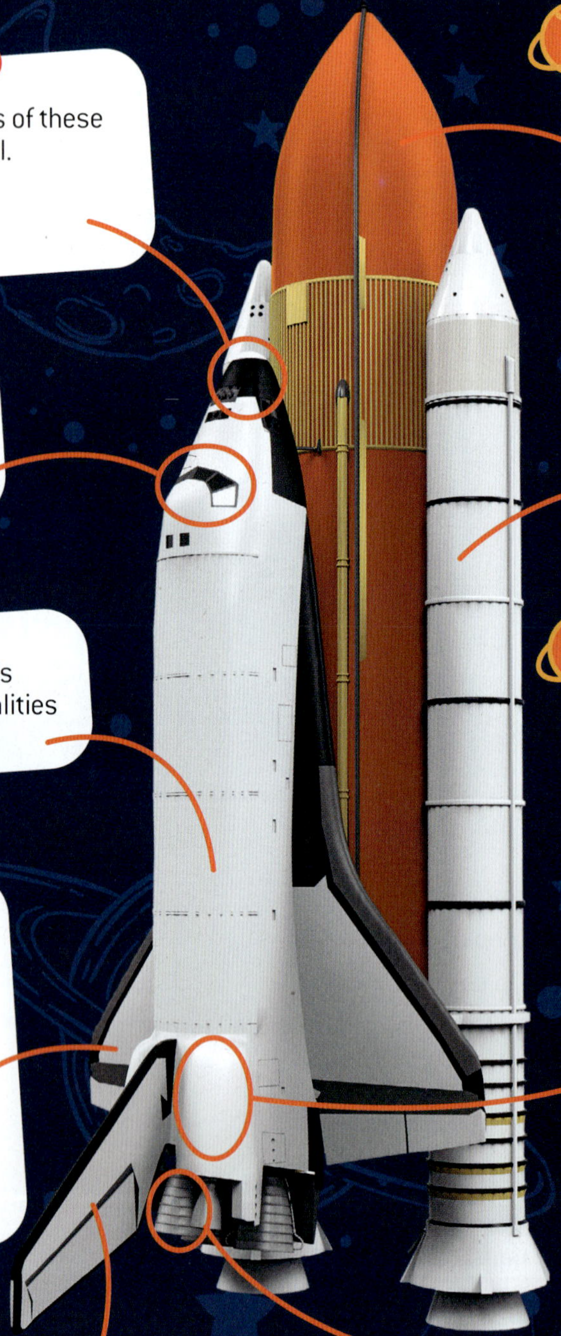

1 The heat shield

Complete the names of these sci-fi films and novel.

- *... to the Future*
- *Ready ... One*
- *A Fall of ...*

2 The flight deck

What is the name of the Captain in *Star Trek*?

3 The spacelab

You have 30 seconds to name 3 functionalities of a smart watch.

4 The wings

Put the letters in the right order to find the name of 3 very famous sci-fi films.

- VARAAT
- SANUIGRAD FO HET AGLYXA
- RATS ARWS: HET STAL JEID

5 The rudder

Give the names of 2 science-fiction film heroines.

6 The main engine

What is the name of the technology that replaces green screens to shoot film scenes?

7 The fuel tank

Match each film with the invention where it first appeared.

a *Metropolis* (1927)	1 The videophone
b *Star Trek* (1966)	2 Animal cloning
c *Star Wars* (1977)	3 The automatic translator
d *Jurassic Park* (1993)	4 The prosthetic hand

8 The rocket booster

What is the name of the NASA mission that sent the first humans to the Moon?

9 The external fuel tank

You have 30 seconds to write the longest list of sci-fi films!

GRAMMAR

EXERCISES → p. 173

A Évoquer des faits irréels à l'aide du conditionnel

Grammar tuto

Le **conditionnel**, exprimé grâce au modal ***would***, permet d'évoquer un fait ou une action soumis à une condition.

CONDITION NON RÉALISÉE
(dans le passé)

***If* + past perfect**

If I **had lived** in 1969,...
If I **had been** on the Moon...

FAIT IRRÉEL
(dans le passé)

***would have* + V-en**

...I **would have watched** the Moon landing.
...I **would have loved** it!

CONDITION HYPOTHÉTIQUE

***If* + prétérit**

If I **could**,...
If I **had** the time,...
If scientists **knew** how to travel in time,...

FAIT IRRÉEL
(dans le présent)

***would* + BV**

...I **would travel** to space.
...I **would read** more sci-fi books.
...they **would launch** a programme.

PAST — PRESENT — FUTURE

1 Associe les propositions ci-dessous deux par deux pour reconstituer les phrases.

People would buy tickets for space travel | if they hadn't had special space suits. | Many people wish | I would get inspiration from sci-fi films. | Astronauts wouldn't have survived on the Moon | if they could afford it. | If I were a scientist | sci-fi inventions would become real life inventions.

2 Termine les phrases de façon logique.

a. If I could fly a spaceship, ...
b. We wouldn't have travelled to space if ...
c. Would engineers invent new things if... ?
d. If I had the opportunity, ...

HOW TO SHINE IN GRAMMAR → p. 151

B Évoquer des faits futurs avec *will*, *may*, *be going to* et *be* + *V-ing*

Pour évoquer des faits futurs, tu peux choisir de les montrer de plusieurs façons...

be going to + BV Le fait futur apparaît comme la suite logique du présent.	*This film **is going to become** a reference.*
be + V-ing Le fait futur est prévu, planifié.	*I'**m flying** to Mars in two days.*
will + BV Le fait futur est certain.	*They **will launch** a space travel programme soon.* *I **won't watch** this sci-fi film.*
may + BV Le fait futur n'est pas certain à 100%.	*Space tourism **may be** common **in 2050**.*

3 Complète les phrases suivantes à l'aide de *will*, *won't* ou *be going to*.

a. They're working on it, I'm sure cars ... fly in 2080!
b. For sure, many films ... inspire reality and scientists.
c. After all these studies, they ... send people to space.
d. Space tourism ... become common in a few years.

4 Termine les phrases suivantes avec *may* et *will* selon le sens des phrases. N'oublie pas les formes négatives.

a. James Cameron's next film...
b. I guess that in the 22nd century, people...
c. To my mind, smart glasses...
d. Within a few years, film makers...

HOW TO SHINE IN GRAMMAR → p. 151

Build your English!

VOCABULARY

EXERCISES ➜ p. 173

1 Wordsearch: how many words can you find in one minute?

U	Y	W	Y	W	P	C	R	H	O
E	G	Y	E	K	R	L	C	E	R
Z	X	R	O	O	U	E	Y	L	H
G	C	P	U	W	Y	E	F	I	E
U	O	C	L	Q	M	N	F	C	A
E	H	G	D	O	K	K	T	O	D
E	S	N	G	P	R	T	Y	P	S
W	A	R	D	L	M	E	J	T	E
E	G	I	X	L	E	U	R	E	T
G	L	I	D	E	F	S	J	R	N

2 Let's match! Find at least five compound words.

smart · green · watch · screen · glasses · touch · reality · virtual

3 Find the odd word out.

a. device • crawl • jump • kneel • tiptoe

b. phenomenal • standalone • feature • immersive • autonomous

c. explore • helicopter • mission • crew • rocket

d. breakthrough • filmmaking tech • goggles • headset • broadcast

4 Find the words corresponding to these definitions. Use the wordmap!

a. ... : (n.) an important discovery in science or technology.

b. ... : (adj.) which surrounds the player or viewer and makes them feel part of a game or a film.

c. ... : (n.) a special type of glasses that lets you see things in 3D or augmented reality.

d. ... : (v.) send a transmission to a large audience via radio or TV.

HOW TO SHINE IN VOCABULARY ➜ p. 160

PHONOLOGY

A La prononciation de la graphie <ea>

- Souvent en anglais, les lettres ne se prononcent **pas comme en français**, et leur prononciation **diffère** selon le mot où elles figurent. C'est le cas de la graphie **<ea>**.

/ɑː/ h**ea**rt — /iː/ dr**ea**m
/ɜː/ **ea**rth — /e/ h**ea**dset
/ɪə/ app**ea**r — /eɪ/ br**ea**kthrough

1 Écoute et répète ces mots en veillant à la prononciation de <ea>. AUDIO

real • early • sea • year • feature • idea • head • gear • research • heartbreaking • great

2 Écoute-les à nouveau et classe-les selon leur prononciation. AUDIO

HOW TO SHINE IN PHONOLOGY ➜ p. 156

B L'accentuation des mots composés

- Dans les **noms composés** (nom + nom, adj + nom, verbe + nom...) l'accent tonique est souvent placé sur la syllabe accentuée du premier mot : *a **mo**bile phone* • ***scien**ce fiction*
- L'accent est important car il permet de distinguer le nom composé du nom accompagné d'un adjectif, par exemple : *a **green**house* (une serre) ≠ *a green house* (une maison verte)
- L'accent tonique des **adjectifs composés** est généralement placé sur le deuxième mot : *life-**chang**ing* • *well-de**signed***

3 Anticipe l'accentuation de ces mots, puis écoute et répète-les. AUDIO

smart watch • touch screen • smart glasses • well-known • newly-designed • homemade

4 Anticipe l'accentuation des mots composés dans ces phrases puis écoute et répète-les. AUDIO

a. Bradbury is a world-famous sci-fi writer, who wrote eye-opening novels.

b. Most filmmakers are visionary and imagine life-changing and smartly-designed artefacts.

c. Smart glasses and touch screens are all the rage at the moment and they appeal to tech-oriented fans.

HOW TO SHINE IN PHONOLOGY ➜ p. 158

WORDMAP

WB → p. 125

SCIENCE AND FICTION

Space exploration
AUDIO

- crew = team
- ex**plo**rer
- glide /glaɪd/
- **heli**copter
- **pass**enger
- ride /raɪd/
- **ro**cket
- round-trip **miss**ion

Gadgets
AUDIO

- de**vice** /dɪ'vaɪs/ = e**quip**ment
- **gogg**les
- **head**set
- LED dis**play**/wall
- smart **glass**es
- touch screen
- **stand**alone = au**to**nomous

From fiction to reality
AUDIO

- **vir**tual rea**li**ty
- bring **some**thing to life = make **some**thing real
- cre**a**te in **vir**tual rea**li**ty
- **dive** /daɪv/ in
- im**merse one**self
- **step** into = enter
- con**vin**cingly
- **mass**ively = e**nor**mously

Technological functionalities
AUDIO

- **break**through /'breɪkˌθruː/: *avancée technologique*
- **fea**ture /'fiːʧə/
- inno**va**tion
- phe**no**menal /fənɒmɪnəl/
- **ans**wer calls
- call for help
- de**tect**
- fold up: *replier*
- in**spire** /ɪn'spaɪə/
- pre**dict** the **wea**ther
- **res**cue **peo**ple

Video games
AUDIO

- enter**tain**ment: *divertissement*
- gear /gɪə/ = e**quip**ment
- **sys**tem = **con**sole
- crawl
- crouch /kraʊʧ/: *s'accroupir*
- draw
- jump
- kneel /niːl/
- **tip**toe

Cinema
AUDIO

- **co**medy
- **film**making tech
- green screen
- **in**dustry
- (film/movie) set
- im**mer**sive
- **life**-size /'laɪf saɪz/
- be re**leased**
- **broad**cast: *diffuser*
- per**form**
- shoot

NOUN · ADJECTIVE · VERB · ADVERB

YOUR FINAL MISSION

Design and present an invention that could be inspired by science fiction for the Imagine Cup Junior!

WB → p. 138

→ Imagine Cup Junior provides students aged 13 to 18 the opportunity to learn about technology and how it can be used to change the world positively. This year's challenge is based on science-fiction gadgets.

→ **Design** and **present** a new gadget inspired by science fiction.

Website college.nathan.fr/**3sb130**

STEP 1 ▶ **Design** a brand new gadget inspired by science fiction. You can **use** a book, film or TV series that you like or that you discovered in the unit.

STEP 2 ▶ **Describe** your gadget and its technological functionalities. **Think** about the compound words you discovered in the unit.

STEP 3 ▶ **Say** what people will be able to do with your gadget. **Explain** why your gadget is useful.

STEP 4 ▶ **Explain** what your gadget would change in people's lives. **Imagine** how different life could be!

YES YOU CAN! Present an innovative gadget.

1 Le gadget

Choisis une œuvre de science fiction dans laquelle tu peux trouver un gadget qui n'a pas encore vu le jour dans la réalité.

Hoverboards in Back to the Future, *flying cars in* The Fifth Element, *teleportation devices in* Star Trek, *lightsabers in* Star Wars, *jetpacks in* Iron Man…

Video

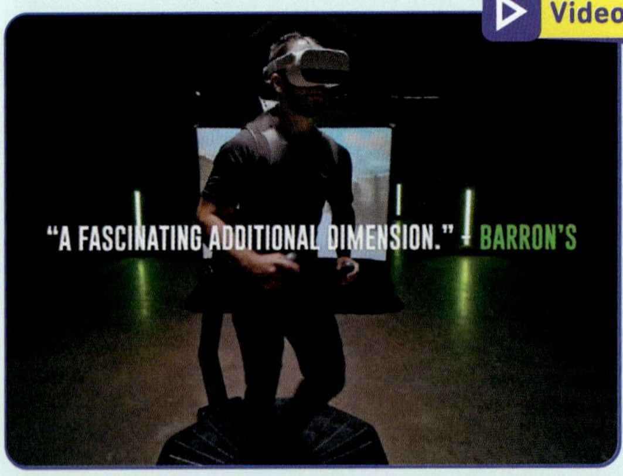

2 La description

Présente ton gadget et ses particularités technologiques.

Omni One is a breakthrough in VR treadmill technology. It includes a standalone VR headset without any cables.

3 Les fonctionnalités du gadget

Explique ce qu'il sera possible de faire avec ton gadget.

It will enable freedom of movement including crouching, kneeling and jumping. It will feature its own game store.

4 Les possibilités du gadget

Explique au jury ce qu'il pourrait faire avec ton gadget s'il le choisissait.

If you tried the Omni One, you would be fascinated! You could…

5 La présentation orale

Parle sans lire tes notes et pense à accentuer correctement les mots composés.

It is optimised for ***home*** *use. It's a complete* ***entertainment*** *system.*

HOW TO SHINE IN SPEAKING → p. 144

Test your skills!

Compréhension de l'oral

B1 OBJECTIF Comprendre un reportage vidéo

Video

A2
1. **Say** what event is presented.
2. **Identify** the people.

A2+
3. **Give** information about the event.
4. **List** details about the main participant.

B1
5. **Explain** why this mission is incredible.

Compréhension de l'écrit

B1 OBJECTIF Comprendre un article de presse

Science fiction as fact: how desires drive technologies

Several sci-fi films and novels have very accurately[1] predicted and paved the way[2] for many of the pieces of technology we enjoy today. This isn't a new phenomenon either – the inventor of the first liquid-fuelled rocket, American Robert H. Goddard, was inspired by H.G. Wells' science-fiction novel *War of the Worlds* (1898). More recent examples include the 3D gesture-based user interface used by Tom Cruise's character in *Minority Report* (2002), which is found today in most touch screens and the motion-sensing capability of Microsoft's Kinect. Similarly, the tablet computer actually first appeared in Stanley Kubrick's *2001: A Space Odyssey* (1968) and the communicator – which we've come to refer today as the mobile phone – was first used by Captain Kirk in *Star Trek* (1966).

The value of science fiction has been also recognised in the rise of a new method for designing technology, called design fiction. If science fiction stimulates the imagination about extraordinary views of the future, design fiction explores the futures that ordinary people would prefer. Design fictions – like short sci-fi films, prototypes and graphic novels – are provocative and engage people, encouraging them to envision[3], explain and raise questions about the direction of future technology and society.

Emmanuel Tsekleves, *theguardian.com*, 2015

A2
1. **Read** the text and **identify** its nature and the topic.
2. **Find** at least three gadgets inspired by science fiction and **say** what specifically inspired each one.

A2+
3. **Describe** science fiction's role in the development of new technologies.

B1
4. **Explain** what design fiction is.

1. precisely
2. open the way for
3. imagine

QUIZ Test de positionnement
college.nathan.fr/3sb131

DISCOVER TREASURE

1 Dive into Stevenson's book!

WB → p. 139

AUDIO VERSION

The Old Sea Dog at the 'Admiral Benbow'

Squire[1] Trelawney, Dr Livesey and the rest of these gentlemen having asked me to write down the whole particulars about Treasure Island, from the beginning to the end, keeping nothing back but the bearings[2] of the island, and that only because there is still treasure not yet lifted, I take up my pen in the year of grace 17–, and go back to the time when my father kept the 'Admiral Benbow' inn[3], and the brown old seaman, with the sabre cut, first took up his lodging[4] under our roof.

I remember him as if it were yesterday, as he came plodding[5] to the inn door, [...] a tall, strong, heavy, nut-brown man; his tarry[6] pigtail[7] falling over the shoulders of his soiled blue coat; his hands ragged and scarred[8], with black, broken nails; and the sabre cut across one cheek, a dirty, livid white. I remember him looking round the cove[9] and whistling to himself as he did so, and then breaking out in that old sea-song that he sang so often afterwards:

'Fifteen men on the dead man's chest –
Yo-ho-ho, and a bottle of rum!'

1. Mr 2. geographical position 3. small hotel 4. bedroom 5. walking slowly 6. dirty and sticky 7. *natte* 8. marked with cuts 9. *crique*

Read Jim's opening lines and **draw** a portrait of Billy Bones, the Old Sea Dog.

A LITTLE EXTRA
Watch the video and **explain** what the Golden Age of Piracy is.

Video

◄ Extracts from the original edition of *Treasure Island*, 1883. ►

2 Meet the characters!

WB → p. 140

Audio

Who is who? **Listen** and **find out**.

ISLAND

3 Step into the story!

WB → p. 140

AUDIO VERSION

The Captain's Papers

The paper had been sealed[1] in several places with a thimble[2] by way of seal; the very thimble, perhaps, that I had found in the captain's pocket. The doctor opened the seals with great care, and there fell out the map of an island, with latitude and longitude, soundings[3], names of hills and bays and inlets[4], and every particular that would be needed to bring a ship to a safe anchorage[5] upon its shores. It was about nine miles long and five across, shaped, you might say, like a fat dragon standing up, and had two fine land-locked harbours[6], and a hill in the centre part marked "The Spyglass". There were several additions of a later date; but above all, three crosses of red ink – two on the north part of the island, one in the south-west, and beside this last, in the same red ink, and in a small, neat hand, very different from the captain's tottery characters, these words: 'Bulk[7] of treasure here.' […]

That was all; but brief as it was and to me incomprehensible, it filled the squire and Dr Livesey with delight.

'Livesey', said the squire […]. 'Tomorrow I start for Bristol. In three weeks' time – three weeks! – two weeks – ten days – we'll have the best ship, sir, and the choicest crew[8] in England. Hawkins shall come as a cabin boy. You'll make a famous cabin boy, Hawkins. You, Livesey, are ship's doctor; I am admiral. We'll take Redruth, Joyce and Hunter, we'll have favourable winds, a quick passage and not the least difficulty in finding the spot, and money to eat – to roll in – to play duck and drake[9] with ever after'.

1. closed securely 2. *dé à coudre* 3. figures indicating the depth of the sea 4. *criques* 5. place to stop a boat 6. ports 7. the largest part 8. *équipage* 9. *faire des ricochets*

▲ Map published in the original edition of *Treasure Island*, 1883.

Read Jim's account of the scene and **identify** the document they have found. What do they decide?

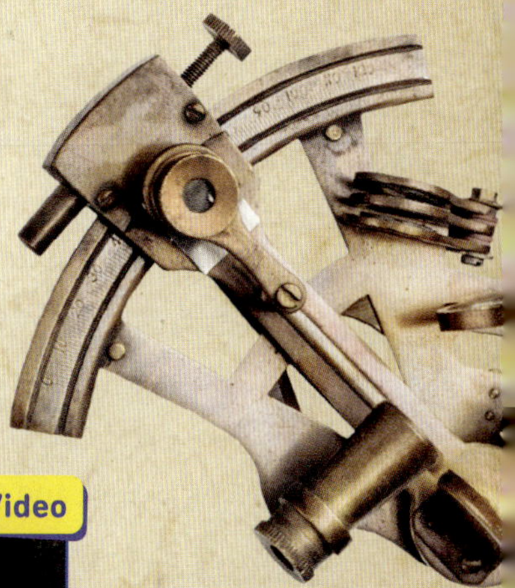

4 All aboard!

WB → p. 142

After finding Captain Flint's treasure map, Jim Hawkins, Squire Trelawney and Doctor Livesey charter a ship and set sail for Treasure Island. One day, Jim Hawkins finds out who Long John Silver really is…

Video

Read the text on the left, **watch** the video and **explain** Long John Silver's plan.

QUIZ Test college.nathan.fr/3sb133

ESCAPE FROM THE

Fifteen men on a dead man's chest—
Yo-ho-ho, and a bottle of rum!
Drink and the devil had done for the rest—
Yo-ho-ho, and a bottle of rum!
But one man of her crew alive,
What put to sea was seventy-five.

Pirate song from Treasure Island (1883) by Robert Louis Stevenson.

The Union Jack

Jim tells the story.

Suddenly with a loud huzzah (= shout), a little cloud of pirates leapt from the woods on the north side and ran straight on the stockade. At the same moment, the fire was once more opened from the woods, and a rifle-ball sang through the doorway and knocked the doctor's musket (= gun) into bits. [...]

The log house (= house made of wood) was full of smoke, to which we owed our comparative safety. Cries and confusion, the flashes and reports of pistol shots and one loud groan (= noise) rang in my ears.

'Out, lads (= boys), out, and fight 'em in the open! Cutlasses (= knives)!' cried the captain. [...]

When I had first sallied (= ran out) from the door, the other mutineers had been already swarming up (= climbing up together) the palisade to make an end of us. One man, in a red nightcap, with his cutlass in his mouth, had even got upon the top and thrown a leg across. Well, so short had been the interval, that when I found my feet again all was in the same posture, the fellow with the red nightcap still halfway over, another still just showing his head above the top of the stockade. And yet, in this breath of time, the fight was over, and the victory was ours.

Extract from Treasure Island (1883) by Robert Louis Stevenson.

ISLAND !

(with the treasure!)

Video

Feuille de route

TREASURE ISLAND

Flint's map after Robert Louis Stevenson's description

The Jolly Roger

PIRATE LINGO

- **black spot:** message given to a condemned pirate
- **buccaneer:** pirate
- **crew:** the people working on a same boat
- **landlubber:** person who doesn't know about sailing
- **matey:** friend
- **mutiny:** rebellion of the crew against the captain
- **rum:** pirates' favourite drink
- **sea dog:** old experienced sailor
- **ship:** large sea boat
- **shipwreck:** ship destroyed at sea
- **be shipwrecked:** survive a ship being destroyed at sea
- **be marooned:** be abandoned on an island

HOW to shine in... READING

Afin de t'aider à bien lire et comprendre différents types d'écrits, voici quelques conseils à suivre.

STEP 1
Chercher des indices

- **Émettre des hypothèses** sur ce que l'on s'apprête à lire grâce au **paratexte** (source du document, auteur, date, titre, illustration, couverture de livre, etc.).
- **Déterminer le type de document** dont il s'agit grâce aux indices repérés : extraits de roman, d'article de presse, de script ; poème, etc.
- **Lire le texte dans son intégralité** sans s'arrêter sur les mots inconnus pour dégager le thème du document.

STEP 2
Effectuer les premiers repérages

- **Les noms propres et les noms commençant par une majuscule** : que représentent-ils ? (noms de lieux, de personnages, nationalités, pays, titres de films ou de romans, etc.)
- **Les nombres** : à quoi font-ils référence ? (âge, date, quantité, etc.)
- **Les pronoms personnels** (*I, he, her, them* ...) : à quelle(s) **personne(s)** font-ils référence ?
- **Les mots transparents** : s'aider de leur **ressemblance** avec le français.
- **Les mots de liaison** : faire le **lien** entre les différents éléments du texte (association, opposition, succession, etc.).

ONLY THE STRONG SURVIVE

CHERUB agents are highly trained, extremely talented – and all under the age of seventeen. For official purposes, these agents do not exist. They are sent out on missions to spy on terrorists, hack into critical documents, and gather intel[1] on global threats – all without gadgets or weapons. It is an extremely dangerous job, but these agents have one crucial advantage: Adults never suspect that teens are spying on them.

James is the latest CHERUB recruit. He's a bit of a troublemaker[2], but he's also brilliant. And CHERUB needs him. James has no idea what to expect, but he's out of options. Before he can start in the field, he must first survive one hundred gruelling[3] days of basic training, where even some of the toughest recruits don't make it to the end...

WILL YOU ACCEPT THE NEXT MISSION?

Robert MUCHAMORE, *The Recruit*, 2004

1. *recueillir des informations* 2. agitator 3. *épuisants*

▲*Snapfile* 1, p. 13

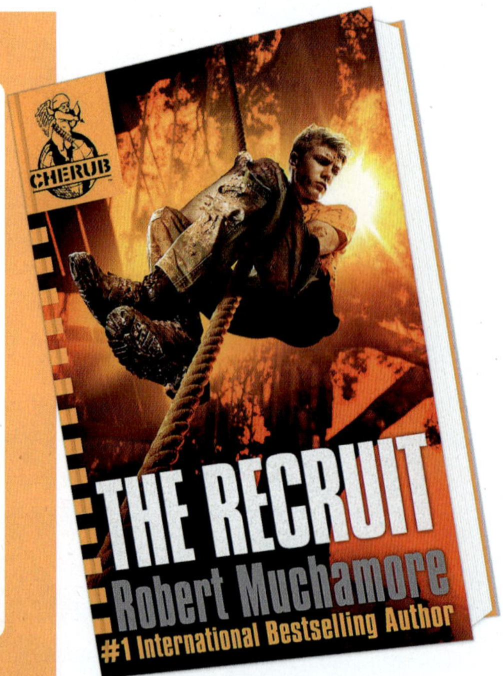

TIPS

- Ne t'arrête pas sur les mots que tu ne connais pas ! Ils ne t'empêcheront pas de comprendre **l'essentiel**.
- Si besoin, appuie-toi sur le **contexte**. Demande-toi si le mot a un sens positif ou négatif.
  talented → sens positif • *troublemaker* → sens négatif
- Analyse la **formation** des mots en partant de ce que tu connais :
  extremely → adjectif *extreme* + ***-ly*** = extrêmement
  trained → verbe *train* + ***-ed*** = entraîné
  toughest → adjectif *tough* + ***-est*** = le plus fort/solide

STEP 3
Mettre en lien les informations

- **S'approprier le texte :** surligner, souligner, entourer, relier les mots importants, etc.
- Utiliser tous les éléments que l'on a appris à repérer pour parvenir à **reconstruire le sens**.
- **S'appuyer sur la structure du texte :** différents paragraphes, mots de liaison, conjonctions de subordination, etc.

Your turn to shine!

À toi de jouer ! Suis les étapes indiquées pour bien lire et comprendre le document suivant.

Kingsman: The Golden Circle falls short of predecessor

Bigger is not always better.

In 2014, a film called *Kingsman: The Secret Service* was released, and it took everyone by surprise. Delivering great action, a witty script and notable performances, *The Secret Service* did what James Bond hasn't been able to do in years: make spy films fun again.

Now, two years later, comes *The Golden Circle*, which takes place directly after the events of the original. This follow up seemed to be everything that made the first one so fun, just turned up to eleven.

However, it is disappointing to say that although *The Golden Circle* tries to be louder and bigger than its predecessor, it never quite comes close, and in the end, loses the qualities that made the original so new and fresh.

Jarrod FLAHERTY, *The Hudsonian Student Newspaper*, 2017

STEP 1

- Observe le **paratexte** : quels sont les mots-clés du titre ?
- Que peux-tu anticiper à partir du **visuel** en lien avec ce titre ?
- Que t'apporte la **source** sur le **type** de document ?
- Lis le texte une première fois. Quel en est le **thème** ?

STEP 2

- Repère les **mots-clés** : les noms propres, les mots en italique, les nombres, les pronoms personnels et ce à quoi ils correspondent, les mots transparents.
- Confirment-ils tes **hypothèses** ?
- Quelles **informations supplémentaires** t'apportent-ils sur le thème du document ?

STEP 3

- Lis le texte une seconde fois.
- Repère les **champs lexicaux** utilisés, notamment les mots négatifs et positifs.
- Identifie aussi les **mots de liaison** utilisés.
- Quelle **opinion** émet l'auteur ?

Now recap!

What have you understood? Write or record a recap. Use the questions below to guide you if necessary.

1. What type of document is it? What is its topic?
2. What does the author compare this film to?
3. What opinion does he express?

HOW to shine in… LISTENING

Pour t'améliorer en compréhension de l'oral, gagner en confiance et devenir plus autonome, voici une méthode que tu peux utiliser.

STEP 1
Mobiliser ses connaissances avant d'écouter

- Utiliser tous les éléments (titre, images, dates, légende, thématique de séquence…) pour **anticiper**.
- Mobiliser les **idées** et le **lexique** associés afin de préparer l'écoute.
- Faire des **hypothèses** sur le contenu de l'enregistrement.
- **Préparer** une feuille de brouillon et un stylo ou un crayon.
- Adopter une **position d'écoute active** afin de ne rien perdre du document dès la première écoute.

1 London's Little India

Doc 1 — Video

▲ Southall, London's Little India.

▲ *File* 2, p. 20

- **Lis le titre** et mets-le en lien avec l'image.
  What is "Little India"? Is this about a place in London?
- **Regarde l'image** et commence à faire des hypothèses.
  It's a street. People are shopping/walking. There are Indian shop names. It looks cold and grey. People are wearing western clothes…
- **Lis la légende**, qui donne des informations complémentaires.
  It looks like "Little India" is a nickname for an area in London. Maybe the document is about this area…

STEP 2
Accéder au sens global (1re écoute)

- Ne pas prendre de notes à la première écoute. Utiliser tous les **indices sonores** (accents, intonations, bruits) pour comprendre et mémoriser la situation.
- Repérer les éléments nécessaires à la **compréhension globale** pour confirmer ou infirmer tes hypothèses :
  – le **nombre de voix** et les caractéristiques des locuteurs : *a woman/a presenter, introducing other people (2 men).*
  – l'**intonation** et le **ton** employés, qui donnent des indications sur l'émotion ou l'intention : *joyful, excited, happy, cheerful…*
  – les **bruits ambiants**, qui peuvent donner des informations sur le lieu ou le contexte : *Oriental music in the background.*
  – la **nature** du document : s'agit-il d'un reportage, d'un extrait de film, d'un entretien, etc. ? *Welcome to Southall! Meet Aadil…*
  – les **dates**, les **lieux**, les **nombres** : *Southall, Punjab, London, India, 40 years ago.*
  – les **mots répétés** (les mots les plus importants) : *Southall, London, Indian, jalebi, Punjabi, music.*
  – les **mots accentués porteurs de sens** : *first corner shop, London, Southall, Aadil's grandfather.*

Si le document est une vidéo, l'image soutiendra la compréhension !

STEP 3
Affiner sa compréhension (autres écoutes)

- Prendre des **notes** et les compléter au fur et à mesure.
- Valider ou invalider les **hypothèses**.
- Ajouter toute **information** pertinente, en partant de ce qui est connu pour comprendre ce qui ne l'est pas.
- Commencer à faire **le lien entre les idées**.

STEP 4
Préparer sa restitution

- Associer les mots et expressions notés pour **reconstruire le sens**.
- Se préparer à **restituer ce que tu as compris**.

TIPS

Lorsque tu prends des notes :
- Prends tes notes sous forme de **mots-clés** ou d'**expressions courtes directement en anglais**.
- Organise tes notes sous forme de **carte mentale** ou de **tableau**.

Your turn to shine!

À toi de jouer ! Suis les étapes indiquées pour bien écouter et comprendre le document suivant.

1 One of Britain's Secret Homes

Doc 1 — Video

▲ Anita Rani in an episode of *Britain's Secret Homes*, a five-part TV documentary which reveals the remarkable stories behind the UK's most secret and surprising homes.

STEP 1

- Regarde **l'image** et lis le **titre**. Quelle est la **nature** du document que tu vas écouter ?
- Quels sont les **mots-clés** dans la **légende** ?
- Commence à faire des **hypothèses** : sur quoi portera le document ? Quel type de lexique t'attends-tu à entendre ?
- **Prépare-toi** à visionner le document pour la première fois.

STEP 2

- Regarde la vidéo et repère les **personnes qui parlent**. Combien sont-ils ? Qui sont-ils ? Que font-ils ?
- Repère les **lieux**. Où se déroule l'action ?
- Écoute ce qui est dit. Quel **ton** est employé ? La globalité du message correspond-elle à tes **hypothèses** ?
- À la fin du visionnage, **note** ce que tu as compris. Laisse de la place pour pouvoir compléter tes notes lors des visionnages suivants.

STEP 3

- Regarde à nouveau la vidéo et écoute attentivement tout en prenant des **notes**. Certains mots sont-ils **répétés** ? **accentués** ? Lesquels ?
- Entends-tu des **dates** ? des **lieux** ? des **nombres** ? À quoi correspondent-ils ?
- **Complète tes notes** en ajoutant des informations à chaque écoute.
- Les nouveaux éléments **confirment**, **contredisent** ou **modifient**-ils le message que tu avais initialement compris ?

Now recap!

What have you understood ? Get ready to recap the information.

1. What type of document is it? Where was it filmed?
2. Who is speaking? What about? Why?
3. What have you learnt?

HOW to shine in... WRITING

Tu vas être amené(e) à rédiger différents types d'écrits. Voici quelques étapes à suivre pour bien répondre aux sujets.

You are a member of the team organising Purple Power Week in your school. Write the life story of an inspiring English-speaking woman for the school's newspaper.

▲ *Snapfile* 3, p. 35

STEP 1 – Comprendre le sujet

Lire attentivement la **consigne** et repérer :

- **le type d'écrit attendu** : s'agit-il d'un article de presse ? d'une lettre ? d'un extrait de fiction ? etc.
- **le sujet et l'objectif de cet écrit** : s'agit-il de convaincre ? de raconter ? d'expliquer ? etc.
- **des informations sur les personnes auxquelles on s'adresse** : les lecteurs sont-ils des adolescents ? des adultes ? des spécialistes du sujet traité ? etc.

STEP 2 – Noter ses idées

- Partir du thème à traiter et écrire **toutes ses idées et le lexique** qui émergent suite à l'étude des documents en classe.
- Organiser ses idées par **grands thèmes** (sous forme de tableau ou de carte mentale).

Inspiring New Zealand woman = Jacinda Ardern

Biographical information
Born in 1980

Achievements
• Elected Prime Minister in 2017

Personality
Determined
Strong
Empathetic

Inspiring facts about her
• World's youngest female head of government
• Had a baby while being Prime Minister

STEP 3 – Faire un plan

- Structurer, **organiser ses idées** en se focalisant sur le type d'écrit attendu et son objectif.

Type d'écrit : a life story → déroulé chronologique
Objectif : décrire une femme inspirante → mettre en exergue ce qu'elle a fait ou dit d'inspirant

Plan :
1) Beginning of her life until her election
2) Her election and why it is a symbol for women/feminism
3) How she is inspiring

STEP 4 – Rédiger son texte

- **Développer les idées notées** en les illustrant par des **exemples** : *Feminists can change the world. For example, Kate Sheppard protested against inequalities between men and women.*
- **Structurer son texte** en utilisant des **mots de liaison appropriés** : des connecteurs chronologiques pour raconter des événements qui se succèdent (*first, then, finally…*), des connecteurs de cause ou de conséquence pour expliquer (*because, so, as a consequence…*), des connecteurs d'ajout ou d'opposition (*moreover, but…*).
- **Respecter la forme du texte attendu** : structurer en paragraphes, respecter la ponctuation, ajouter les formules d'usage (*ex.* : salutations dans une lettre), etc.

STEP 5 – Relire sa production

- **Faire plusieurs relectures ciblées** pour vérifier :
  – la **conjugaison** des verbes et la concordance des temps ;
  – l'**orthographe** (*ex.* : noms pluriels avec un "s", adjectifs invariables, majuscules aux noms propres, etc.) ;
  – la **ponctuation**.
- **Vérifier que toutes ses idées sont bien traitées** dans le texte.

TIPS

• Si tu ne connais pas un mot, cherche **des expressions équivalentes ou des synonymes**. Il vaut mieux écrire quelque chose d'un peu différent mais dont tu es sûr(e) : *a successful singer = a famous singer.*

Your turn to shine!

▶ **À toi de jouer ! Suis les étapes indiquées pour rédiger le texte demandé.**

Your school is organising Purple Power Week this year and Lorde is invited. Write a speech to open the ceremony and introduce your famous guest.

▲ Lorde in a concert, Mexico City, 2018.

STEP 1

▶ Lis le sujet et interroge-toi :
– Quel **type d'écrit** est demandé ?
– Quel est le **thème** du texte ?
– Quels sont les **objectifs** ?
– À **qui** s'adresse-t-il ? Dans quel **contexte** ?

STEP 2

▶ Fais une liste des **formulations** que tu peux utiliser pour débuter un discours.

▶ Prends des notes sur **ce que tu sais de l'événement** organisé et des **objectifs**.

▶ Écris tout **ce que tu sais sur Lorde** et fais le lien entre elle et l'événement. Note des **adjectifs** et des **adverbes positifs** pour la décrire.

STEP 3

▶ Organise tes idées sous forme d'un **plan logique** :

Accueil	Présentation de l'événement	Présentation de la personnalité invitée

STEP 4

▶ Commence ton texte avec une **formule d'accueil**.

▶ Utilise des **connecteurs logiques** pour relier les parties de ton plan et les idées à l'intérieur de chaque partie : ***First****, Lorde listened to music.* ***Then****, she wrote 'Royals'.*

▶ Si tu n'es pas sûr(e) de toi, privilégie les **phrases simples** (sujet + verbe + complément) pour éviter les erreurs : *We have invited Lorde for Purple Power Week. We will honour her.*

▶ Si tu es plus à l'aise, ose les **phrases plus complexes** : *We have invited Lorde to honour her.*

▶ N'hésite pas à donner **ton opinion** : *I (strongly) believe that boys and girls should be equal*.

▶ Pense à donner des **exemples** pour illustrer, en les introduisant correctement : *Girls must stick to their dreams. For example/instance, Lorde has always wanted to be a singer*.

STEP 5

▶ **Relis ton texte** : as-tu bien **traité le sujet** ?

▶ Quels **temps** as-tu utilisés ? Vérifie que les verbes sont correctement conjugués.

▶ Relis ton **brouillon** : n'as-tu rien oublié ?

HOW to shine in… INTERACTING

Savoir interagir avec autrui est central dans la pratique d'une langue. Voici des stratégies que tu peux mettre en place pour t'y entraîner.

Act out a conversation with your best friend about opening a lemonade stand.
Partner A Try to convince your partner to open a lemonade stand.
Partner B Listen to the arguments and ask questions to make your own decision.

▲ *File* 4, p. 41

STEP 1 Comprendre le sujet

Lire attentivement le sujet et repérer :

- **le contexte** : est-ce une émission de radio ou de télévision, une conférence de presse, une interview journalistique, un débat scolaire, une conversation, etc. ?
- **l'enjeu de cette interaction** : échanger des informations, convaincre, débattre, etc. ?
- **les participant(e)s** : quel registre sera utilisé (familier ou soutenu) ? Quels codes doivent être respectés dans l'échange (salutations, remerciements, etc.) ?

STEP 2 Préparer ses idées

- En fonction du rôle choisi dans l'interaction, noter au brouillon toutes les **idées et informations utiles** pour poser des questions riches et variées, donner des arguments et des exemples pour défendre un point de vue, etc.
- **Anticiper** la manière dont les interlocuteurs(trices) pourraient répondre et prendre des notes en vue des réponses éventuelles à donner.

⚠ Ne pas rédiger des phrases complètes au brouillon, mais simplement noter des mots et expressions.

Partner A Opinions

– easy to start
– make money
– do what you want with the profits > give money to a charity or save money to buy something
– start your own business = become an entrepreneur

Partner B Questions possibles

– location/where ?
– material/what ?
– cost/how much ?
– duration/how long ?
– weather conditions/when ?
– recipe/how ?

STEP 3 Interagir

- **Animer et participer à l'interaction** en fonction de son rôle :
  – accueillir et remercier les participant(e)s à l'échange ;
  – exposer brièvement le sujet ;
  – donner son point de vue ;
  – poser des questions ou y répondre avec précision ;
  – relancer la discussion, etc.
- **Écouter attentivement** ce que disent les autres :
  – montrer de l'intérêt ;
  – réagir aux propos tenus, en exprimant son approbation, son désaccord, sa surprise ;
  – reformuler sans couper la parole pour s'assurer d'avoir bien compris, etc.
- **Adapter son attitude et sa posture** :
  – articuler ;
  – veiller à adopter une intonation adéquate ;
  – faire des pauses et utiliser des *gap fillers* pour rester naturel(le) ;
  – regarder ses interlocuteurs(trices) dans les yeux ;
  – rester souriant(e) et courtois(e).

TIPS

Voici des amorces qui peuvent t'aider pour :

- Exprimer clairement ton **point de vue** : *I personally believe that… • In my opinion… • I think that… • I'm convinced that… • To my mind… • It seems to me that…*
- Exprimer ton **accord** : *I agree with you… • You're right when you say… • It is true that…*
- Exprimer ton **désaccord** : *I don't think so. • I (totally) disagree with you! • I don't share your opinion.*
- **Reformuler** : *What did you mean when you said that…? • Did you really mean that…? • May I ask you why you said…?*
- Dire que tu n'as **pas compris** : *I'm sorry, I didn't hear… • Could you repeat please? • Do you mean that…? • I'm not sure I understand what you mean…*
- Utiliser des ***gap fillers*** : *Let me think… • Well… • So… • I mean… • You know…*

Your turn to shine!

À toi de jouer ! Suis les étapes indiquées pour participer au débat proposé.

Your school is taking part in a talk show about teen entrepreneurs organised by the producers of the TV show *Shark Tank*. The topic of the debate is: "Should entrepreneurship be taught at school?"

STEP 1

Lis le sujet et interroge-toi :

- Quel est le **contexte** ?
- Quel est **l'enjeu** de cette interaction ?
- Qui sont les différents **participant(e)s** et quel est leur **rôle** dans l'interaction ?

STEP 2

Choisis ta place dans le débat et prends des notes pour préparer tes interventions.

Tu dois mener le débat.

- Analyse ton **rôle**.
- Assure-toi d'adapter ton **registre de langue** au contexte.
- Sois prêt(e) à **présenter le sujet et les différent(e)s intervenant(e)s**.

Tu es en faveur ou contre l'affirmation avancée.

- Prends des notes sur ce que tu sais du **thème** traité.
- Note des **arguments** pour appuyer ton point de vue.
- Utilise des **exemples** précis pour les illustrer.
- **Anticipe les arguments des autres participant(e)s** pour mieux les contrer.

STEP 3

Introduction

- **Accueille** tes invité(e)s et **remercie-les** d'accepter de participer au débat.

Welcome to this special Shark Tank *talk show! Thank you for joining us today!*

- **Expose** brièvement le sujet.

Let's talk about entrepreneurship.

Animation

- Pose des **questions** sur le sujet et maintiens le fil du débat.
- **Relance tes invité(e)s** si nécessaire.

I would like to come back to what you said…

Attitude

- **Écoute** attentivement les propos de tes invité(e)s.
- Réagis à leurs propos sous forme **d'affirmations** ou de **questions**.

That's right… • Don't you think…?

Salutations

- **Remercie** l'animateur(trice) pour son accueil.

Thank you for having us. Good afternoon!

Opinion

- Présente ton **point de vue** et **réagis** à celui des autres participant(e)s.

In my opinion, entrepreneurship should be taught in primary schools.

- N'oublie pas de t'appuyer sur des **exemples**.
- Exprime ton **accord** ou ton **désaccord**.

I don't share your viewpoint because teenagers are too young to start a business.

- **Concède** certains arguments pour mieux affirmer tes positions.

Sure, but still… • And yet… • Yes, I suppose so… However…

Posture

- **Regarde** tes interlocuteurs(trices) et parle **haut et fort**.
- **Écoute** la personne qui parle sans lui couper la parole et reste **courtois(e)**.

HOW to shine in… SPEAKING

Prendre la parole en anglais demande confiance en soi et entraînement. Voici des stratégies à adopter pour une prise de parole réussie ! Elles te serviront aussi lors de l'oral du brevet.

As a volunteer for Barbados Sea Turtle Project, make a two-minute video to encourage tourists to protect the marine environment in Barbados.

▲ *Snapfile 7*, p. 75

STEP 1 Comprendre le sujet

Lire la consigne et repérer :

- **la nature de la tâche** : est-ce un discours ? une présentation ? une vidéo ? etc.
- **l'objectif et le contenu de l'intervention** : s'agit-il d'expliquer ? de convaincre ? d'encourager ? Quel est le contexte ? etc.
- **l'auteur et la cible du message** : qui parle et à qui parle-t-on ? Quel niveau de langue utiliser ?
- **la durée de l'intervention.**

STEP 2 Rassembler ses idées et ses outils

Récapituler les **connaissances culturelles et linguistiques utiles** à la tâche en revoyant le chapitre. Par exemple, dans le sujet ci-dessus :

– les subordonnées en *if* et le futur en *will* pour décrire des situations hypothétiques ;

– *must* ou *have to* pour expliquer aux touristes ce qu'ils doivent faire et *should* pour les inciter à agir ;

– le lexique incontournable pour parler des problèmes écologiques (voir *wordmap* p. 77).

STEP 3 Organiser sa prise de parole

Préparer un **plan précis mais simple** à retenir, sous forme de notes.

⚠ Ne surtout pas écrire de phrases entières car ce ne serait plus une prise de parole, mais de la lecture ou de la récitation ! Noter simplement quelques mots et amorces de phrases.

1. Présenter le sujet	2. Répondre au sujet	3. Terminer l'intervention
= expliquer brièvement ce dont on va parler	*= exposer les idées et exemples permettant de répondre au sujet*	*= donner une réponse claire à la question du sujet*
- Présenter la Barbade, île paradisiaque des Caraïbes. - Expliquer les problèmes écologiques actuels. - Mentionner ce qui se passera si on ne fait rien.	- Présenter l'association. - Expliquer aux touristes ce qu'ils doivent ou ne doivent pas faire à la Barbade. - Les encourager à rejoindre l'association pour aider sur les plages.	- Résumer ce qui a été dit en quelques mots. - Indiquer la fin de l'intervention et remercier l'auditoire.

STEP 4 Se lancer !

- Commencer avec des **phrases simples** pour être clair(e) et trouver son rythme.
  Today, I'm going to talk about… • Barbados is an island country in…
- Entrer ensuite dans le vif du sujet : donner des **explications** en utilisant des **connecteurs logiques** pour structurer les idées.
  Turtles are endangered because… • If we don't do anything, turtles will…
- Encourager et convaincre grâce à l'utilisation des **modaux et équivalents**, et de **l'impératif** dans des phrases courtes percutantes.
  All tourists must understand that… • Do not disturb them!

STEP 5 Garder son auditoire intéressé

- Ne parler **ni trop vite ni trop lentement** et **respecter la durée**.
- Éviter de lire ses notes pour garder un **discours naturel et fluide**.
- Penser aux **gap-fillers** :
  um, well, let me think, I mean…
  et éviter le français !

Your turn to shine!

À toi de jouer ! Suis les étapes indiquées pour prendre la parole sur le sujet demandé.

As a volunteer for CORALL Barbados, make a two-minute speech for an international youth conference about climate change. Make people aware that coral reefs in Barbados are under threat.

▲ A coral reef in Barbados.

STEP 1

▶ Lis le sujet et repère les mots-clés dans la consigne.

– Quel **rôle** incarnes-tu ? De **quoi** vas-tu parler ? À **qui** ?

– Quel **format** doit prendre ton intervention (forme, durée) ?

– Quel est son **objectif** ?

STEP 2

▶ **Rassemble des informations** sur l'association, ainsi que sur le problème. Tu peux aller sur le site *corallbarbados.org*.

▶ **Fais une liste d'expressions** ou de mots qui te permettront d'alerter l'opinion sur le problème évoqué. Tu peux le faire sous forme de nuage de mots :

coral reef endangered coral restoration barrier fish ecosystem preserve healthy beautiful snorkelling bleach turn white climate change global warming

▶ **Revois également le lexique** qui te permettra d'organiser ta présentation.

STEP 3

Fais un **plan rapide** avant de prendre la parole.

1. Présente le sujet

- La barrière de corail à la Barbade, une merveille pour la nature et le tourisme.

2. Expose les enjeux

- Le problème écologique : les coraux deviennent blancs et meurent à cause du réchauffement climatique.
- La prise de conscience nécessaire.

3. Termine ton discours

= Résumé du problème.
= Remerciements.

STEP 4

▶ **Salue ton auditoire**, puis présente-toi et introduis ton sujet : *Hello everyone! Thank you for having me. My name is... and I am going to speak to you today about coral reefs in Barbados. As you know, Barbados is…*

▶ **Explique le problème** et souligne la nécessité d'agir : *I want to raise awareness about… People need to take action…*

▶ N'oublie pas de **conclure** et de **remercier** : *We have to protect… Thank you for your attention.*

STEP 5

▶ Pour parler de façon naturelle et convaincante, **regarde les personnes à qui tu parles** et évite de lire ton brouillon. Tu peux jeter un coup d'œil à tes notes de temps en temps, mais ne lis surtout pas un texte rédigé entièrement à l'avance.

▶ Emploie un **ton déterminé et positif**. Même si le sujet est préoccupant, donne envie à ton auditoire de t'écouter et de te suivre !

Le groupe nominal

Pour construire une phrase, tu as besoin de noms que tu vas préciser et caractériser. Tu peux ajouter des éléments pour donner davantage de précisions.

Le nom

→ Il peut être **dénombrable** ou **indénombrable**.
a chair — *butter*

→ S'il est **dénombrable**, il peut être au **singulier** ou au **pluriel**.
a pupil — *pupils*

Pour former un **pluriel**, on ajoute un **-s** à la fin du mot, sauf pour les exceptions : *bus**es**, match**es**, part**ies**, wol**ves**, fish, m**e**n, wom**e**n, child**ren**, f**ee**t, t**ee**th…*

→ Il peut être **simple** ou **composé**.
coat — *raincoat*

This | friend | of mine | is | so | cool!

Les articles et les démonstratifs

Ils **précèdent** le nom pour apporter une information supplémentaire.

→ On emploie **l'article indéfini *a*** (ou ***an*** devant un son voyelle) pour désigner **un élément isolé**.

- ***a** story / **an** apple*

→ On n'utilise **pas d'article (Ø)** pour désigner **plusieurs éléments indéfinis**.

- *I have **Ø** friends in London.*

→ On emploie ***the*** pour parler d'un élément ou de plusieurs éléments dont on a déjà parlé.

- ***The** friends who live in London come from India.*

→ Pour désigner une **généralité**, on n'utilise **pas d'article** (**Ø**).

- *He likes **Ø** photography!*

→ Lorsque tu veux être très **précis** pour désigner quelque chose, tu peux utiliser un **démonstratif**.

- ***this** friend → **these** friends* (proximité)
- ***that** time → **those** times* (éloignement)

La possession

Pour exprimer une **relation** entre deux éléments, on utilise :

→ Des **adjectifs possessifs** devant un nom : *my, your, his/her/its, our, your, their* ou des **pronoms possessifs** : *mine, yours, his, hers, its, ours, yours, theirs*.

→ Le **génitif** : *Harry's car*
possesseur ┘ └ ce qui est possédé

- *the doctor's car* (singulier)
- *the doctors' office* (pluriel)

→ La **structure avec *of*** = *the top of the building.* La structure en ***of*** existe mais est moins utilisée en anglais. ***Top*** est mis en relief.

Les adjectifs

→ Ils donnent une **indication sur le nom**.

→ Ils sont **invariables**.

→ Ils peuvent être **simples** ou **composés**.
cool *good-looking*

→ Lorsqu'ils sont associés à un nom, ils se placent toujours **devant le nom** selon la règle **TAFCOM** : **T**aille – **Â**ge – **F**orme – **C**ouleur – **O**rigine – **M**atière

→ Ils sont utilisés dans le **comparatif** et le **superlatif** :

Comparatif	Superlatif
less cool than... (moins cool que...) *as cool as...* (aussi cool que...) *cooler than...* (plus cool que...) *more relaxed than...* (plus détendu que...)	*the least cool boy* (le garçon le moins cool) *the coolest boy* (le garçon le plus cool) *the most relaxed boy* (le garçon le plus détendu)

adjectif court

adjectif long

adjectif court

adjectif long

Les degrés

Pour exprimer le **degré**, on utilise :

→ Des **adverbes** qui servent à nuancer les adjectifs (***very** good*, ***so** interesting*) et les noms (***such** a cool person*).

→ Des **quantifieurs** avec des noms :

	Noms indénombrables	Noms dénombrables
Quantité nulle	*no money*	*no trains*
Petite quantité	*little milk* (peu) *a little milk* (un peu)	*few eggs* (peu) *a few eggs* (un peu)
Quantité incertaine	*some work* *any work*	*some/several days* *any day*
Grande quantité	*a lot of water*	*many biscuits* *a lot of biscuits*

Train and memorise!

Ma fabrique de noms

Crée des groupes nominaux pour décrire cette situation en utilisant des articles, des démonstratifs, des quantifieurs, des adjectifs, des noms...

Je m'entraîne :
SNAPFILE 1 p. 16 • **SNAPFILE 5** p. 56 • **SNAPFILE 9** p. 96 • **FILE 10** p. 107

Le groupe verbal

Pour construire une phrase, tu as besoin de verbes que tu vas modifier pour rendre compte des actions.

La base verbale, l'infinitif et le gérondif

→ La **base verbale** est la forme la plus simple du verbe.
• dance • adapt • link
Elle s'utilise après les **modaux, et les verbes *help*, *let* ou *make***.
*• He helped him **settle** in London.*
*• She must **see** this beautiful Indian palace!*

→ **L'infinitif** est la base verbale précédée de ***to***.
Elle s'utilise après **les verbes de volonté** : ***expect***, ***want***, ***would like***, ***ask***....
*• I would like **to visit** it with you!*

→ Le **gérondif** est la base verbale suivie de ***-ing***.
Il s'utilise après les expressions ***prefer, don't mind, look forward to, like...***
*• I prefer **eating** in this restaurant. Their curry tastes better!*
*• I like **playing** cricket.*

Rai wanted to know what it would be like to bring all of that music together. Using his own money, he bought a sampler and began making loops. He effectively revolutionised the traditional genre to make it music people could dance to in clubs.

Les énoncés affirmatifs

→ Ils suivent l'ordre : **Sujet Verbe Complément**
• He bought a sampler.

→ On peut utiliser l'auxiliaire ***do*** (***did*** au prétérit) pour donner du poids à ce que l'on dit.
*• I **do** like this palace!* (J'aime vraiment ce palais!)

Les énoncés exclamatifs

Ils se forment :

→ avec ***what*** + groupe nominal (introduit par ***a/an*** au singulier).
*• **What a** delicious curry!*
*• **What** delicious desserts!*

→ avec ***how*** + adjectif.
*• **How** beautiful this show is!*

La négation

→ Les énoncés négatifs se forment grâce à un **auxiliaire**. C'est sur cet auxiliaire que porte la négation.
*• I **don't** like this restaurant.*
*• She **did not** go there.*
*• I **am not** dancing.*

→ Je peux utiliser des mots comme ***no***, ***nobody***, ***nothing*** ou ***never***. Le verbe est à la forme affirmative.
*• I play **no** instrument.*
*• I **never** went there.*
*• She met **no one** there.*

→ Je peux garder la négation avec ***any*** et ses composés.
*• I **do not** play **any** instrument.*
*• I **didn't** meet **anyone**.*

Les questions

Il y a plusieurs types de questions :

→ Les questions **fermées** ou ***yes-no questions*** : elles appellent une réponse commençant par oui ou non. Elles se construisent selon le schéma : **Auxiliaire Sujet Verbe**
• *Do you know the Durbar room?*

→ Les questions **ouvertes** ou ***wh- questions*** : elles demandent une information et sont introduites par un **pronom interrogatif**.
What = nature d'un objet : ***What*** *do you like?* • ***What instrument*** *do you play?*
Which = quel(le) ? ***Which restaurant*** *is your favourite?*

Who = identité d'une personne : ***Who*** *is this musician?*
Whose = identité du possesseur : ***Whose book*** *is it?*
Where = lieu : ***Where*** *is this palace?*
When = date, heure : ***When*** *do you want to go there?*
Why = cause : ***Why*** *did they leave India?*

How = manière : ***How*** *did they travel?*
ou associé à un adjectif pour une demande de renseignement : ***How much*** *is it?* (prix)
How long *have you been in England?* (durée)
How often *do you go back to India?* (fréquence)

Les adverbes

→ Pour qualifier, intensifier ou nuancer une action, on peut utiliser des **adverbes**.
Leur position dans la phrase peut varier.

Adverbes	Position dans la phrase
Lieu : *here, there…*	Généralement en fin d'énoncé : *The restaurant is **nearby**.*
Temps : *yesterday, now, today, soon…*	Début ou fin d'énoncé : *They will celebrate it **tomorrow**.*
Fréquence : *never, sometimes, often, always…*	Généralement entre le sujet et le verbe : *I **rarely** celebrate Diwali festival.*
Degré : *so, too, almost, enough…*	Avant l'adjectif sauf *enough* : *This shop is **very** exciting and it's big **enough**.*
Manière : *quickly slowly, beautifully…*	Généralement après le verbe : *They are dancing **gracefully**.*

La voix passive

→ Pour attirer l'attention sur **l'objet** ou **la victime de l'action**, on peut utiliser la voix passive.

→ La voix passive se forme grâce à l'auxiliaire ***be*** (conjugué au temps voulu) et au **verbe au participe passé**. Lorsque l'agent (l'auteur de l'action) est mentionné, il est introduit par la préposition ***by***.

Voix active	Voix passive
*The city **organises** the Diwali festival.*	*The Diwali festival **is organised by** the city.*
*The city **is organising** the Diwali festival.*	*The Diwali festival **is being organised**.*
*The city **organised** the Diwali festival.*	*The Diwali festival **was organised**.*
*The city **has organised** the Diwali festival.*	*The Diwali festival **has been organised**.*
*The city **will organise** the Diwali festival.*	*The Diwali festival **will be organised**.*

Train and memorise!

Ma fabrique de phrases

Fabrique le plus de phrases possibles pour décrire cette situation.

The Diwali festival in London.

Je m'entraîne :
FILE 2 p. 27 • **FILE 4** p. 47 • **FILE 6** p. 67 • **FILE 8** p. 87 • **SNAPFILE 9** p. 96

HOW to shine in... GRAMMAR

Les temps

Pour construire une phrase ou un paragraphe, tu as besoin de décrire des actions au moyen de verbes. Tu conjugueras les verbes au temps qui convient.

Le présent simple

→ Il se forme avec la **base verbale** à laquelle on ajoute un ***-s*** à la 3e personne du singulier.
- *I **encourage** women to do it.*
- *She **encourages** them to be pilots.*

→ Pour former une **question** ou un énoncé **négatif**, on utilise l'auxiliaire ***do***, ou l'auxiliaire ***does*** à la 3e personne du singulier.
- *When **do** you **start** working?*
- *When **does** she **start** working?*
- *I **don't work** as a flight attendant!*
- *She **does not work** as a flight attendant!*

→ Il est employé pour **caractériser** quelqu'un ou quelque chose ou évoquer une **habitude**.
- *She **lives** in New Zealand.*
- *She **likes** flying.*
- *She **goes** to the training centre every week.*

Le present perfect

→ Il se forme avec l'auxiliaire ***have* au présent** et le **participe passé** du verbe.
- *She **has heard** it a lot.*

→ Pour former une **question**, ***have*** conjugué au **présent** est placé avant le sujet.
- *What **has** she **heard**?*

→ Pour former un énoncé **négatif**, on ajoute ***not*** à l'auxiliaire.
- *They **have not seen** a Maori woman pilot yet!*

→ Il fait le **bilan** d'une situation **passée** ou présente les **résultats présents** d'une action **passée**.
- *The situation **has changed** over the years.*

L'impératif

→ Aux **2e personnes** du **singulier** et du **pluriel**, il se forme avec la **base verbale**.
- ***Look**! I'm a pilot.* • ***Listen** carefully!*

→ À la forme **négative**, on ajoute ***don't*** devant le verbe.
- ***Don't be** afraid!*

→ À la **1re personne du pluriel**, le verbe est précédé de ***Let's***.
- ***Let's listen** to her!*

→ À la forme **négative**, on ajoute ***not*** à ***let's***.
- ***Let's not forget** what she did!*

→ On utilise l'impératif pour donner un **ordre** ou une **consigne**.

Le présent en *be* + V-*ing* et le prétérit en *be* + V-*ing*

→ On utilise l'auxiliaire ***be* au présent** ou au **prétérit + V-*ing***.
- *She **is answering** the journalist's questions.* (présent)
- *She **was answering** the journalist's questions.* (passé)

→ Pour former une **question**, on place ***be***, conjugué au présent ou au prétérit, avant le sujet.
- *What **is** she **doing**?* (présent)
- *What **was** she **doing**?* (passé)

→ Pour former un énoncé **négatif**, on ajoute ***not*** à l'auxiliaire ***be*** conjugué au **présent** ou au **prétérit**.
- *She **is not complaining** about her situation!* (présent)
- *She **was not complaining** about her situation!* (passé)

→ Il est utilisé pour insister sur le fait que l'action est ou était **en cours de déroulement**.
- *Right now she **is answering** his questions.* (présent)
- *She **was answering** his questions when she realised she had to go.* (passé)

Le prétérit simple

- Il se forme en ajoutant ***-ed*** à la base verbale. Les **verbes irréguliers** ont des formes particulières qu'il faut connaître par cœur (→ p. 174-175).
  - *I just* ***assumed*** *that you were a flight attendant.*
- Pour former une **question** ou un énoncé **négatif**, on utilise l'auxiliaire ***did***.
  - *What* ***did*** *you* ***say****?*
  - *I* ***didn't give up****!*
- Il est employé pour exprimer un **fait passé et terminé**. Il peut être associé à des repères temporels passés.
  - *Twenty years ago, she* ***was*** *the first Maori woman to become a pilot.*

Le *past perfect* (ou *pluperfect*)

- Il se forme avec l'auxiliaire ***have*** au **prétérit** et le **participe passé** du verbe.
  - *She said she* ***had failed*** *to get in.*
- Pour former une **question**, ***have*** conjugué au **prétérit** est placé avant le sujet.
  - *What* ***had*** *she* ***failed****?*
- Pour former un énoncé **négatif**, on ajoute ***not*** à l'auxiliaire.
  - *He* ***had not seen*** *a Maori woman pilot before meeting Angela.*
- Il marque **l'antériorité** d'un fait par rapport à d'autres faits **passés**.
  - *He* ***had not seen*** *a Maori woman pilot before he met Angela.*

Angela: I said: "Oh, no, look. I'm a pilot." He goes: "Oh, I just assumed that you were a flight attendant."

Journalist: It's something 44-year-old pilot Angela Swan Cronin has heard a lot. Twenty years ago, she was the first Maori woman to become a pilot in the New Zealand Air Force.

Angela: I had failed to get in for the first two times but I was extremely determined so I got in on the third attempt. I encourage other women to consider aviation as a career.

Journalist: Indeed, they will succeed if they believe in it!

L'expression du futur ou du conditionnel

En anglais le futur n'est **pas un temps**.
Il peut être exprimé :

- Avec le modal ***will*** pour prédire l'avenir grâce à une **certitude personnelle**.
  - *She* ***will*** *become a pilot!*
- Avec ***be going to*** + BV pour prédire l'avenir grâce à des **critères objectifs**.
  - *Look at the plane! It****'s going to*** *take off!*
- Avec ***be about to*** + BV pour dire ce qui est **sur le point de se réaliser**.
  - *Hurry up! The plane* ***is about to*** *take off!*
- Le conditionnel, ou **futur dans le passé** est exprimé grâce à ***would***.
  - *She said she* ***would*** *become a pilot.*

Train and memorise!

Ma fabrique de phrases

Décris ce récit à l'aide des différents temps.

Je m'entraîne :

FILE 2 p. 27 • **SNAPFILE 3** p. 36 • **SNAPFILE 5** p. 56 • **FILE 6** p. 67 • **SNAPFILE 7** p. 76 • **FILE 8** p. 87 • **FILE 12** p. 127

Les modaux ou équivalents

Pour construire une phrase, tu as besoin de verbes que tu vas modifier pour rendre compte des actions.

Informations sur le sujet

La capacité

- On utilise ***can*** + **BV** pour exprimer la **capacité** physique ou intellectuelle **au présent**.
  - *He **can run** very fast.*
- On emploie ***could*** + **BV** pour exprimer la **capacité** physique ou intellectuelle **au passé.**
  - *She **could read** when she was four.*
- **L'incapacité** sera exprimée par ***cannot*** (***can't***) au présent ou ***could not*** (***couldn't***) + **BV** au passé.
  - *She **cannot catch** him.*
  - *He **could not teach** her how to read.*
- On utilise aussi l'expression ***be able to*** + **BV**, notamment **au futur.**
  - *He **is able to run** very fast.*
  - *She **was able to read** when she was four.*
  - *He **will be able to come**.*

L'obligation, l'interdiction

- On utilise ***must*** + **BV** pour exprimer **l'obligation**.
  - *He **must do** his homework before going to the spy club.*
- On emploie ***mustn't*** + **BV** pour exprimer **l'interdiction**.
  - *He **mustn't go** there alone. It's too dangerous!*
- **L'obligation** peut également être exprimée par **un équivalent *have to*** + **BV**, notamment **au futur.**
  - *She will **have to help** him if he is in danger.*
- Lorsque **l'obligation** est liée à une nécessité, on peut utiliser ***need to*** + **BV.**
  - *He **needs to see** his instructor before leaving.*

He can speak four different languages and decipher codes. He must leave school earlier. He may be a spy.

La permission et la suggestion

- On utilise ***may*** + **BV** pour demander la **permission**.
  - ***May I use** this gadget?*
- On peut utiliser ***might*** + **BV** pour suggérer.
  - *You **might want** to ask the boss first.*

Le conseil

- On utilise le modal ***should*** + **BV** pour **conseiller** quelqu'un.
  - *You **should train** more before going on this difficult mission.*
- On emploie l'équivalent ***ought to*** + **BV** pour exprimer un **devoir moral.**
  - *He **ought to help** his partner.*
- On utilise aussi l'expression ***If I were you, I would*** + **BV.**
  - ***If I were you, I would** help my partner.*

Informations sur les chances de réalisation d'un fait

La probabilité

→ Les modaux de probabilité indiquent les **chances de réalisation** d'un fait.

Certitude →	**must:** *They **must be** training for this new mission.*
Possibilité logique →	**can:** *This **can happen** tonight!*
Possibilité moindre →	**may:** *She **may learn** that he is a spy.*
Possibilité moindre →	**could:** *That **could happen** tonight.*
Probabilité restreinte →	**might:** *He **might be** interested in this new mission.*

Les adverbes de probabilité

→ La probabilité peut également s'exprimer grâce à des **adverbes** : *certainly, surely, probably, maybe, perhaps…*
• ***Maybe** he is training to be a spy.*

Certitude →	*They are **certainly** training for this new mission.*
Possibilité logique →	***Surely** this will happen tonight!*
Possibilité moindre →	*That will **probably** happen tonight.*
Probabilité restreinte →	***Maybe/Perhaps** he is training to be a spy.*

La probabilité au passé

→ Pour exprimer une probabilité d'un fait passé, on peut utiliser un **modal de probabilité** + ***have*** **V-EN**.
• *He **may have lied** to hide his secret.*
= ***Perhaps** he lied to hide his secret.*

Train and memorise!

Ma fabrique de phrases

Exprime des hypothèses pour décrire ces deux situations.

Je m'entraîne :
SNAPFILE 1 p. 16 • **SNAPFILE 7** p. 76 • **SNAPFILE 11** p. 116

La phrase complexe

Pour construire un paragraphe, tu as besoin de lier des idées entre elles. Pour cela, tu peux utiliser des phrases complexes.

Les propositions relatives

→ Les **propositions relatives** sont introduites par un **pronom relatif** qui a pour antécédent un **groupe nominal** ou une **proposition**. Elles permettent d'éviter une répétition.

Groupe nominal :
- *Girls have to wear uniforms. The uniforms are composed of a skirt, a blouse and a tie.*

→ *Girls have to wear uniforms, which are composed of a skirt, a blouse and a tie.*
- *The UK is a country. In the UK, pupils have to wear uniforms.*

→ *The UK is a country where pupils have to wear uniforms.*

Proposition :
- *He wants to wear shorts, which is impossible.*

→ Les **pronoms relatifs** :

Fonction du pronom relatif	Antécédent humain	Antécédent non-humain	Antécédent exprimant le lieu, le temps, la cause
Sujet	***who*** • *The designer* ***who*** *worked for the protection of the planet is Vivienne Westwood.*	***which*** • *The uniform* ***which*** *is gender-neutral was popular.*	
Complément	***Ø, that*** • *Vivienne Westwood is the designer that she prefers.*	***Ø, which, that*** • *The symbol* ***that*** *she chose for this dress is the Union Jack.*	***where, when, why*** • *The country* ***where***… • *The time* ***when***… • *The reason* ***why***…

Les mots de liaison

→ Les mots de liaison permettent de **relier deux éléments**.
- *He went to the school in shorts,* ***and / that's why / so*** *he was not accepted in class.*

→ Les mots de liaison expriment différents sens :
Le temps : *then, afterwards…*
L'opposition : *but*
La concession : *however, yet…*
L'addition : *and, moreover, also…*
La précision : *indeed, in fact, actually…*
La conséquence : *so, that's why…*
La cause : *for…*

She said, "I have called the school several times **and they have told me that if I send my son to school in shorts** then he will be sent to the isolation room all day and if I keep him off school then it'll be an unauthorised absence."

Les propositions subordonnées

→ La **proposition principale** et la **proposition subordonnée** sont reliées entre elles par une **conjonction de subordination**.
Le sens dépend de la conjonction :
La condition : *if* (si)
- ***If*** *they are creative, they will make a new uniform.*

Le temps : *when* (quand), *while* (pendant que), *as soon as* (dès que), *until* (jusqu'à)
- *She will become a fashion designer* ***when*** *she is older.*

La cause : *because*
- *He likes this jacket* ***because*** *the material is organic.*

Le but : *in order to, to*
- *They used this material* ***to*** *create a new uniform.*

L'opposition : *while, whereas* (alors que)
- *He likes punk rock* ***while*** *his sister likes pop music.*

La concession : *although* (bien que)
- ***Although*** *they do not like it, they must wear this uniform.*

Les discours direct et indirect

LE DISCOURS DIRECT

→ Une personne rapporte directement la parole de quelqu'un en utilisant des **guillemets**.
- ***She said,*** *"I've called the school several times."*

LE DISCOURS INDIRECT

→ Une personne rapporte les paroles de quelqu'un en **faisant des modifications.**
- ***She said that*** *she had called the school several times.*

→ Quand le verbe introducteur est **au présent**, les changements affectent seulement la **ponctuation** (disparition des guillemets, du point d'interrogation), les **pronoms**, les **possessifs**, **l'ordre des mots** et parfois l'ajout de ***that*** (affirmation) ou de ***if*** (question fermée).
- *She says, "I've called the school several times."*
→ *She says (**that**) **she** has called the school several times.*
- *He asks his daughter, "Do you like your uniform?"*
→ *He asks his daughter **if she** likes **her** uniform.*

→ Quand le verbe introducteur est **au prétérit**, les changements affectent aussi **les temps, les démonstratifs** et **les repères de temps ou de lieu.**
- *She said, "I called the school yesterday."*
→ *She said that she **had called** the school **the day before**.*

Changements :

Discours direct	Discours indirect passé
présent simple / en *be + ing*	prétérit simple / en *be + ing*
prétérit simple / en *be + ing*	*past perfect* / en *be + ing*
present perfect	*past perfect*
will	*would*
can	*could*
here	*there*
yesterday / tomorrow	*the day before / the day after*

Verbes introducteurs :
say to somebody, tell somebody, ask somebody, answer, reply…

Train and memorise!

Ma fabrique de phrases

Fabrique le plus de phrases complexes possibles pour décrire cette situation.

Je m'entraîne :
FILE 3 p. 36 • **SNAPFILE 7** p. 76 • **FILE 10** p. 107 • **SNAPFILE 11** p. 116

HOW to shine in… PHONOLOGY

Les sons

Voici les symboles phonétiques de l'anglais.

Il existe des sons longs et des sons courts en anglais. Les sons longs sont signalés par les deux points : Prononce bien les voyelles courtes et les voyelles longues, autrement le sens du mot n'est pas le même !

Elles sont plus « explosives » qu'en français. Mais certaines peuvent être muettes : *climb, doubt, subtle, muscle, handkerchief, Wednesday…*

VOYELLES (AUDIO)

/æ/	hat	/hæt/
/ɑː/	car	/kɑː/
/ə/	ago	/ə'gəʊ/
/e/	bed	/bed/
/iː/	sea	/siː/
/ɪ/	fill	/fɪl/
/ɒ/	not	/nɒt/
/ɔː/	door	/dɔː/
/ʊ/	put	/pʊt/
/uː/	moon	/muːn/
/ʌ/	sun	/sʌn/
/ɜː/	burn	/bɜːn/

= 2 sons voyelles à la suite !

DIPHTONGUES (AUDIO)

/eɪ/	page	/peɪdʒ/
/aɪ/	five	/faɪv/
/ɔɪ/	boy	/bɔɪ/
/əʊ/	no	/nəʊ/
/aʊ/	now	/naʊ/
/ɪə/	hear	/hɪə/
/eə/	hair	/heə/
/ʊə/	sure	/ʃʊə/

= 3 sons voyelles à la suite !

TRIPHTONGUES (AUDIO)

/aɪə/	fire	/faɪə/
/eɪə/	player	/'pleɪə/
/ɔɪə/	royal	/'rɔɪəl/
/aʊə/	flower	/'flaʊə/
/əʊə/	lower	/'ləʊə/

CONSONNES (AUDIO)

/p/	peace	/piːs/
/b/	bug	/bʌg/
/t/	tea	/tiː/
/d/	doll	/dɒl/
/k/	colour	/'kʌlə/
/g/	great	/greɪt//
/m/	machine	/mə'ʃiːn/
/n/	new	/njuː/
/ŋ/	song	/sɒŋ/
/f/	fool	/fuːl/
/v/	village	/'vɪlɪdʒ/
/θ/	thin	/θɪn/
/ð/	there	/ðeə/
/s/	son	/sʌn/
/z/	zero	/'zɪərəʊ/
/ʃ/	shop	/ʃɒp/
/tʃ/	change	/tʃeɪndʒ/
/ʒ/	leisure	/'leʒə/
/dʒ/	journalist	/'dʒɜːnəlɪst/
/r/	root	/ruːt/
/h/	hello	/he'ləʊ/
/w/	well	/wel/
/j/	yellow	/'jeləʊ/
/l/	lie	/laɪ/

Consonnes sonores : /b/ /d/ /g/ /v/ /ð/ /z/ /ʒ/ /dʒ/ /w/ /m/ /n/ /ŋ/ /r/ /j/ /l/

Consonnes sourdes : /p/ /t/ /k/ /f/ /θ/ /s/ /ʃ/ /tʃ/ /h/

Évite le piège du **<th>** : jamais /s/ ni /z/, mais toujours la langue contre les dents… Avec un peu d'entraînement, c'est facile !

Prononce le **<h>** au début des mots sauf dans *honour, hour, honest*.

ACCENT DE MOT (AUDIO)

Accent principal : /'/ → /ɪk'strɔːdɪnri/ extra**or**dinary

Accent secondaire : /ˌ/ → /ˌɪntə'fɪə/ <u>in</u>ter**fere**

Your turn to shine!

Tu penses que tu ne sais pas prononcer correctement ? Suis ces conseils pour t'entraîner et tu verras, ce n'est pas si difficile !

STEP 1

Pour bien prononcer l'anglais, il est utile d'apprendre les **symboles phonétiques**. Observe-les p. 156 et entraîne-toi à les **répéter** en écoutant les audios.

STEP 2

Anticipe la prononciation des mots que tu rencontres ! Il y a quelques règles pour deviner la prononciation des sons voyelles notamment.

- Par exemple, le **<i>** dans *write* se prononce /ai/ alors que dans *written* il se prononce /ɪ/. Pourquoi ? Car dans *written*, le **<i>** est suivi de deux consonnes, ce qui l'empêche de diphtonguer ! Alors que dans *write*, **<i>** est suivi d'une consonne et du **<e>** final.
- La lettre **<a>** se prononce /ɑː/ lorsqu'elle est suivie d'un **<r>** sans lettre après elle comme dans *car*, *bar*, *far*… Lorsqu'elle est suivie d'un **<e>** comme dans *care*, *bare*, *fare*, elle diphtongue.
- Tu peux repérer les combinaisons de lettres qui reviennent souvent, comme les lettres **<ower>** qui se prononcent presque toujours /aʊə/ comme dans *flower*, *power*, *tower*… (mais pas dans *lower* /ˈləʊə/ dont le radical est *low* !).

STEP 3

N'aie pas peur de te lancer ! **Entraîne-toi devant un miroir** à prononcer des mots et regarde les **mouvements** que font ta bouche et tes lèvres. Exagère ces mouvements et garde-les en mémoire lorsque tu t'exprimes en anglais.

Train and memorise!

1 Anticipe la prononciation des lettres en rouge, puis écoute et classe les mots en fonction de leur prononciation. AUDIO

/ɪ/	/ɪə/	/iː/	/aɪ/

screen • cheer • dive • ride • chill • year • reel • fiction • science • here • please • teen • drive

2 Recopie les mots et entoure d'une même couleur ceux dont les lettres en rouge ont la même prononciation, puis écoute pour vérifier. AUDIO

third • later • meet • sweet • moon • please • skate • bird • rumour

3 Écoute et identifie le mot qui est prononcé dans chacune des ces paires minimales. AUDIO

a. chip • ship
b. shop • chop
c. cheap • chip
d. sheep • ship
e. sheet • cheat
f. chair • share
g. boat • bought
h. leave • live
i. sail • sell

Attention à la prononciation, cela peut changer le sens ! Observe bien les premiers mots. Une frite (*chip*) n'est pas un bateau (*ship*) ! ☺
Répète ce *tongue-twister* de plus en plus vite : *I bought cheap chips in the shop on the ship.*

HOW to shine in… **PHONOLOGY**

L'accent tonique

Comme dans toutes les langues, les mots en anglais sont accentués sur une syllabe en particulier. On appelle cela l'accent tonique.

Les spécificités de l'accent tonique

AUDIO

- Contrairement au français, la syllabe accentuée en anglais **varie selon les mots**.
  • *uniform* • *Internet* • *computer* • *education*
- Quand tu apprends un mot, **mémorise aussi son accent**. L'accent tonique est très important car le déplacer peut **changer le sens** du mot !
  dessert /dɪ'zɜːt/ ≠ *desert* /'dezət/
- Les **suffixes, préfixes**, le **nombre de syllabes** et parfois même la **nature** du mot peuvent avoir un impact sur le placement de l'accent tonique.
- L'accent tonique est marqué par un **accent vertical** /'/ dans les dictionnaires. Écoute les audios pour savoir où placer l'accent dans les mots des *wordmaps*. Tu peux aussi utiliser des **dictionnaires en ligne** tels que dictionary.cambridge.org/fr/dictionnaire/anglais/ pour écouter le mot et repérer l'accent tonique !

Les noms et les verbes

AUDIO

- L'accent tonique dans les **noms** de deux syllabes se place généralement sur la première syllabe alors que les **verbes** sont accentués sur la dernière syllabe.
  • *record* (nom : disque)
  ≠ *record* (verbe : enregistrer)
  • *object* (nom : objet)
  ≠ *object* (verbe : objecter, protester)
  • *progress* (nom : progrès)
  ≠ *progress* (verbe : progresser)
- Mais il peut y avoir des **exceptions** ! Par exemple :
  • *comment* (nom : commentaire)
  ≠ *comment* (verbe : commenter)
  • *award* (nom : prix)
  ≠ *award* (verbe : attribuer un prix)

Les mots dérivés

AUDIO

- L'accent tonique porte en général sur la **première syllabe** du mot, mais lorsque l'on ajoute un **suffixe**, l'accent peut parfois se **déplacer**. Par exemple :
  • *icon* → *iconic*
  • *experiment* → *experimental*
- Certains suffixes comme ***-ing***, ***-ly***, ***-hood***, ***-ness***, ***-ment***, ***-ship***, ***-less***, ***-ful***, etc. ne changent pas la position de l'accent. Par exemple :
  • *happy* → *happiness*
  • *extraordinary* → *extraordinarily*

Les mots composés

AUDIO

- Dans les **noms composés**, l'accent tonique principal porte en général sur la syllabe accentuée du premier mot.
  • *swimming pool*
  • *bookshop*
  • *coffee table*
- L'accent tonique principal des **adjectifs composés** porte en général sur le deuxième mot.
  • *homemade*
  • *old-fashioned*
  • *well known*

Train and memorise!

AUDIO

Lis les mots suivants et anticipe leur prononciation en repérant les suffixes par exemple. Écoute et répète ces mots en faisant attention au placement de l'accent tonique.

America • formula • tradition • entrepreneurship • opportunity • involvement • charity

L'intonation des phrases

Puisque les mots sont accentués, cela produit un rythme particulier dans la phrase. La phrase elle-même est accentuée, créant une mélodie.

Les schémas intonatifs

AUDIO

L'anglais comporte plusieurs schémas intonatifs.

→ L'intonation **descendante** : la voix descend d'une note haute sur le premier accent de mot vers une note basse sur le dernier accent de mot.
- *She will open an Asian restaurant.* ↘

→ L'intonation **ascendante** : la voix s'élève d'une note basse jusqu'à une note assez élevée sur le dernier mot accentué.
- *Will she open it in London?* ↗

→ L'intonation **descendante-ascendante** : la voix descend sur la partie la plus importante de la phrase et remonte sur la syllabe accentuée d'un mot qui la suit.
- *I think she will!* ↘↗

L'accentuation des mots

AUDIO

→ De manière générale, l'anglais accentue les mots **porteurs de sens**, c'est à dire les **verbes**, les **noms** et les **adjectifs**. Les mots grammaticaux sont peu accentués (déterminants, prépositions) et sont donc réalisés sous leur forme faible.
- *She's a **teenpreneur** and she **started** at **12**.*

→ On peut parfois **choisir** d'accentuer certains mots afin **d'attirer l'attention** de son interlocuteur/trice sur un mot en particulier. Le sens de la phrase diffère en fonction du mot accentué.
- ***I** watched a sci-fi movie.* → C'est moi qui ai regardé un film de science-fiction (et pas quelqu'un d'autre).
- *I watched a **sci-fi** movie.* → J'ai regardé un film de science-fiction (et non d'aventure ou autre).

Les questions

AUDIO

→ L'intonation des *yes/no questions* est ascendante.
- *Do you like fashion?* ↗

→ Celle des questions en *wh-* en revanche est descendante.
- *Who are the volunteers cleaning the beaches?* ↘

Les phrases exclamatives

AUDIO

→ En général, l'intonation des phrases exclamatives est **descendante**.
- *Come with me!* ↘

→ Mais elle est **montante** quand on veut marquer la surprise ou l'étonnement.
- *I can't believe it!* ↗

Les phrases déclaratives

AUDIO

→ En général, l'intonation des phrases déclaratives est **descendante**.
- *Science fiction is sometimes close to reality.* ↘

→ Pour des phrases un peu longues, l'intonation **monte puis descend**.
- *They created their own business* ↗ *when they were teenagers.* ↘

Train and memorise!

1 Anticipe l'intonation de ces phrases, puis écoute, répète et vérifie. AUDIO

a. When did you start your business?
b. Are you a superhero fan?
c. I'm really impressed!
d. They help preserve their environment by cleaning beaches.
e. It was a good movie indeed!

2 Anticipe quels mots sont accentués et inaccentués dans ces phrases, puis écoute et vérifie. AUDIO

a. This is the sci-fi novel I prefer.
b. We volunteer in an association to help save the environment.

3 Écoute ces phrases et explique leur sens en fonction du mot accentué. AUDIO

a. I wore a **skirt** yesterday.
b. **I** wore a skirt yesterday.
c. I wore a skirt **yesterday**.

HOW to shine in... VOCABULARY

Comprendre le sens des mots

Lorsque tu lis un texte ou que tu écoutes un document audio, il est normal de ne pas connaître tous les mots. En revanche, il y a des méthodes pour en déduire le sens.

TIP 1

Sers-toi du **contexte** et de la **thématique** du document pour comprendre le sens global du mot.

• *I can't believe this parody. It looks real one, it's **breathtaking**!* → Avec le début de la phrase, tu comprends que la personne est surprise : elle n'en croit pas ses yeux, *breathtaking* est certainement en lien avec l'idée d'étonnement.

TIP 2

Sers-toi de la **place** du mot dans la phrase afin de déterminer sa **catégorie grammaticale** : s'il est devant un nom, c'est un adjectif ; s'il vient après un pronom sujet, c'est un verbe.

• *Every year, they **broadcast** the same sci-fi movies.* → Ici, *broadcast* suit *they* qui est un pronom, il y a de fortes chances pour que ce soit un verbe.

TIP 3

Décompose le mot : si tu connais son radical (sa racine) ou le sens du préfixe ou du suffixe, tu pourras utiliser ces éléments pour comprendre le mot.

• *This debate is **endless**!* → Tu reconnais le mot *end* et le suffixe *-less* qui indique le manque, l'idée de « sans ». *Endless* fait donc référence à quelque chose qui est sans fin, interminable.

TIP 4

Tu peux bien sûr **combiner les trois techniques** pour déduire le sens d'un mot inconnu.

• ***Disrespectful** behaviour will not be tolerated in the classroom.*

1. On parle de quelque chose de négatif qui n'est pas accepté en classe.
2. Le mot *disrespectful* est placé devant un nom, c'est donc un adjectif.
3. On peut décomposer le mot en trois parties : le préfixe *dis-* (idée d'opposition, de contraire), le radical *respect* et le suffixe *-ful* (« plein de »). On peut le traduire par « irrespectueux ».

Les préfixes et les suffixes

Les préfixes et les suffixes s'ajoutent au radical des mots pour former des mots dérivés. La **dérivation** permet de nuancer le sens du radical, en fonction du sens des préfixes et des suffixes choisis.

Préfixes

- Idée de contraire, d'opposé : ***un**happy* • *__im__possible* • *__ir__regular* • *__il__legal* • *__in__discreet* • *__dis__agree* • *__de__motivate*
- Idée d'élévation ≠ abaissement : *__up__stairs* ≠ *__down__stairs*
- Idée de surpassement : *__over__view* • *__out__live*
- Idée d'erreur : *__mis__understanding*
- Idée de répétition : *__re__build*

Suffixes

- Formation d'un nom abstrait : *child__hood__* • *happi__ness__* • *friend__ship__* • *capital__ism__*
- Formation d'une catégorie de personnes : *employ__ee__* • *prison__er__* • *creat__or__* • *act__ress__*
- Idée de faisabilité : *teach__able__*
- Formation d'un adjectif : *care__ful__* • *rain__y__* • *child__ish__* • *econom__ic__* • *magic__al__*
- Idée de manque : *home__less__*
- Formation d'un adverbe : *sincere__ly__*

Train and memorise!

Entraîne-toi à trouver le sens des mots dérivés du radical *use* !
useless • misuse • reuse • useful • usual • uselessly • usefully • usefulness

Your turn to shine!

À toi de jouer ! Lis ce texte et observe les mots surlignés. Suis les conseils pour deviner leur sens.

Ethical Fashion series: the legendary Vivienne Westwood

A grande dame of the fashion world, famous for her designs that play with the codes of punk and Britishness, Vivienne Westwood is also renowned as a pioneer of sustainable clothing. [...]

Westwood has ceaselessly worked for the protection of the planet and its ecosystems, seeking to raise awareness. [...] Over time, her commitment has intensified, to the point where today she is just as well known for her historically inspired collections as for her ecological militancy. One of her best known slogans, "*Buy less, choose well, make it last,*" calls for balanced[3] consumption, whether of fashion or any other resources.

Lea ZETLAOUI, *numero.com*, 2019

▲ *File* 10, p. 105

Ce mot est placé avant le nom *fashion*, c'est donc certainement un adjectif. Tu reconnais le mot transparent *ethic*. Tu peux penser que *ethical* signifie « éthique ».

Le mot est formé de l'adjectif *British* et du suffixe *-ness* utilisé pour former des noms. *Britishness* désigne donc certainement le fait d'être britannique.

Au radical *aware* qui signifie « être conscient » est accolé le suffixe *-ness* servant à former un nom. Le mot semble donc exprimer le fait d'être conscient.

Le mot se termine par *-ed* et il est placé après *is*. Il s'agit donc du participe passé d'un verbe conjugué à la forme passive. D'après le contexte, notamment le mot *famous* (l. 1) et l'utilisation de *also*, tu peux déduire que *renowed* veut dire « connue, reconnue ».

Le mot contient deux suffixes : *-ly* qui indique la formation d'un adverbe et *-less* qui veut dire « sans ». Tu peux déduire le sens de *cease*, qui ressemble un peu au français « cesser », en fonction du contexte : Westwood a travaillé « sans cesse ».

Tu peux reconnaître *intense* dans le mot. La terminaison *-ed* et le fait qu'il suit l'auxiliaire *has* indiquent qu'il s'agit d'un verbe au *present perfect*. C'est un verbe transparent, qui correspond au français « intensifier ».

Les mots composés

La langue anglaise contient de nombreux mots composés et elle permet d'en créer très facilement.

→ Ils s'écrivent en **deux mots** distincts reliés par un **trait d'union** ou bien en **un seul mot**. Le premier mot donne **un renseignement, une précision** sur le second mot qui désigne **l'objet** ou **la personne** en question.
- *bedroom* : une pièce (*room*) où il y a un lit (*bed*) → une chambre
- *washing machine* : une machine pour laver → un lave-linge

→ Les possibilités d'associations de mots de **natures grammaticales différentes** sont multiples.
- *bookshop* (nom + nom) • *greenhouse* (adjectif + nom) • *haircut* (nom + verbe) • *swimming pool* (verbe + nom) • *grown-up* (adjectif + adverbe) • *overcome* (adverbe + verbe)

Train and memorise!

Entraîne-toi à trouver le sens de ces mots composés !
traffic lights • moonlight • fireworks • alarm clock • headquarters • seaside • blood donor

Mémoriser le lexique

Pour apprendre de nouveaux mots, tu peux utiliser les techniques suivantes.

MAKE IT EASY

- En utilisant des couleurs différentes, **note sur ton cahier** les mots à apprendre par cœur. Organise-les sous forme de **carte mentale** si cela t'aide et trouve ton propre **code couleur** pour repérer les noms, les adjectifs, les verbes, etc.

- Apprends chaque mot nouveau **en contexte**, c'est-à-dire intégré dans une phrase vue en cours. Tu retiendras mieux ce mot car tu l'associeras à la thématique de l'unité étudiée.

- Observe la **formation** du mot que tu veux retenir : par exemple, note que le mot *unhappily* contient le **radical** *happ(y)* ainsi que le **préfixe** *un-* qui indique le contraire et le **suffixe** *-ly* qui sert à former des adverbes.

- Associe des **images** aux mots que tu apprends. Tu peux par exemple dessiner des smileys pour symboliser les adjectifs de sentiments ou bien représenter des couverts en plastique à côté de *single-use plastic cutlery*.

- Pour être sûr(e) de te souvenir du mot, tu peux **l'écrire**, le **prononcer** à voix haute, le **mimer**… Lorsque tu auras besoin d'utiliser ce mot, tu le retrouveras plus facilement dans ta mémoire grâce au **geste** associé.

MAKE IT EFFICIENT

- Sois **régulier/ère** dans tes apprentissages : fixe-toi **cinq minutes dans la journée**, tous les jours, pour apprendre le vocabulaire. Mets un minuteur et de la musique douce si cela t'aide, et reste concentré(e) sur ton objectif d'apprentissage pendant ces cinq minutes.

- Apprends toujours la **prononciation** du mot en même temps que son **orthographe** car tu peux avoir besoin d'utiliser ce mot pour communiquer à l'écrit comme à l'oral ! Si besoin, utilise un dictionnaire en ligne ou l'appli live! pour écouter la prononciation. La **phonétique** des mots difficiles est précisée dans les cartes mentales de vocabulaire de ton manuel.

MAKE IT FUN

- Lis les mots nouveaux **à voix haute** et **enregistre-toi** à l'aide de ton téléphone. N'oublie pas **d'épeler** ces mots. Écoute ensuite cet enregistrement pendant que tu te prépares le matin, dans le bus ou en marchant jusqu'au collège…

- **Rappe** ou **chante** les mots nouveaux en accentuant la prononciation qui te pose problème. Quel rythme mettrais-tu sur cette phrase : *This digital spoof is unreliable!* ?

- Crée un **jeu de cartes** : prépare des fiches recto-verso avec un dessin sur une face et le mot écrit sur l'autre face. Joue ensuite seul(e) ou à plusieurs, en inventant tes propres règles !

- Avant un test, **réécris les mots nouveaux** sur des post-it et colle-les un peu partout dans ta chambre pour réviser sans t'en rendre compte ! *Smuggle* sur le placard, *threaten* sur le miroir, *robbery* sur la lampe de bureau… Ces mots rentreront tout seuls dans ta mémoire !

Your turn to shine!

À toi de jouer ! Entraîne-toi à apprendre quelques mots figurant sur la carte mentale du *File* 12 page 129, qui répertorie le vocabulaire lié aux liens entre science et fiction.

MAKE IT EASY

- Commence par **lire** les mots et **note** sur un cahier de brouillon ceux qui te posent problème à cause de l'orthographe ou du sens. Pense à utiliser un **code couleur**. Tu peux utiliser la **carte mentale vierge** à compléter dans ton *workbook*. WB → p. 125
- Tu peux apprendre les mots dans une **phrase** extraite d'un document de l'unité, par exemple : *Marty McFly's kids wear* ***smart glasses*** *that let them watch TV and* ***answer calls***.
- Réfléchis à la **formation** des mots. Observe par exemple *headset*, *standalone*, *breakthrough* : comment peux-tu les découper ?
- Si cela t'aide, tu peux **dessiner** chaque gadget à côté de son nom.
- **Recopie** et/ou **répète** les mots plusieurs fois en faisant des gestes : par exemple, tu peux mimer *crouch*, *draw*, *jump*, *kneel*.

SCIENCE AND FICTION

Space exploration (AUDIO)
- crew = team
- explorer
- glide /glaɪd/
- helicopter
- passenger
- ride /raɪd/
- rocket
- round-trip mission

Gadgets (AUDIO)
- device /dɪ'vaɪs/ = equipment
- goggles
- headset
- LED display/wall
- smart glasses
- touch screen
- standalone = autonomous

From fiction to reality (AUDIO)
- virtual reality
- bring something to life = make something real
- create in virtual reality
- dive /daɪv/ in
- immerse oneself
- step into (enter)
- convincingly
- massively = enormously

Technological functionalities (AUDIO)
- breakthrough /'breɪkˌθruː/: *avancée technologique*
- feature /'fiːtʃə/
- innovation
- phenomenal /fɪ'nɒmɪnl/
- answer calls
- call for help
- detect
- fold up: *replier*
- inspire /ɪn'spaɪə/
- predict the weather
- rescue people

Video games (AUDIO)
- entertainment: *divertissement*
- gear /gɪə/ = equipment
- system = console
- crawl
- crouch /kraʊtʃ/: *s'accroupir*
- draw
- jump
- kneel /niːl/
- tiptoe

Cinema (AUDIO)
- comedy
- filmmaking tech
- green screen
- industry
- (film/movie) set
- immersive
- life-size /'laɪf saɪz/
- be released
- broadcast: *diffuser*
- perform
- shoot

NOUN ADJECTIVE VERB ADVERB

MAKE IT EFFICIENT

- Choisis un moment de la journée où tu peux consacrer cinq minutes à l'étude du vocabulaire et fais-le **tous les jours**.
- N'oublie pas d'écouter **l'audio** des mots, surtout ceux qui te posent problème. Tu peux t'appuyer sur la phonétique indiquée en rouge pour les termes *device*, *breakthrough*, *feature*, *phenomenal*, *inspire*, etc.

MAKE IT FUN

- Choisis un des conseils de l'encadré *Make it fun* p. 162 et mets-le en application. Utilise tes talents en **dessin**, **chant**, **théâtre** pour t'enregistrer, créer des cartes, chanter ces mots !
- Note les mots sur des **post-it** et colle-les dans ta chambre !

Train and memorise!

Maintenant, utilise les conseils donnés pour apprendre le vocabulaire du chapitre de ton choix !

HOW to shine in… **VOCABULARY**

Trouver le mot juste

Lorsque tu veux t'exprimer à l'écrit ou à l'oral, il te manque parfois le mot exact à utiliser pour dire ce que tu souhaites. Voici quelques techniques qui te permettront de trouver le mot juste !

TIP 1 – Les préfixes et les suffixes

Tu as vu p. 160 que les préfixes et les suffixes s'ajoutent au **radical** des mots pour former **des mots dérivés**.

care + *less* = *careless* (négligent, insouciant)
radical (attention, soin) – **suffixe** (idée de manque)

un + ***happy*** = *unhappy* (malheureux)
préfixe (idée de contraire, d'opposé) – **radical** (heureux)

friend + *ship* = *friendship* (amitié)
radical (ami) – **suffixe** (formation d'un nom)

final + *ly* = *finally* (finalement)
radical (final) – **suffixe** (formation d'un adverbe)

Le mot que tu recherches est peut-être le dérivé d'un radical que tu connais !

TIP 2 – Les mots composés

Tu as vu p. 161 que la langue anglaise permet très facilement la création de **mots composés**. Penses-y !

swimming pool (piscine)
information sur l'objet (nage) – **objet** (bassin)

policewoman (policière)
information sur la personne (police) – **personne** (femme)

TIP 3 – Les synonymes et les antonymes

Pour trouver le mot juste, tu peux réfléchir aux **synonymes** et aux **antonymes** (ou contraires) d'un mot. Dans ton cahier ou sur des fiches, crée des **boîtes de synonymes** qui peuvent être différents selon le contexte.

good	***bad***	***important***
great	*dreadful*	*paramount*
marvellous	*squalid*	*essential*
pleasant	*nasty*	*huge*
tasty	*poor*	*etc.*
adequate	*etc.*	
impressive		
etc.		

Tu peux aussi écrire **un mot et son antonyme** sur la même ligne. Utilise un **code couleur** pour noter sur tes fiches les mots nouveaux et leurs synonymes d'une couleur et leurs antonymes d'une autre.

big ≠ ***small* • *short* • *tiny***
enormous
huge
long
tall
fat

TIP 4 – Les collocations

Une **collocation** est la combinaison de deux ou plusieurs mots qui vont bien ensemble. Utiliser des collocations rendra ton anglais plus authentique.

tense	situation	right	number
wide	choice	sound	advice
sharp	rise	deep	concern
relevant	information	pretty	bad
get	angry	make	friends

TIP 5 – Phrasal verbs

Les ***phrasal verbs***, ou verbes à particules, rendront aussi ton anglais plus authentique. Ce sont des verbes suivis d'une particule qui change le sens du verbe.

look up to = admire (admirer)
verbe (regarder) – **particule** (vers le haut)

Voici quelques exemples de *phrasal verbs* avec leur équivalent.

- *find out = discover*
- *put up with = tolerate*
- *look for = seek*
- *give up = abandon*
- *look down upon = despise*
- *fill out = complete*

Your turn to shine!

EXERCICE 1

▶ **Ajoute** des suffixes et préfixes à ces mots pour créer des mots dérivés.

happy · power · forget · help · possible · honest

EXERCICE 2

▶ **Associe** les mots afin de créer des mots composés. **Explique** le sens des mots ainsi créés.

class · horse · bed · car · room · work · art · street · home · race

EXERCICE 3

a. Remplace le mot en bleu par le synonyme approprié selon le contexte.

- The meal was **good**.
- We had a **good** weekend.
- I think it's **important** to believe in your dreams.
- This idea is an **important** part of the concept.
- This is **bad** quality.
- She had a **bad** behaviour.

b. Trouve le contraire de chaque mot.

artificial · late · similar · presence · buy · accept · cheap · awake · open · after

before · different · early · close · natural · asleep · refuse · sell · absence · expensive

EXERCICE 4

▶ **Associe** les mots pour retrouver des collocations.

reach · cause · pay · highly · heavy · get · take

rain · competitive · home · trouble · an agreement · attention · a look

EXERCICE 5

▶ **Associe** chaque *phrasal verb* à son synonyme.

carry on · call off · account for · back up · blow up · figure out · get away · show up

understand · cancel · explode · escape · explain · support · continue · appear

SNAPFILE 1 Join the Spy School

GRAMMAR Le superlatif de supériorité

➜ p. 16

1 Mets ces adjectifs au superlatif de supériorité.

a. I'm (big) fan of the CHERUB series in the class.

b. Training is not (hard) part, being discreet is (difficult) challenge for a secret agent.

c. Who is (strong) spy? I don't know, but James Bond is (athletic).

d. Only (good) agents will be recruited.

2 Remets les lettres dans l'ordre pour retrouver les superlatifs de supériorité et traduis-les.

THE AFTSETS
THE ILIELSTS
THE SALTLET
THE SRABVET
THE FNIEUSTN

GRAMMAR La capacité au présent

➜ p. 16

3 Reformule les phrases suivantes à l'aide des expressions suggérées.

a. He can dive into deep waters. → be capable of

b. She is able to decipher codes in a few seconds. → be good at

c. He masters spying to perfection. → can

d. He cannot fly a plane. → be able to

4 Écris ce que James Bond est capable de faire en utilisant les verbes proposés et en variant les expressions.

dive
ride a motorcycle
swim
drive
hack computers
break codes
fly a plane

VOCABULARY The world of spies

➜ p. 17

5 Retrouve les huit mots cachés dans la grille.

X	F	I	T	S	S	I	A	U	R	V
A	B	G	H	C	O	Q	R	D	Z	F
R	D	K	R	W	L	D	X	E	G	Z
E	G	L	I	F	V	O	M	C	E	O
C	H	A	L	L	E	N	G	I	N	G
R	P	D	L	U	V	J	N	P	I	R
U	D	M	I	G	F	R	E	H	U	O
I	P	Q	N	B	R	A	V	E	S	I
T	E	H	G	H	Y	W	T	R	G	U

6 Trouve l'intrus dans chaque série de mots.

a. swim • smug • drive • dive • fly

b. sporty • strong • brave • host • fast

c. extremely • funny • highly • really

d. arrogant • spy • genius • mastermind

FILE 2 British Indian fusion

GRAMMAR Le présent simple et le présent en *be* + V-ing

➜ p. 27

7 Complète ces phrases en utilisant les marqueurs temporels proposés.

today | every year | right now | usually

a. ... British Indians celebrate Diwali in London.

b. For Diwali, I ... visit the Hindu temple with my family.

c. ... the Indian community is celebrating Diwali in Trafalgar Square.

d. I'm in Trafalgar Square ..., the Mayor of London is giving a speech.

8 Conjugue les verbes au présent simple ou au présent en *be* + V-ing selon la situation.

a. At the moment I (listen) to bhangra music and I really (like) it.

b. Every year we (buy) a different costume and we (attend) the parade, but this year I (wear) last year's costume because it still (look) good.

c. People in England (appreciate) Indian food.

d. Meera often (cook) Indian food because her parents (live) in London but they (come) from Mumbai.

GRAMMAR Les tournures exclamatives

➜ p. 27

9 Reconstitue ces phrases exclamatives.

a. a • what • festival • fantastic • !
b. an • dancer • incredible • she • such • is • !
c. athletic • cricket • this • is • so • player • !
d. my • delicious • how • is • curry • !

10 Réagis positivement à ces situations à l'aide d'une tournure exclamative en *what*, *how*, *so* ou *such*.

a. You are watching a Bollywood dance performance.
b. You are listening to bhangra music.
c. Your friend cooked curry.
d. You are visiting a Hindu temple.

VOCABULARY *Indian Britain*

➜ p. 28-29

11 Associe les étiquettes pour former des mots.

MINO • IMMI • COMMU • POPU • INTE • ARCHI • FU • LEGA • TRA • CELE

CY • TECTURE • SION • DITION • GRATION • GRATION • NITY • RITY • LATION • BRATION

SNAPFILE 3 Go New Zealand girls

GRAMMAR Le prétérit simple et le prétérit en *be* + V-ing

➜ p. 36

12 Choisis la forme du verbe au prétérit qui convient le mieux.

a. Many women wore / were wearing white ribbon bows to symbolise protest while they demonstrated / were demonstrating.
b. These pioneers empowered / were empowering the next generations of women.
c. As she sang / was singing, people understood / were understanding the feminist message.
d. During the demonstration, protesters followed / were following their leaders and they chanted / were chanting their hymn.
e. These activists showed / were showing the way and later, many people followed / were following their example.

13 Mets le verbe entre parenthèses au prétérit simple ou au prétérit en *be* + V-*ing*.

a. They (protest) to get equal rights and they finally (get) them.
b. As she (demonstrate), she (become) a role model and she (meet) other leaders.
c. Many women (grow up) without any rights a few decades ago.
d. Supporters (cheer) and (encourage) women as they (march) to Parliament.

GRAMMAR Les pronoms relatifs

➜ p. 36

14 Complète les phrases avec le bon pronom relatif. Justifie ton choix.

a. Jacinda Arden is the Prime Minister who / which went to Parliament with her baby.
b. New Zealand is the country who / where women got the right to vote in the early 20th century.
c. The song that / who she wrote is a feminist one.
d. This is the reason that / why they signed the treaty.

15 Transforme ces deux phrases indépendantes en une seule phrase composée d'une principale et d'une relative.

a. They signed the petition. The petition was a turning point in history.
b. Dame Cooper was a leader. Dame Cooper made things change.
c. Activists had the courage to stand up. I find it impressive.
d. New Zealand is a country. In this country, women have power.

▲ Jacinda Ardern

VOCABULARY *Gender equality in NZ*

➜ p. 37

16 Complète les phrases avec les mots correspondant aux définitions données.

a. The first person to do something is a p _ _ _ _ _ _.
b. When you start a campaign, you l _ _ _ _ _ it.
c. Trying to do something is an a _ _ _ _ _ _ _.
d. When you make someone realise something, you raise a _ _ _ _ _ _ _ _ _.
e. When you give more freedom or power to a group of people, you e _ _ _ _ _ _ them.
f. When you talk positively about something so people want to do it too, you p _ _ _ _ _ _ it.

FILE 4 Teen entrepreneurs

GRAMMAR Poser des questions (1)

→ p. 47

17 Remets les mots dans l'ordre pour obtenir des questions.

a. did • when • start • you • your business • ?

b. you • do • what • sell • ?

c. she • a • does • idea • have • business • new • ?

d. this • business • launched • who • successful • ?

18 Pose une question dont la réponse sera l'élément surligné.

a. She opened her first lemonade stand in Indianapolis.

b. He gave an interview last year.

c. He wrote a book because he wanted to share his tips to succeed.

d. Mikaila is a successful businesswoman.

GRAMMAR Les propositions infinitives

→ p. 47

19 Associe les étiquettes pour former les phrases. Attention au sens et à la construction des verbes.

Reading this book made her

Feeling supported enables

Many parents encourage

Many people expect teenpreneurs

people to succeed.

their children to be teenpreneurs.

think about creating a business.

to share their experience.

20 Termine ces phrases avec des propositions infinitives.

a. She has a lot of ideas, she wants…

b. After the show, his parents let him…

c. I don't expect my teenage daughter…

d. This business enabled me…

e. Our teachers allowed us…

VOCABULARY Teen entrepreneurs

→ p. 48-49

21 Retrouve les neuf mots cachés dans la grille.

A	W	A	R	D	A	B	S	I
D	C	D	G	E	J	M	U	N
V	E	F	K	H	L	O	C	S
I	N	F	R	W	S	P	C	P
C	H	A	R	I	T	Y	E	I
E	T	I	U	L	I	V	S	R
W	X	L	Y	L	P	Z	S	E
A	Q	U	C	I	C	F	H	D
J	I	R	K	N	D	E	G	L
P	O	E	N	G	O	A	L	M

SNAPFILE 5 A winning formula

GRAMMAR Le *present perfect*

→ p. 56

22 Choisis une étiquette de chaque couleur pour faire des phrases.

drivers F1 cars fans Great Britain

have been popular

have become greener

have admired drivers

has hosted a Grand Prix

for since

decades the 2000s many years 1950

23 Mets le verbe au *present perfect* et ajoute *already* ou *not … yet* comme indiqué.

a. Too bad for him: he (win a race / not … yet)!

b. He knows this race track very well: he (already / attend) the Grand Prix.

c. One lap to go… Hamilton (cross / not … yet) the finish line.

d. Engineers (improve/ already) the engines. I am convinced they will do better in a few years.

e. I (attend a race / not yet), but I'm going to Silverstone next month!

f. Women (compete / already) in many races and even more will in a few years!

GRAMMAR Les articles

➜ p. 56

24 Choisis l'article qui convient dans chaque phrase.

a. Look at an / the F1 car: it's crossing the / Ø finish line!
b. I've never met an / the F1 driver.
c. The / Ø British Grand Prix is a / the perfect place for the / Ø drivers to test their skills.
d. The / Ø campaign for reducing CO2 emissions has had a / the great impact on the / Ø fans and the / Ø drivers.
e. The / Ø engineers have worked on the / Ø eco-friendly engines that have been used in the / Ø past races.

25 Complète avec *the*, *a/an* ou *Ø*.

a. ... experts have worked on ... pollution issues for years.
b. ... F1 races in ... UK are very popular.
c. ... racism is ... real issue in ... F1 world.
d. ... environmental issues have changed ... design of ... engines and ... cars.

▲ Lewis Hamilton

VOCABULARY *Formula One*

➜ p. 57

26 Remets les lettres dans l'ordre pour trouver les mots correspondant aux définitions.

a. FCEFITINE = using energy without wasting it (for an engine)
b. AEBSRK = elements that make a car go slower or stop
c. ENILCUISV = that allows all kinds of people, rather than just one kind of person
d. RYEST = pieces of rubber that are fitted on the wheels of a car
e. YBDHIR = using both petrol and electricity (for an engine)

27 Ajoute les lettres manquantes pour former des mots.

a. T_C__OL__Y	G N E O H
b. _EC__NI_	H A C M
c. ST__RING_HE__	E E L E W
d. IN__LV__EN_	M E V O T
e. S_S_AIN_B_LIT_	A T U Y I

FILE 6 Move on up

GRAMMAR Le prétérit et le *present perfect*

➜ p. 67

28 Associe les phrases avec le marqueur de temps qui convient.

They have sung to celebrate their ancestors
Slaves sang in fields
in the 19th century.
The civil rights movement started
since the abolition of slavery.
in the 1950s.
The fight for equal rights has been going on
for centuries.

29 Mets le verbe entre parenthèses au *present perfect* ou au prétérit.

a. She (join) the BLM movement last year.
b. They (protest) to obtain the end of segregation.
c. Activists and artists (defend) equal rights for many years.
d. Many African-American artists (sing) protest songs.

GRAMMAR La voix passive

➜ p. 67

30 Mets en avant l'élément surligné à l'aide de la voix passive.

a. Slave owners exploited black people.
b. Many different singers have sung this song.
c. Some people created the BLM movement in the 2000s.
d. They captured many young Africans.

31 Utilise les éléments suggérés pour rédiger des phrases au passif.

a. demonstrations • lead • artists
b. the lyrics • remember • everyone
c. the civil rights movement • help • music
d. MLK • assassinate • a criminal

VOCABULARY *African-American music*

➜ p. 68-69

32 Associe les étiquettes pour former des mots.

PRO, UPLIFT, GATION, RUS, SEGRE, ANCES, ING, RY, STRI, CHO, KE, TEST, CENTU, LY, RICS, TORS

SNAPFILE 7 Dive into Barbados

GRAMMAR Le conseil et l'obligation (*should, must, have to* et *need to*)

→ p. 76

33 Crée des phrases en choisissant un élément dans chaque encadré.

volunteers • tourists • The Prime Minister of Barbados • everyone

need • must • should • have

to • Ø

clean the beaches • alert public opinion • be aware of the situation • help

34 Tu es bénévole pour une association environnementale à la Barbade. Exprime deux conseils en utilisant *should* et deux obligations avec *must, have to* ou *need to*.

GRAMMAR L'hypothèse avec *if* et *will*

→ p. 76

35 Mets les verbes entre parenthèses au présent et ajoute *will* quand c'est nécessaire.

a. If we (stop) polluting, sea turtles (reproduce) more easily in the future.

b. People (help) clean beaches if we (invite) them to do so.

c. Green tourism (develop) if people (understand) its importance.

d. I (be) happy to help if an association (suggest) I take part.

36 Termine ces phrases en *if*.

a. If I go to Barbados, ...

b. Volunteers will collect less plastic if ...

c. Corals won't die if ...

d. If the government bans plastic bags, ...

VOCABULARY Ecology in Barbados

→ p. 77

37 Trouve le mot correspondant à chaque définition.

a. Someone who does work without being paid: ... (n)

b. Process trash (plastic or paper) to produce useful materials that can be used again: ... (v)

c. Endangered, that could stop existing: ... (adj)

d. Things you throw away: ... (n)

38 Retrouve l'intrus dans chaque liste de mots et justifie ton choix.

a. swimming • cleaning • snorkelling • diving

b. coastline • beach • island • jellyfish

c. turtle • crab • jellyfish • bird

d. clean • garbage • dumping • debris

FILE 8 America's most wanted

GRAMMAR Le prétérit et le *past perfect*

→ p. 87

39 Mets les verbes entre parenthèses au prétérit ou au *past perfect*.

a. By the time they (go) to prison, they (steal) a lot of money.

b. The FBI (arrest) them after they (escape) from prison.

c. Gangsters (be) famous in real life before they (be) famous on screens.

d. They (rob) banks before they (start) bootlegging.

40 Complète ce texte avec les verbes proposés conjugués au prétérit ou au *past perfect*.

know • become • murder • be killed • get caught

Bonnie Parker ... one of America's most famous outlaws during the 1930s. She ... Clyde Barrow for four years when they ... in a police ambush. Before they ..., they ... at least nine police officers and four civilians.

GRAMMAR Poser des questions (2)

→ p. 87

41 Ajoute le *question tag* qui convient.

a. He robbed many banks, ... ?

b. The FBI didn't catch him, ... ?

c. They had smuggled alcohol, ... ?

d. He was Public Enemy number one, ... ?

e. They haven't heard about Machine Gun Kelly, ... ?

42 **Reformule ces questions comme dans l'exemple.**

Ex : Why do you think you ended up in Alcatraz?
→ In your opinion, why did you end up in Alcatraz?

a. Why do you think people admired him so much?
b. How do you think they arrested him?
c. Who do you think helped him?
d. When do you think he started his activity?

VOCABULARY *American gangsters*

→ p. 88-89

43 **Remets les lettres dans l'ordre pour trouver les mots correspondant aux définitions.**

a. RTEHNATE = menace (verb)
b. GLUGESM = take something to or from a place illegally
c. RSREAT = catch someone and take him or her to a police station
d. HINEDALE = title of a newspaper article, printed in large letters

SNAPFILE 9 Captain America: born in the USA

GRAMMAR Le gérondif

→ p. 96

44 **Complète les phrases suivantes avec les verbes ci-dessous (base verbale ou gérondif).**

ensure | become | hesitate | fly | save | rescue

a. Superman is capable of ... and he can ... people.
b. ... the world is the goal of most super heroes.
c. Before ... movie characters, most superheroes were comics characters.
d. They save innocent people without ... in order to ... peace.

45 **Reconstitue ces phrases.**

watching the latest Marvel movie. | Going to the movies is | my favourite activity. | They fight evil in order | Most children start | I feel inspired after | reading comics at a young age. | to protect every citizen.

GRAMMAR Le comparatif de supériorité, d'égalité et d'infériorité

→ p. 96

46 **Écris les comparatifs à la forme demandée.**

a. athletic <
b. big >
c. famous =
d. funny >
e. tall =
f. heroic <

47 **Écris au moins quatre phrases en utilisant des adjectifs pour comparer ces superhéros.**

Muscleman	Red Flash
STRENGTH ////	STRENGTH ///
SPEED ///	SPEED ////
INTELLIGENCE ///	INTELLIGENCE ///
COURAGE ///	COURAGE ////

VOCABULARY *Captain America*

→ p. 97

48 **Reconstitue ces mots.**

PATRI | STRA | WEA | PROPA | FREE | MORA

DOM | OTIC | GANDA | LITY | TEGIC | PON

49 **Trouve les lettres manquantes dans chaque mot. Aide-toi des indications données.**

a. D_CT_ _OR_ _L = non-democratic
b. BUL_E_-P_O_F = that can resist bullets
c. D_ _ _NSI_E = the contrary of "offensive"
d. A_ _EG_A_CE = a synonym for "loyalty"

FILE 10 All dressed up!

GRAMMAR Les quantifieurs

➔ p. 107

50 Complète ces phrases avec les quantifieurs donnés.

many | every | much | a few | a lot of | any

a. Dressing up and changing clothes is so ... fun.

b. There are ... different styles but I only like ... and I don't have ... favourite ones.

c. ... designer has a special style that you can identify.

d. ... singers and artists become icons for famous brands.

51 Complète ces phrases avec le quantifieur qui convient.

a. There were too ... people at the fashion show, I couldn't see ... of the outfits!

b. I've never seen ... artist wearing a Union Jack shirt!

c. I like my Dandy style so much! I see ... reason to change my style.

d. ... people think it's weird, but we get ... positive comments on our style.

GRAMMAR L'opposition et la concession ; la cause et la conséquence

➔ p. 107

52 Choisis le mot de liaison qui convient dans chaque phrase.

a. I love fashion whereas / therefore my sister doesn't care!

b. She is a designer while / that's why she has a fashion sense.

c. She has a very modern style despite / because of her age.

d. Since / Although he makes very bold fashion choices, people look at him weirdly.

53 Forme des phrases en utilisant les propositions suivantes et des mots de liaison.

a. he is a dandy / he has his own style

b. many artists wear Union Jack clothes / they are not British

c. they have to wear a uniform / it's compulsory at school

d. he's original / the rest of his friends are classical

VOCABULARY *Fashion and identity*

➔ p. 108-109

54 Trouve 12 mots dans la grille.

B	Z	B	Y	T	R	E	N	D	W
L	P	O	R	S	T	W	X	R	E
A	O	L	F	M	W	T	I	E	A
Z	S	D	H	A	O	N	V	S	R
E	I	V	I	R	D	R	E	S	S
R	N	N	E	T	T	W	D	C	W
S	C	A	S	U	A	L	O	O	A
R	N	A	C	E	N	X	E	D	L
L	H	A	L	E	A	T	H	E	R
U	G	L	Y	R	D	B	O	O	M

SNAPFILE 11 Twist and tell

GRAMMAR La probabilité (*must*, *may*, *could*, *might* et *can't*)

➔ p. 116

55 Complète les phrases avec le modal qui convient.

a. Look at this poster! It ... be a fake, I'm sure!

b. This organisation ... make things change but I doubt it.

c. Deepfake is dangerous because people ... think what they see is real.

d. Don't underestimate the risks: these ads ... deceive you!

56 Reformule ces phrases à l'aide d'un modal + BV ou modal + *have* V-*en* pour exprimer la probabilité.

a. I'm certain you've seen this advert.

b. I guess many people believe what they see.

c. I don't know if this picture is a fake, but it's possible.

d. I'm sure that is not the Queen in the poster, it's impossible!

GRAMMAR Les discours direct et indirect

➔ p. 116

57 Mets les phrases suivantes au style indirect.

a. I don't trust these ads! ➔ He said he...

b. Fake news spreads so fast, it's incredible! ➔ She says...

c. Where did you see this poster? → She asks me…

d. Do you believe everything you see? → He asked him…

58 **Remets ces phrases au style direct.**

a. She told me she had seen the ad on TV.

b. They asked her if she was aware of the dangers of deepfake.

c. They explained they tried to inform people since they worked for an organisation.

d. She says she thought the ad she saw yesterday was a real one.

VOCABULARY *Twist and tell*

→ p. 117

59 **Associe par deux ou par trois les mots ayant le même sens.**

alter · amazing · change · exchange · modify · fascinating · parody · swap · reliable · spoof · trustworthy

60 **Trouve les mots correspondant aux définitions.**

a. The board on which ads are displayed: …

b. Eliminate something: …

c. An ad slogan or catchphrase everyone remembers: …

d. When you worry about something: …

e. Something dangerous: …

FILE 12 From reel to real

GRAMMAR Le conditionnel

→ p. 127

61 **Mets les verbes entre parenthèses au prétérit, au *past perfect* ou au conditionnel (*would* + BV ou *would have* + V-en).**

a. If I (have) more time, I (read) sci-fi novels!

b. Jim (love) to travel to space if it (be) possible.

c. Sci-fi authors (change) the world if their ideas (exist) for real.

d. If science (get) inspiration from sci-fi novels, our lives (be) crazy!

e. If they (exist) twenty years ago, people (use) smart watches!

f. Today's technology (help) space explorers if they (have) it in the 1960s.

62 **Utilise les verbes ci-dessous pour rédiger au moins quatre phrases en *if* (au conditionnel). Tu peux ajouter des éléments selon ton inspiration.**

SUBJECTS
sci-fi authors • engineers • people • reality • daily life • designers

VERBS
be • fly cars • change our habits • wear special gear • invent gadgets • predict the weather

GRAMMAR L'expression du futur

→ p. 127

63 **Choisis la forme qui convient le mieux selon la situation. Justifie ton choix.**

a. I'm sure engineers will / are going to fly cars by 2050.

b. I suppose this film will / is going to be a blockbuster.

c. Why not? This technology is becoming / may become common in a few years.

d. I think this film is inspiring / may inspire engineers.

64 **Termine les phrases de ce garçon.**

a. I guess explorers…

b. I'm sure that one day, …

c. It's obvious that this scientific breakthrough…

d. After this research, scientists…

VOCABULARY *Science and fiction*

→ p. 128-129

65 **Trouve l'intrus dans chaque série de mots.**

a. headset • crouch • device • goggles

b. scientists • engineers • film-makers • breakthrough

c. jump • features • kneel • crouch

d. crew • ride • explorer • passenger

66 **Associe les synonymes deux par deux.**

dive · invent · forecast · influence · inspire · predict · immerse oneself · design

LE MARCHÉ DES VERBES IRRÉGULIERS

Apprendre les verbes irréguliers n'est pas si difficile : à toi de faire ton marché !

3 POUR LE PRIX D'UN !

AUDIO

BV	prétérit	participe passé	🇫🇷
cost /kɒst/	cost	cost	*coûter*
cut /kʌt/	cut	cut	*couper*
hit	hit	hit	*frapper*
hurt /hɜːt/	hurt	hurt	*blesser, faire mal*
let	let	let	*laisser, permettre*
put /pʊt/	put	put	*mettre*
read /riːd/	read /red/	read /red/	*lire*

Attention, la prononciation change !

2 POUR LE PRIX D'UN !

AUDIO

BV	prétérit	participe passé	🇫🇷
find	found	found	*trouver*
have	had	had	*avoir*
hear /hɪər/	heard /həːd/	heard /həːd/	*entendre*
make	made	made	*fabriquer*
pay	paid /peɪd/	paid /peɪd/	*payer*
say	said /sed/	said /sed/	*dire*
sell	sold /səʊld/	sold /səʊld/	*vendre*
tell	told	told	*raconter*
understand	understood	understood	*comprendre*
win	won /wʌn/	won /wʌn/	*gagner*

2 POUR LE PRIX D'UN AVEC UN -T FINAL BONUS !

AUDIO

BV	prétérit	participe passé	🇫🇷
build /bɪld/	built	built	*construire*
burn /bɜːn/	burnt	burnt	*brûler*
dream /driːm/	dreamed / dreamt /dremt/	dreamed / dreamt /dremt/	*rêver*
feel	felt	felt	*ressentir*
get	got	got	*obtenir*
keep	kept	kept	*garder*
learn	learned / learnt	learned / learnt	*apprendre*
leave	left	left	*laisser, partir, quitter*
lose	lost	lost	*(se) perdre*
mean /miːn/	meant /ment/	meant /ment/	*signifier*
meet	met	met	*rencontrer*
send	sent	sent	*envoyer*
shoot	shot	shot	*tirer (fusil)*
sit	sat	sat	*s'asseoir, être assis(e)*
smell	smelled / smelt	smelled / smelt	*sentir (odeur)*
sleep	slept	slept	*dormir*
spend	spent	spent	*dépenser, passer du temps*

2 POUR LE PRIX D'UN : « J'AI ACHETÉ » (GHT) !

AUDIO

BV	prétérit	participe passé	🇫🇷
bring	brought /brɔːt/	brought	*apporter*
buy	bought /bɔːt/	bought	*acheter*
catch	caught	caught	*attraper*
fight	fought	fought	*(se) battre*
teach	taught	taught	*enseigner*
think	thought	thought	*penser*

PACK SPÉCIAL VOYELLES i/u • a • u

AUDIO

BV	prétérit	participe passé	🇫🇷
begin	began	begun	*commencer*
drink	drank	drunk	*boire*
ring	rang	rung	*sonner*
run	ran	run	*courir*
sing	sang	sung	*chanter*
swim	swam	swum	*nager*

Base verbale en u

UN BONUS -EN POUR LE PARTICIPE PASSÉ

AUDIO

BV	prétérit	participe passé	🇫🇷
bite	bit	bitten	*mordre*
break	broke	broken	*casser*
choose	chose	chosen	*choisir*
drive	drove	driven	*conduire*
eat	ate	eaten	*manger*
fall	fell	fallen	*tomber*
forbid	forbade	forbidden	*interdire*
forget	forgot	forgotten	*oublier*
forgive	forgave	forgiven	*pardonner*
freeze	froze	frozen	*geler*
hide	hid	hidden	*(se) cacher*
ride	rode	ridden	*monter, aller à (cheval)*
see	saw	seen	*voir*
steal	stole	stolen	*voler (dérober)*
take	took	taken	*prendre*
wake	woke	woken	*(se) réveiller*
write /raɪt/	wrote	written /ˈrɪtən/	*écrire*

PACK SPÉCIAL -ew • -awn / -own

AUDIO

BV	prétérit	participe passé	🇫🇷
draw	drew	drawn	*dessiner*
fly	flew	flown	*voler (oiseau)*
know	knew	known	*savoir, connaître*
throw	threw	thrown	*lancer, jeter*

PACK FAMILY « COME »

AUDIO

BV	prétérit	participe passé	🇫🇷
become	became	become	*devenir*
come	came	come	*venir*
overcome	overcame	overcome	*surmonter*

PACK BONUS MULTIFORMES

AUDIO

BV	prétérit	participe passé	🇫🇷
be	was, were	been	*être*
do	did	done /dʌn/	*faire*
go	went	gone /gɒn/	*aller*

Crédits photographiques

Couverture : h ADOBE STOCK PHOTO/Daniel ; **b** ADOBE STOCK PHOTO/Lighfield Studios

Garde IV : SHUTTERSTOCK/Random Illustrator (reprise garde V, garde VI) ; **Garde V :** SHUTTERSTOCK/Panda Vector ; SHUTTERSTOCK/Beresnev ; ISTOCK/Anastasiia Krasavina ; ISTOCK/mage_masher (reprise garde VI) ; **Garde VI :** SHUTTERSTOCK/Turkan Rahimli ; SHUTTERSTOCK/VectorPot ; SHUTTERSTOCK/Macrovector ; SHUTTERSTOCK/Little.Kalu ; SHUTTERSTOCK/danceyourlife

12-13 SHUTTERSTOCK/Natalia80 (reprise p. 14-15) ; **12** CHRISTOPHE L COLLECTION/ Prisma/© Zodiak/CITV (reprise p. 4 h) ; **13 h** *The Recruit* Robert Muchamore © Reproduced with permission of the Licensor through PLSclear ; **13 b** CHRISTOPHE L COLLECTION/© Universal Pictures/Relativity Media/StudioCanal (reprise p. 16-1) ; **14 h** ISTOCK/Nerthuz ; **14 m** TCD/BOUTEILLER/Prod DB © Danjaq/MGM/Columbia Pictures/ Eon Prod/DR (reprise p. 16-3) ; **14 b** CHRISTOPHE L COLLECTION/© Kudos/BBC (reprise p. 16-2) ; **14 hg** © Kickresume / Trend Hunter, 2015 / DR ; **15** CHRISTOPHE L COLLECTION/ Prisma/© The Weinstein Company (reprise p. 16-4) ; **17** CHRISTOPHE L COLLECTION/© Zodiak ; **18** PHOTO12.COM/ALAMY/Matthew Chattle (reprise p. 4 m) ; **19** PHOTO12.COM/ALAMY Live News/Stephen Chung ; **20 h** PHOTO12.COM/ALAMY/Imageplotter Travel (reprise p. 138) ; **20 b** PHOTO12.COM/ALAMY/Peter Lane (reprise p. 30) ; **21 mg** © Mandavi Kaushik, 2018 ; **21 md** © Government of India, 2015 / DR ; **22** AGE FOTOSTOCK/ ImageBROKER/Mara Brandl ; **22 bd** BRIDGEMAN IMAGES/MEPL ; **22 bg** PHOTO12.COM/ ALAMY/David Gee ; **23 h** © Anglophenia, 2015 / DR ; **23 b** ABACA PRESS/PA Wire/PA Images/Adam Davy ; **24 h** © Sheba Brick Lane, 2014 ; **24 m** PHOTO12.COM/ALAMY/ Imagedoc ; **24 b** SHUTTERSTOCK/Nelea33 ; **25 h** ITV/Fremantle UK/DR ; **25 b** GETTY IMAGES/Jack Vartoogian ; **26** SHUTTERSTOCK/ViSnezh ; **29** PHOTO12.COM/ALAMY/ Shakeyjon ; **31** AFP/Getty Images Europe/Dan Kitwood ; **32** © Lorna Hallett, 2020 ; **32-33** SHUTTERSTOCK/Patthamapong (reprise p. 34-35) ; **33 h** © Maria Gill and Marco Ivancic / Scholastic, 2018 ; **33 b** NZ Herald Archive/Michael Tubberty ; **34 hg** © Focus Magazine, 2021 ; **34 hd** REUTERS/Carlo Allegri ; **34 bd** REUTERS/Carlo Allegri ; **35** PHOTO12. COM/ALAMY/UPI/Corey Sipkin ; **37** SHUTTERSTOCK/krakenimages.com (reprise p. 4 b) ; **38** ADOBE STOCK PHOTO/Denisismagilov (reprise p. 5 h) ; **39** © TRUiC, 2021 / DR ; **40 h** CALVIN AND HOBBES © 1993 Watterson. Reprinted with permission of ANDREWS MCMEEL SYNDICATION. All righs reserved. ; **40 b** © Rachel and Avery Huggins ; **41 h** © Aladdin, Simon & Schuster Children's Publishing, 2012 / DR ; **41 b** © business.org, 2019 / DR ; **42 h** © Me & the Bees, 2017 / DR ; **42 b** GETTY IMAGES/© ABC/Walt Disney Television/Michael Desmond ; **43 h** © Mahsa Riar Limitless Limb ; **43 m** © Adom Appiah Ball4Good ; **44 h** GETTY IMAGES/Kidzcon/Michael Bezjian ; **44b** © Whistle, 2019 / DR ; **45 g** © The Yummy Brothers ; **45 d** ISTOCK/Bortonia ; ISTOCK/Bortonia ; **46** ISTOCK/ DragonTiger ; ISTOCK/Yuoak ; **48** ISTOCK/VanReeel ; **49** ISTOCK/Mediaphotos ; **50** © Fox News, 2018 / DR ; **51** © Angel Valentin ; **52-53** SHUTTERSTOCK/Jamesteohart (reprise p. 53-54) ; **52** REUTERS/Peter Cziborra (reprise p. 5 m) ; **53 h** © FIA, 2021 / DR ; **53 b** SHUTTERSTOCK/Hafiz Johari ; **54 h** PHOTO12.COM/ALAMY/James Moy ; **54 b** PANORAMIC/ Motorsport Images/Sam Bloxham ; **55 g** PHOTO12.COM/ALAMY/Motorsport Archive Images ; **55 d** © Formula 1 / DR ; **56** AFP/Getty Images North America/Mark Thompson ; **57** SHUTTERSTOCK/Tcharts ; **58** AFP/Getty Images/Getty Images North America/Larry Busacca ; **59** ©National Museum of African American Music / DR ; **60 h** © US Embassy Vienna, 2015 / DR ; **60 b** © Atheneum Books, Simon & Schuster US, 2006 / DR ; **61 h** AKG-Images/North Wind Picture Archives (reprise p. 66) ; **61 b** AURIMAGES/Mary Evans/ AF Archive/MGM (*Queimada: Burn!*, film by Gillo Pontecorvo, 1969) ; **62 h** GETTY IMAGES/ Charlie Gillett Collection/Redferns ; **62 b** Bridgeman Images **63 h** SHUTTERSTOCK/The LIFE Picture Collection/Francis Miller ; **63 b** AFP Photo/Timothy A. Clary ; **64 h** SIPA PRESS/Sipa NY/Alex Milan Tracy ; **64 b** SIPA PRESS/AP/Invision for Essence/Adrienne Battistella (reprise p. 5 b) ; **65 h** © Keedron Bryant / DR ; **66 h** ADOBE STOCK PHOTO/ Dash ; **66 bd** DALLE/Avalon/CC/GB ; GETTY IMAGES/FilmMagic/Jason LaVeris ; GETTY IMAGES/FilmMagic/Paul Archuleta ; GETTY IMAGES/Hulton Archives/Evening Standard ; **66 b g** Toppng ; **68** MAXPPP/Newscom/EPA/Etienne Laurent ; **69** ADOBE STOCK PHOTO/ Prostock-studio ; **70 b** © RCA Records / DR ; **71** BRIDGEMAN IMAGES/© Chicago History Museum/© Estate of Archibald John Motley Jr. All reserved righs 2021 ; **72-73** ISTOCK/ Deejpilot (reprise p. 74-75) ; **72** © From Barbados Dive Map & Reef Creature Guide, copyright Franko Maps Ltd. Used with permission. ; **73 h** © Carla Daniel / The Barbados Sea Turtle Project, 2019 ; **73 m** © HEY Campaign ; **73 b** ISTOCK/Czekma13 (reprise p. 74 m, 77) ; **74 h** GETTY IMAGES/Photodisc/Maremagnum ; **74 b** © Barbados Government Information Service / DR ; **75 h** © Barbados› International Coastal Cleanup, 2019 / DR ; **75 m et b** © The Barbados Sea Turtle Project ; **76** ISTOCK/FilippoBacci ; **78** Gabriel Moskolis ; **79** CHRISTOPHE L COLLECTION/© AMC ; **80** AKG-Images ; **81 g** AURIMAGES/ The Advertising Archive ; **81 d** ROGER-VIOLLET (reprise p. 90) ; **82 h** AURIMAGES/Everett Collection/© A&E/Adam Taylor ; **82 b** AURIMAGES/BBQ_DFY/Universal Pictures ; **83 g** PHOTO12.COM/ALAMY/GL Archive ; **83 d** © Broadway, 2009 / DR ; **84 g** AKG-Images/ World History Archive ; **84 d** AURIMAGES/Everett Collection/Netflix ; **85** SHUTTERSTOCK/ Ingus Kruklitis ; **86 g** BRIDGEMAN IMAGES ; **86 d** BRIDGEMAN IMAGES/Granger ; **88** © 2016, 2022 Colin Wilson ; **89** AURIMAGES/Everett Collection/© Universal Pictures ; **91** AURIMAGES/Mary Evans/© Paramount ; **92** CHRISTOPHE L COLLECTION/© Marvel Studios ; **93** PHOTO12.COM/ALAMY/Vint1 ; **94 hd** CHRISTOPHE L COLLECTION/© Marvel Studios ; **94 hm** CHRISTOPHE L COLLECTION/© 2014 Marvel/DR ; **94 hg** CHRISTOPHE L COLLECTION/© Jay Maidment/Marvel Studios (reprise p. 6 b) ; **94 b** CHRISTOPHE L COLLECTION/© Marvel Enterprises ; **95** CHRISTOPHE L COLLECTION/© Disney+/Marvel Studios ; **96** CHRISTOPHE L COLLECTION/© Marvel Entertainment/Marvel Studios/Studio Babelsberg ; **97** CHRISTOPHE L COLLECTION/© Marvel Studios ; **98** GETTY IMAGES/Track5 (reprise p. 7 h) ; **99** AFP/Pool/Aaron Chown ; **100 g** PHOTO12.COM/ALAMY/True Images ; **100 d** © Research conducted by Trutex Schoolwear, 2017 ; **101 h** © SWNS, 2018 ; **101b** © Birmingham TV, 2019 / DR ; **102-103** SHUTTERSTOCK/Tomas Ragina ; **102 hd** PHOTO12. COM/ALAMY/horst friedrichs ; **102 hg** PHOTO12.COM/ALAMY/horst friedrichs ; **102 b** © Highsnobiety, 2016 / DR ; **103 h** GAMMA RAPHO/Robert Van der Hilst ; **103 b** PHOTO12. COM/ALAMY/Chris Davies ; **104 h g** GETTY IMAGES/Dave J Hogan ; **104 hd** GETTY IMAGES/ JMEnternational/Redferns ; **104 b** PHOTO12.COM/ALAMY/horst friedrichs ; **105h** © Zack Pinsent, 2019 / DR ; **105 d** GETTY IMAGES/BFC/Mike Marsland (reprise p. 161) ; **106** ADOBE STOCK PHOTO/Siberian Art ; SHUTTERSTOCK/Vasran ; ADOBE STOCK PHOTO/ dimon_ua ; ADOBE STOCK PHOTO/bigmouse108 ; **108 g** PHOTO12.COM/ALAMY/Borna øavrag ; **108 d** ABACA PRESS/PA Archive/PA Images/Daniel Leal-Olivas ; **109** ISTOCK/ JohnnyGreig ; **110** © NBC News, 2013 / DR ; **111** SHUTTERSTOCK/View Apart ; **112-113** ISTOCK/Kateryna Bereziuk (reprise p. 114-115) ; **112** © The Advocacy Academy / DR ; **113** © Brandalism ; **114h et m** © Malaria No More UK ; **114 b** ISTOCK/AndSim ; **115 h** © Channel 4 ; **115 b** ISTOCK/AndSim ; **117** SHUTTERSTOCK/Stanislav Photographer ; **118** CHRISTOPHE L COLLECTION/© Marvel Studios (reprise p. 7 b) ; **119** © Fw:Thinking, 2014 / DR ; **120 hd** AURIMAGES/courtesy Everett Collection/Universal Picture/Amblin/U Drive Productions ; **120 hg** CHRISTOPHE L COLLECTION/© Universal Picture/Amblin/U Drive Productions ; **120 b** REA/Zuma/Google ; SHUTTERSTOCK/Charnsitr ; © Digital Information World ; **121 h** SHUTTERSTOCK/DenPhotos ; **121 b** GETTY IMAGES/CBS ; **122h** © *A Fall of Moondust* Arthur C. Clarke © Reproduced with permission of the Licensor through PLSclear. ; **122 b** Image Science and Analysis Laboratory, NASA-Johnson Space Center ; **123 h** REA/Zuma Press Wire/Blue Origin ; **123 b** AURIMAGES/Everett/20th Century Fox/ Genre Films/International Traders/Mid Atlantic Films ; **124 h** CHRISTOPHE L COLLECTION/© Disney - Lucasfilm - Walt Disney Studios ; **124 b** CHRISTOPHE L COLLECTION/© Disney - Lucasfilm - Walt Disney Studios ; **125h** © Future of StoryTelling, 2015 / DR ; **125 b** AURIMAGES/BBQ_DFY/Amblin Entertainment/Warner Bros ; **126** ISTOCK/ Nerthuz ; **129** ISTOCK/Franz12 (reprise p. 163) ; **130** © Virtuix Omni, 2020 / DR ; **131** REA/Zuma Press Wire/Blue Origin ; **132-133** SHUTTERSTOCK/Zhukov Oleg (reprise p. 134-135) ; **132 h** SHUTTERSTOCK/Triff (reprise p. 8 d) ; **132 b** Prod DB © Kindle Entertainment - MNG Films - Parallel Film Productions (reprise p. 8 g) ;*Treasure Island* Robert Louis Stevenson © Reproduced with permission of the Licensor through PLSclear. ; **133 h** PHOTO12.COM/ALAMY/Old Paper Studios ; **133 m** SHUTTERSTOCK/Triff ; **133 b** Prod DB © Kindle Entertainment - MNG Films - Parallel Film Productions ; **137** AURIMAGES/BBQ_DFY+20th Century Fox ; **141** SIPA PRESS/AP/Eduardo Verdugo ; **143** ADOBE STOCK PHOTO/Prostock-studio ; **145** SHUTTERSTOCK/Bcampbell65 ; **146** SHUTTERSTOCK/Biletskiyevgeniy.com ; **147** SHUTTERSTOCK/Walnut Bird ; **149** PHOTO12.COM/ALAMY/Dinendra Haria ; **151** ADOBE STOCK PHOTO/Igor Zakowski ; **153 g** SHUTTERSTOCK/Anna Demianenko ; **153 d** SHUTTERSTOCK/Elnur ; **155** SHUTTERSTOCK/ Baon ; **157** SHUTTERSTOCK/KPDMedia ; **166** AURIMAGES/BBQ_DFY/MGM/Danjaq ; **167** PHOTONONSTOP/Picture Alliance/Photoshot ; **168** ISTOCK/SDI Productions ; **169** ABACA PRESS/PA Wire/Tim Goode ; **170** PHOTONONSTOP/Sime/Pietro Canali ; **171** SHUTTERSTOCK/ Virinaflora ; **172** SHUTTERSTOCK/Elena Rostunova ; **173** SHUTTERSTOCK/Volha Hlinskaya

Crédits des textes

13 © Robert Muchamore / Simon & Schuster Books For Young Readers, 2004 / DR ; **14** © https://mihigh.fandom.com/wiki/Daisy_Milla ; **15** © Anthony Horrowitz, 2019 ; **20** © The Marble Arch London, 2016 / DR ; **21** © Jeremy Mancino / Jetset Times, 2019 ; **23** © The Times of India, 2021 / DR ; **25** © Shivaani Shashi, 2016 / DR ; **31** © Shompa Lahiri / History Extra, 2017 ; **32** © Hariette Boucher and Lorna Hallett / Stuff, 2020 / DR ; **33** © Rachel Sayers / corpus.nz, 2018 / DR ; **35** © Barbara Else, *Go Girl : A Storybook of Epic NZ Women*, by Barbara Else, 2018 ; **40** © Maureen C. Gilmer – USA TODAY NETWORK ; **42** © Christina Izzo / rachaelraymag.com, 2020 / DR ; **43** © Samantha Swann – USA TODAY NETWORK ; **51** © Kieran Goodwin / Huffington Post, 2016 / DR ; **52** © Chris Medland / Formula 1 / DR ; **53** © Chase Carey / Formula 1 / DR ; **54** © Joe Saward / autoweek.com, 2021 / DR ; **55** © Daniel Mora / Mortorlat, 2020 ; **60** © Sharon M. Draper / Atheneum Books, Simon & Schuster US, 2006 / DR ; **62** A Change Is Gonna Come (Sam Cooke) ©ABKCO Music Inc, 1964. Avec l'aimable autorisation d'EMI Music Publishing France. Droits protégés. ; **64** © James McNair / The National, 2016 / DR ; **65g** © Keedron Bryant / Warner Publishing, 2020 / DR ; **65d** © Beyoncé, 2020 / DR ; **71** © 2019 National Public Radio, Inc. Excerpt from news report titled "Nina Simone's 'Lovely, Precious Dream' For Black Children" by Noel King and Walter Ray Watson was originally published on npr.org on January 8, 2019, and were used with the permission of NPR. Any unauthorized duplication is stricly prohibited. ; **73** © HEY Campaign ; **74** © Craggy Nook Villas / DR ; **75** © The Barbados Sea Turtle Project ; **83** © Black Barrel Media, 2021 / DR ; **84** © Federal Bureau of Investigation ; **85** Excerpt from AL CAPONE DOES MY SHIRTS by Gennifer Choldenko, copyright © 2004 by Gennifer Choldenko, text. Used by permission of G. P. Putnam's Sons Books for Young Readers, an imprint of Penguin Young Readers Group, a division of Penguin Random House LLC. All rights reserved. ; **91** © John A. Beineke / IHS, 2014 ; **93** © John R. Parker / ComicsAlliance ; **100 - 101** © Mirrorpix ; **102-103** © Simply Chic Blog Boutique, 2017 / DR ; **104h** © Geri Halliwell, 2021 / DR ; **104b** © London Hut ; **105** © Léa Zetlaoui / Numéro, 2019 / DR ; **111** © Amy Sherlock / Frieze, 2019 / DR ; **112** © Alice Snape / Oh Magazine, 2018 / DR ; **113** © Alexandre Courbat ; **113** © Alexandre Courbat ; **114** © BBC, 2020 / DR ; **115** © Rhett Jones / Gizmodo, 2020 / DR ; **121** © Hiawatha Bray / The Boston Globe, 2021 / DR ; **122** *A Fall of Moondust* by Arthur C. Clarke (Gollancz), reproduced by permission of David Higham Associates. ; **124** © Doit Vision ; **131** © Copyright Guardian New & Media Ltd 2021

Direction éditoriale : Marie Lucas
Édition : Pauline Gaberel, assistée de Margaux Von Der Marck
Édition numérique : Pauline Boyeau, assistée de Juliette Josse
Relecture : Seonaid Cruickshank
Iconographie : Geoffroy Mauzé
Conception de la maquette et de la couverture : Élise Launay
Mise en pages : Laure Gros, Anne-Danielle Naname
Illustrations : Alain Boyer, Johanna Crainmark, Antoine Levesque
Infographies : Marie Van Der Marlière

N° de projet 10293117 Dépôt légal : Avril 2022 Achevé d'imprimer en Juin 2023 par Rotolito S.p.A. en Italie

THE ENGLISH-SPEAKING WORLD

Interactive map

THE UNITED STATES OF AMERICA
CANADA
WASHINGTON
OREGON
IDAHO
MONTANA
WYOMING
NORTH DAKOTA
SOUTH DAKOTA
MINNESOTA
WISCONSIN
MICHIGAN
NEW YORK
MAINE
VERMONT
NEW HAMPSHIRE
MASSACHUSETTS
RHODE ISLAND
CONNECTICUT
New York City
PENNSYLVANIA
NEW JERSEY
DELAWARE
MARYLAND
Washington, D.C.
OHIO
INDIANA
ILLINOIS
Chicago
IOWA
NEBRASKA
NEVADA
UTAH
COLORADO
KANSAS
MISSOURI
WEST VIRGINIA
VIRGINIA
KENTUCKY
NORTH CAROLINA
TENNESSEE
SOUTH CAROLINA
San Francisco
CALIFORNIA
ARIZONA
NEW MEXICO
OKLAHOMA
ARKANSAS
GEORGIA
ALABAMA
MISSISSIPPI
TEXAS
LOUISIANA
FLORIDA
Miami
ATLANTIC OCEAN
PACIFIC OCEAN
MEXICO
THE BAHAMAS
CUBA
N
W
E
S
RUSSIA
CANADA
ALASKA
HAWAII